Against the Cottonwood Tree

By Linda Jensen

Cover designed by
Blue Valley Author Services

Prairie Wind Press, North Platte, Nebraska

Linda Jensen

Dedication

To my family, with love and memories:
My wonderful husband *Leslie*
My daughter *Lacey*
My son *Landon*
and his family *Kimmera* and *Lillian*
All of you are my reason for living.

I dedicate this novel to my dearest friend,
Kathy Marks.
This novel would never have been completed without your diligence.
You are a gem!

Linda Jensen

Acknowledgements

I also want to thank

Elsie Dockweiler

and

Judy Power

Without your help and encouragement, early into this endeavor, I
would not have continued to write this novel at all.

A special shout out goes to

Faith Colburn

of

Prairie Wind Press

Table of Contents

Prologue

Two Years Earlier

Isabelle was annoyed with her sister as she dropped the basket of clothes on the floor in the living room. She sat down on the sofa and picked out the towels to fold. "Mom, where is Maggie? Why can't she help?" She scowled. When the basket was empty, she grabbed it again to get the rest of the clothes off the clothesline. She let the screen door slam shut behind her.

Caroline heard her but had not answered. She knew her daughter Maggie was outside tinkering around the farm as usual. Maggie spent her days tending to the garden, petting their shepherd dog Casey, or just lying in the grass under the big cottonwood tree in the back yard reading her books. Caroline thought to herself that Isabelle had the right to complain. Isabelle was the daughter who was always by her side inside the house. It just was easier for Caroline to ask her to do things. Caroline watched her daughter carry in another basket of freshly cleaned laundry from the clothesline as she placed the sausage in the skillet to cook.

Isabelle dropped another basket of clean laundry on the living room floor and proceeded to fold the sheets and pillowcases. She walked through the kitchen to put the stack of kitchen towels in the drawer. "So, what is she doing? I bet she is hiding out reading one of her stupid books again. She always gets by doing nothing!" she said, complaining to her mother.

Maggie came into the house carrying the egg basket with six eggs in it, along with a novel she checked out from the Cleary Public Library. "That's all the eggs I could find," she said, as she put the eggs in the refrigerator and took her book out of the basket. She hung the basket on a nail in the porch.

Isabelle asked sarcastically, "Did you lay those eggs? It sure took you long enough to gather them." Maggie ignored her sister and went to the bathroom to wash up. She knew that Isabelle was mad at her again. The truth was that Maggie hated housework. The two of them just did not see eye to eye. When Maggie came out of the bathroom, Caroline instructed her to set the table. Maggie turned her back away from her mother and stuck out her tongue at Isabelle. She took plates and glasses out of the cabinet and set them around the table. Isabelle saw what Maggie did, but she said nothing. To her there was no point in tattling. It just did not seem to matter.

Henry came into the house wondering if supper was ready. "Yes Dad," said Isabelle. He went into the bathroom to wash his face and hands from a hard day's work on the farm. When he came out of the bathroom, he turned on the radio to hear the six o'clock grain and weather reports. Speaking aloud to himself, Henry said, "We sure could use some more rain. A couple inches wouldn't hurt." He sat down on his chair at the end of the table. Caroline put the food on the table and sat down on the other end. Without asking, Henry lifted his glass for Isabelle to fill it with water.

The announcer on the radio gave the grain market reports. "Corn prices are remaining steady. Soybeans are up four cents per bushel. The price of hay is climbing, but not expected to peak until fall." Henry reached into his overall pocket and took out a small notebook. He picked up the pencil from the table that Maggie placed there when she set the table. He jotted down some notes in the notebook. Every Saturday night Henry made notes as he listened to the radio broadcast. He had not planted soybeans this year, but he was watching the corn prices closely. When the corn prices were up, he would sell his corn that was stored in the corncrib from last fall.

After the grain reports aired, the announcer gave the weather report. "Temperatures are expected to drop as rain is in the forecast tomorrow through Tuesday night." Henry's face lit up when he heard that piece of news. He was pleased to hear that rain was on its way. The corn in the fields was looking good and he knew this year could be a bumper crop. "I'm sure glad to hear that," he said as he rose from his chair and shut off the radio.

When the family finished their supper, Caroline packaged the leftovers and put them into the refrigerator. Isabelle made a face at Caroline pleading, "Why can't Maggie do the dishes? She didn't do anything all day."

"Hey!" Maggie shouted. "It's your turn!"

Caroline interrupted the girls. "Maggie, you can do them. Isabelle did the laundry today." Isabelle smirked at Maggie mouthing, "Ha! Ha!" behind her mother's back. Maggie grunted as she went to the sink and filled it with hot water. She wanted to give Isabelle a piece of her mind by listing all of the things she had done today, but decided not to. She did not want to disrespect her mother.

That night, Henry woke to the sound of the wind howling from the north. He slipped on his overalls and stepped outside. He saw lightening streaks in the distance off to the east and the air felt cold. He knew that sometime during the night the wind had changed its direction. He could smell the rain, but only a few drops had fallen. He went back inside, shut the kitchen window, and headed back to bed.

Daylight was pouring through the windows as Henry awoke again by the weather. He panicked when he heard hail pounding against the windows. Without putting on his overalls, he rushed out the porch door. The hail covered ground horrified Henry. Some of them were nearly two inches in diameter. By the time Henry got dressed, the hail stopped and turned into a heavy rain. He rushed through the rain out to the fields.

Isabelle and Maggie climbed out of bed and slowly plodded down the stairs. Caroline was in the kitchen looking out the window. Isabelle saw the panic in her mother's eyes when she turned to the girls. "Did you girls look outside?"

"Yes, we saw the hail." Isabelle answered softly. She knew that the hail covering the ground was not a good sign. Caroline sat down at the kitchen table to wait for Henry to return. Both of the girls joined their mother. All three of them sat in silence, consumed in their own thoughts.

Henry stepped into the porch, removed his overshoes, and walked into the kitchen with slumped shoulders. Caroline could tell by his body language that it was bad news. Henry sat down at the kitchen table and buried his face in his hands. "It's all gone. The corn is stripped down to nothing." Caroline walked over to him and placed her hands on Henry's shoulders. He continued, "It's too late to replant."

CHAPTER ONE

It had been a hot July in the year of 1961. Isabelle and her sister Maggie were sitting on opposite sides against the cottonwood tree in their back yard. "It's so hot," Isabelle said.

Their shepherd dog, Casey, was lying between them panting. "Even Casey is hot," Maggie said, while fanning herself with the book she was reading. "What time did Mom say she'd be home from work?" Caroline worked as an aid at the hospital in Cleary.

Isabelle lifted her head from the tablet she was drawing on. "I suppose about five thirty. She was going to the store to get groceries before she came home. We will have to start supper by four. We're supposed to fry the chicken and make a salad." She stopped drawing and stretched out on her back in the grass. "I think it's too hot to cook."

Maggie put her book in her lap while keeping her thumb on the page she was reading. 'I know, but dad will be hungry. I wonder what time it is."

Isabelle was seventeen. Just the age when teenage girls dreamed about boys, rock music, and what it would be like after graduating from high school. Summers were boring to her and she missed her friends. She wanted to get a summer job in town to earn money for a car, but she had no way of getting there. The only family car they owned was one that her mother drove back and forth to her job. Isabelle felt trapped on the farm. She could not wait until she was out of high school. Then she could be out on her own. Maggie, on the other hand, loved the lazy days of summer. She liked going barefoot, sitting in the grass with a book in her hands, and feeling the warm breeze blowing through her hair. She could get lost in the make believe fantasy world of books for hours.

Isabelle got up and went into the house to check the time. She panicked when she looked at the clock on the kitchen wall. She yelled out the window at her sister, "It's already a half past four!" Maggie stuffed a bookmarker in her book, grabbed Isabelle's pencils and the tablet, and ran into the house. Isabelle was cutting up the chicken to fry. "Go out in the garden and get some tomatoes. See if there are any cucumbers, too." Maggie took the pail that was hanging on a nail in the porch and headed to the garden. She hated it when her sister told her what to do. Maggie was fourteen and Isabelle was only three years older, but Isabelle thought she was the 'Queen of England'.

Maggie brought the pail full of tomatoes and cucumbers into the kitchen and set them on the counter. She saw that Isabelle had already set the table and she could smell the chicken frying.

"Are you just going to leave the vegetables in the pail?"

"No, I guess not." Maggie retorted.

Isabelle glared at Maggie and said. "Well, do something with them. Mom and Dad will want to eat right away. We don't have that much time to get everything ready." She put the potatoes on the stove to boil for the potato salad.

Maggie just grunted and took the pail to the sink to wash the vegetables. She cut them up into a bowl and put them in the refrigerator. "What else is there to do?" Maggie regretted asking that question as soon as it popped out of her mouth. She was sure Isabelle would order her to do something she did not want to do.

"Go out to the chicken coop and see if there are any eggs. I could use a couple more for the potato salad." Maggie rolled her eyes, but did not respond. Again, she grabbed the pail she had used for the vegetables and headed to the chicken coop. Maggie really did not mind going to gather the eggs, just as long as she did not have to do any of the cooking or the housework. Besides, she could take her sweet time and let her sister finish the supper. It was Isabelle's job to do the cooking and housecleaning anyway. Maggie's job was to take care of the garden, lawn, chickens, and Casey. She preferred it that way.

Maggie brought in the pail that contained two eggs and placed it on the counter. Before Isabelle could boss her around again, she turned towards the porch. "I'm going to give Casey fresh water."

She walked out the door, letting the screen door slam shut behind her.

Isabelle put the eggs on the stove to boil. "Typical!" She said aloud to herself while thinking what a spoiled brat Maggie was.

Caroline drove into the yard. She got out of the family car and yelled for the girls to help her unload the groceries. She was a pretty woman with coal black hair that she tied in a bun at the back of her head. She had good posture and carried her slightly overweight figure well. Caroline looked professional in her white nurse's uniform. Hail destroyed the crops two years ago, that is when Caroline decided to get a job. Even though the crops had been good since, she never gave up her job at Cleary General Hospital.

Maggie opened the back door of the car and took out two grocery sacks. Caroline took the other two sacks from the car. "Did Dad come in from the field yet?' she asked as she walked through the door that Isabelle held open for her and Maggie.

Isabelle replied, "No, we haven't seen him since lunch. He said that he thought he could finish cultivating the north field by the end of today."

Caroline set the sacks of groceries on the counter and lifted the lid from the skillet. "How long has the chicken been frying?"

Isabelle answered, "It should be nearly done, maybe fifteen more minutes or so." She unpacked the groceries and put them away.

"Maggie, go out and signal your father that supper is done. He must be hungry by now." Caroline ordered.

Maggie took the kitchen towel off the rack and headed to the north field. Henry was near the far end cultivating, so she had to wait until her father turned the tractor around and came towards her. She petted Casey, picked up a stick she found in the grove of cottonwood trees, and used it to draw a picture in the brown-caked dirt. She paused and tipped her nose in the air as she drew in a deep breath. She loved the smell of fresh overturned dirt. In the distance, she could see her father sitting on the tractor. Maggie stared at him and realized how similar they were in personality. She enjoyed the outdoors and the peace and quiet it brought her, just like her father. She asked herself the question, "If I had been a boy, would I be on the tractor helping him with the farm work?" She saw her father heading back south towards her. She stood up and waved the towel vigorously until Henry raised his arm to signal back, showing Maggie that he got the message. Maggie turned and slowly walked back to the house.

Henry stopped and scraped the dirt from his shoes on the iron slat by the cement steps before he drudged into the house. He was beat from the heat and went into the bathroom to wash. Henry was a tall average built rugged looking man with a deep farmer's tan. His worn out cap was wet from sweat and grime covered his overalls. The worn out shirt he had on was so thin you could see his chest hairs through it. He had never done anything other than farming in his entire life. Henry and his father farmed together until his parents, Pete and Marie Sims, retired and moved into the town of Cleary. Henry and Caroline moved their family out of a house in Cleary to the family farm. Grandfather Pete passed away four years ago, leaving his wife Marie living alone.

In 1945, Henry and his father had built the farmhouse together. There is a porch, kitchen, living room, dining room, bathroom, and one bedroom on the main level. The upstairs is one big room that Isabelle and Maggie shared. The farmstead consisted of a barn, a tool shed that housed the tractor, a chicken coop, corncrib, and a small smoke house. There is a dilapidated shed in the back yard that Casey uses as a doghouse. It also contains gardening tools and an old lawn mower. There is a grove of apple trees and cottonwoods on the west side of the acreage. The lane leading to the house is long with deep ditches on both sides of it. A creek off the Cleary Loup River in Cleary County separates the Sims farm from the neighbors. The Sims owns a field to the south and another on the north side of the farmstead. Beyond the grove of trees is a hay meadow for the stock cattle. Sometimes Henry thought about hiring help to manage the farm, but so far he had done it all himself.

The family sat down to eat their supper. Isabelle and Maggie kept their silence knowing that their parents were exhausted from the day. Once the evening meal was finished, Caroline got up and started to clear the table. She said to the girls, "Tomorrow, I want you two to get the laundry done. Just wheel the washer outside from the porch, then you won't have to carry the water so far." The family used an old electric wringer washer that their grandparents gave them when they moved to Cleary. The wringer washer had a round tub attached for clothes, soap and water. When the clothes were finished washing, the machine rollers would squeeze out the excess water from the clothes. Clean water rinsed the clothes and put through the rollers again before they were hung up on the clothesline.

Isabelle filled the sink with water to wash the supper dishes, "Mom, why can't we buy one of those new clothes washers? After you put the clothes and soap in, all you have to do is turn the dial to start it. The machine does the rest."

"We might get one before the winter sets in. We'll have to wait and see how the crops produce before we spend money on such luxuries," Caroline replied. Disappointment etched across Isabelle's face.

The next morning, Isabelle and Maggie started the laundry. Maggie rinsed out a washcloth to wipe the bird poop off the clotheslines. Isabelle wheeled the washer from the porch to the back yard and filled it with water and laundry soap. Both of the girls gathered the dirty laundry. Maggie brought out the last of the dirty clothes and asked Isabelle how many loads there were. Isabelle loaded the machine and looked at the piles. "Maybe four or five," she said, "the sheets will be the most work. Did you get all of the dirty clothes from inside?"

Maggie pulled up a chair in the shade, "Yeah. I'll push the clothes through the wringers, if you'll hang them on the clothesline?"

Isabelle joined her sister with another chair and replied, "Okay."

Maggie was surprised that Isabelle agreed so quickly. She had never agreed to anything Maggie suggested. The girls sat in silence listening to the hum of the washing machine. The first load of clothes was finished and ready to put through the wringers. Maggie pulled out the clothes and placed them through the wringers, but instantly the wringers popped apart. Isabelle was standing on the other side waiting to put the clothes in a basket. "You can't put that many through at once," she instructed.

"I know!" Maggie scowled. She set the wringers and started the machine again. The girls finished the first load and waited for the second load to wash.

When the second load was finished, Maggie bent down to retrieve the clothes. All of a sudden, she felt something tugging at her hair. Maggie realized that the wringers grabbed her hair. She tried to reach the trip lever to stop the wringers from turning, but her hand could not find it. Maggie screamed. Isabelle ran back from the clothesline to help. She tripped the lever and instantly the wringers popped apart, but by that time, the wringers wrapped Maggie's hair around them several times.

"Maggie, are you alright?"

"I-I don't know," Maggie stuttered. "Hurry, help me! My neck hurts!"

Isabelle was trying to unwind Maggie's hair without pulling it. "Don't move. Can you hold your head with your hands?"

"No, I don't want to lift my hands off of the washer. Hurry!" Maggie yelled through tears of pain. Slowly Isabelle untangled what she could of Maggie's hair from the wringers. She could see that she was not going to get all of it untangled. She did the best she could without pulling too hard. Isabelle had to pull some of Maggie's hair out of her head. Finally Maggie was freed from the machine that wanted to eat her alive.

Isabelle helped Maggie into the house. Maggie was shook up and she had tears streaming down her face. "How much of my hair is still on those rollers?" she asked terrified.

"I got most of it out. Your hair is uneven on the right side." Isabelle said.

"Let me see!" Maggie said while running up the stairs to look in the mirror. "Oh my God, what am I going to do?"

Isabelle followed her up the stairs, "There's a lot of summer left. Mom will be able to cut your hair and straighten it out. By the time school starts, your hair will grow back. It's not that..."

"No!" Maggie interrupted. "I don't want my hair short. I'll just die! I'm starting high school in the fall. Please don't tell Mom," she pleaded. Maggie started to cry. "She'll make me cut my hair short. I'll just die!"

"Well, let's comb through it and see." Isabelle parted Maggie's hair from the left side and flipped it to the right to hide the damaged hair. She put a barrette in it to hold the newly parted hair in place. "That doesn't look so bad." She said.

Maggie looked in the mirror at the new hairdo. "It's okay. I guess." She turned to face Isabelle with tears still streaming down her face. "Just don't tell Mom. I would look awful with short hair," she pleaded. "Please don't tell. Do you think she will notice?"

Isabelle shrugged her shoulders, "I don't know." Isabelle was sure that Caroline would notice Maggie's hair the instant she saw her.

Maggie put both of her hands on Isabelle's shoulders reinforcing her plea, "Promise me you won't tell her what happened."

"Okay, okay! I won't tell her unless she asks." Isabelle said. The girls finished the laundry in silence. Maggie's head was still throbbing with pain and she was worried that her mother would notice what had happened.

Caroline walked into the kitchen from a long day at the hospital. "I see that you girls got the laundry on the clothesline. Were you able to finish?"

Isabelle was alone in the kitchen. "Yes. After I start the supper, I'll get the clothes off the clothesline."

Caroline sat down on one of the kitchen chairs and took off her shoes. "Where's Maggie?"

"She's upstairs." Isabelle answered.

Caroline went to the steps and hollered up, "Maggie, come down and get the clothes off of the clothesline. They're dry." Maggie hurried down the steps and headed for the door. Caroline turned to look at her. "Your hair looks different."

Maggie stopped in her tracks and turned back towards her mother. "Oh! I decided to comb it a different way," she said, falsifying the truth.

Caroline looked at her daughter puzzled. "It's all right, but I don't think it'll stay parted that way. You'll have to always wear a barrette."

"Oh, I don't care. I just thought I would try something new." Maggie glanced at Isabelle silently begging her not to say anything and ran out of the house.

. . .

The lazy days of summer seemed to drag by. During the day, cotton drifted through the air from the cottonwood trees, falling like snow. At night, the fireflies glowed with their luminescent lights while they flickered in the dark sky.

Maggie and Isabelle attended to their chores. The tomatoes, cucumbers, green beans, and beets in Maggie's garden flourished in the summer heat. The girls spent many mornings washing jars and preparing the vegetables for canning. Maggie gathered the eggs from the chicken coop every day. Whatever extra eggs the family did not use, the girls could package up for the open market in Cleary to sell. Isabelle saved her money for a car someday. Maggie would spend hers on the latest novel. However, this summer the hens were not laying very many eggs, so they did not get enough to sell.

One hot afternoon, Maggie came into the house from doing her chores. Sweat was dripping down her face. She wiped her forehead with the sleeve of her t-shirt. "Isabelle, do you want to take a walk with me? I thought we would go down by the river."

Isabelle put the broom and dustpan in the pantry. "Dad doesn't want us down there. He said the water is too swift to swim in."

"We won't go in the water." Maggie retorted. "It might be cooler there. Besides, the water is too low to be swift." Maggie was disappointed. She knew that Isabelle would not let her go alone. "I just thought it might be fun."

Isabelle looked around the kitchen. "Oh, all right; I'm finished cleaning anyway."

The two girls started down the road with Casey ahead of them. They came to the one room schoolhouse they used to attend. The school taught Kindergarten through eighth grade. Maggie and two boys had just graduated from the eighth grade there. They would be attending Cleary Public School in the fall.

The school looked lifeless. The grass and weeds had grown up around the building. The schoolyard had broken tree limbs strewn here and there from a recent windstorm. One of the swings was broken, dangling on one chain, and it seemed strange not seeing a flag on the flagpole. All but one window had its shade accidently not pulled down. Only a month has gone by since school let out for the summer, but it looked positively destitute.

The girls turned the corner and walked east. The river was half a mile away from the school. Sometimes the boys would take their fishing rods to school. When school let out, they would head towards their favorite fishing hole along the riverbank.

The Cleary Loup River was a small tributary that meandered between the cornfields. When the water was high, it would be swift, especially right after a rainfall or in the spring after the snow melted. This summer the rain had been scarce. The water level was so low the water current was at a standstill. Isabelle crossed the one-lane bridge to the other side. Casey walked ahead of her to go exploring. Maggie went down the bank to see if she could see any fish in the water. Isabelle yelled at her, "Don't get so close to the bank; you'll fall in." She looked upstream and saw Casey heading down the bank on the other side. She yelled, "Casey, come back." Casey turned and walked back with his head down and a look of disappointment in his eyes.

Ignoring her sister, Maggie climbed down the bank further to get a closer look at the water. "Isabelle, the water is really low. I am going to take my shoes off and stick my feet in." She found a place where she could sit and put her feet in the water. She put her shoes and socks on a rock on the riverbank. "The water is cool. It feels good."

Isabelle joined her sister on the bank placing her shoes and socks next to Maggie's. Casey came and found a place to lie down beside them. She petted Casey and admitted, "It is cooler down here by the river."

Maggie was trying to pull a twig that was sticking out of the dirt near her. She finally was able to pull the twig loose. When the dirt fell down the bank, she noticed something partially uncovered in the parched earth. She used the twig to move more of the dirt from the object to see what it was. "Look Isabelle!" Maggie exclaimed. "I think there's something buried here." The two girls dug in the dirt until they uncovered a leather billfold. Isabelle brushed the dirt from the leather. When she unzipped it, she saw a ten-dollar bill. "Wow!" Maggie exclaimed. "I think we can keep it."

Isabelle inspected the billfold. "I don't see any kind of identification." She searched the billfold for any other compartments, but did not find any. The billfold was completely empty except for the money.

"Well then it's ours," Maggie said.

Isabelle proceeded to put her shoes back on. "It must have been buried here for a while, because the leather is pealing and the money is yellowed with age. We should be heading back it's getting late. Come on Casey." Isabelle headed up the bank of the river with the billfold in her hand.

Maggie put her socks and shoes on and started up the bank, "Wait for me," she yelled. Just then, the rock gave way from underneath her right foot and she tumbled down the bank and fell into the water. "Ahhhh!" she screamed. Isabelle turned around and ran back to see what had happened to Maggie. When she looked down the bank, she laughed. Maggie was standing knee deep in the river, soaking wet with mud covering her body. The muddy river water darkened Maggie's light blue shorts. Mud splashed her pink t-shirt, as well as both of her arms and in her hair. "Well don't just stand there, help me out," Maggie scowled. "The river bottom is too muddy to get my feet out and it stinks like dead fish in here."

Isabelle found a long tree branch to help pull Maggie out of the river while still laughing. "That's what you get for getting too close to the bank," she teased.

"Well I didn't think I would fall in." Maggie said, while shaking her hair to get the mud out of it.

The girls took their time walking back home. The mud on Maggie's body was drying. She was scraping it off her arms as she walked. Her shoes squished with every step she took. Isabelle saw mud on Maggie's right cheek and started laughing again. Maggie frowned at Isabelle, "It's not funny!"

"Well, you looked hilarious standing in the muddy river. I was thinking how things always seem to happen to you."

Maggie smiled too, "I know. I'm just lucky that way." She said sarcastically.

The girls discussed how they would each spend their five dollars. Maggie said, "I want a transistor radio."

Isabelle stopped walking, smiled, and looked at her sister. "You might have to spend your share on barrettes and a pair of shoes." She teased.

"Ha, ha, very funny Isabelle."

When they got back home, Maggie's clothes had dried, except for the inside of her shoes. "Isabelle, I'm going to take a bath. What shall I do with my dirty clothes?"

"Just put them upstairs. We will wash them tomorrow. We cannot let Dad know that we were at the river. He'll get mad."

Maggie took off her shoes and asked, "What about these?"

Isabelle took the shoes from Maggie and inspected them. She said, "I think we can wash them off with clean water then let them dry. Just put them upstairs too."

That night at the supper table, the girls did not say anything to their parents about what happened at the river that day, nor did they say anything about the money they found. They decided that would be their secret.

CHAPTER TWO

Tranquility Lutheran Church was having their mid-summer picnic. Isabelle and Maggie came downstairs wearing their shorts and summer shirts. This was the only Sunday Caroline would allow Isabelle and Maggie to wear shorts to the church service.

Caroline was in the kitchen making a pasta salad. "Maggie, go out in the porch and get those two large glass jars. We'll fill them with lemonade."

Isabelle opened the refrigerator to get out the butter. She spread slices of bread with the butter for the ham sandwiches, "What time does the picnic start?" she asked.

"Right after the service," Caroline responded.

Maggie came into the kitchen carrying the glass jars. "How long can we stay at the picnic?"

"I don't know, probably most of the day. Maggie, make sure you wash those jars before you pour the lemonade in them. Isabelle, get the picnic basket from the pantry."

Isabelle came back with the picnic basket for her mother to fill as Henry entered the house. "Maggie, you'll have to check to see if Casey has water before we go. Is everything ready?" Maggie went outside to check on Casey. By the time she came back to the house, the family had the car loaded and ready to go to church.

Cars filled the church lot. The Sims could see that tables and chairs were already set up on the church lawn. It was good to get there early on this Sunday, as Reverend Ahlmann and his wife would provide sweet rolls, juice, and coffee in the church lobby for everyone before the service. When the church bells sounded, the congregation drifted into the church. The same people sat in the same pews Sunday after Sunday. The Sims sat on the third pew next to the Parkers. Doctor and Betty Parker, along with their children

Mark and Sara, lived on Plum Street, just three blocks east of Cleary Public School. Sara was Isabelle's best friend. Mark was one year older than Sara was, and had graduated from high school in May. Behind them were Joe and Alice Miller. They lived three miles north of the Sims. Alice Miller was expecting their first baby soon.

Reverend Ahlmann's sermon always seemed to be longer on this Sunday than any other Sunday. The children were restless. Even the grownups were checking their watches from time to time. When the church service was over the women would spread the tables with tablecloths and set the food out. On one end of the table were filled glasses of lemonade and tea. When everything was ready, Reverend Ahlmann would say the blessing.

Maggie was sitting against an elm tree in the churchyard with a plate of food talking to Joanie and Connie, a couple of younger girls, when Mark came walking towards her. "Can I join you?" he asked.

"Sure." Maggie liked Mark. He always made a point to talk to her whenever he saw her. He would tell her what it was like to go to high school. He told her he was planning on going to the University of Nebraska in the fall to be a math teacher. She was going to miss him.

Mark sat down next to Maggie. "You're wearing your hair different than you used to."

"Yeah, I decided to do something a little different with it." Maggie blushed. She was not about to tell him what really happened earlier that summer, especially when she knew that his family had one of those new washing machines. Joanie and Connie giggled at Mark and Maggie; they ran off. Maggie was embarrassed and tried to ignore them. "When do you leave for the university?" she asked.

"I only have four weeks left of summer vacation. Then I'll be checking into one of the dorms there." Mark took a bite out of his sandwich.

Maggie put her empty glass on the ground beside her. "Wasn't your dad disappointed that you weren't going to be a doctor like he is?"

"Well he was at first, but one night we had a long talk. I told him that I really didn't like the thought of practicing medicine. Besides, I think I would be a good math teacher. I want to be a teacher at a big high school somewhere or even a college professor someday. I like to work with numbers. The Math teacher in Cleary, Mr. Hickson, has been helping me with some of the college prep classes. He said that I was good at it."

Maggie looked down at her plate. "I just can't wait to get out of school, but I have four years to go. I'm worried about going to high school."

"The years will go by fast. They did for me. You will be surprised how much better high school is. There are more kids your age to talk to." Mark assured her.

Maggie smiled back. "That's what Isabelle said."

The men were gathering around the horseshoe pits. Bill Drake nudged Henry, "Look over yonder." Bill pointed towards Maggie and Mark. "Maybe you'll get that son you need." he teased. The rest of the men snickered.

"Bite your tongue Bill, that's my daughter you're talking about, and she's only fourteen." Henry scowled.

Doctor Parker frowned at Bill for talking the way he did. "Yes and that's my son you're referring to."

"What is Mark going to do now that he has graduated?" Joe Miller asked.

Doctor Parker replied, "He's going to college in the fall to be a math teacher."

Joe picked up the horseshoes to start playing the first round. "I'd figure he'd want to be a doctor like you." He pitched the horseshoe, but missed the stake.

Doctor Parker moved a chair closer to the horseshoe pits. "Betty was disappointed, but I say let the boy decide." Henry pitched a horseshoe and it hooked the stake. Doctor Parker said, "Good one Henry."

"Thanks." Henry surprised himself with the pitch. He turned towards Jerry. "Jerry, I'm ready to shell my corn. What's your schedule like?" Last year's corn had been in the corncrib until the corn prices were good enough to sell it. Jerry Shields was the only farmer with a corn-shelling machine in Cleary County.

"I'm shelling corn at Tom Anderson's next Saturday, but the weekend after that should work."

"I'll get back to you." Henry was trying to count the Saturdays in his head. "I think Caroline is off that weekend. Is Tom going to need some help?"

"I don't know. He didn't say. But there's always enough work for one more, if you have the time." Jerry replied.

"Yeah, I'll be there."

The women were packing up the food. Lois picked up her cardboard box from underneath the table and said to Caroline, "The crops have produced well the last two years. I thought you were going to give up your job at the hospital."

Caroline brought her picnic basket from beside an elm tree and set in on a chair. "Well, the money is good and I want to buy some things for the house. I have been eyeing a new dining room set. The girls have been asking for an automatic clothes washer, and Henry thinks Isabelle needs a car for school." She added, "I have to be at the hospital at six o'clock in the morning. Isabelle could drive Maggie and herself to school so Henry doesn't have to."

Lois wrapped up the leftover sandwiches. "Doesn't Henry worry about you out on the road in the winter?"

"It's only six miles. Now that I work the day shift, it isn't so bad. I stayed with Henry's mom, Marie, last winter through the blizzard we had. She didn't mind the company."

"How is Marie?" Betty asked. "We haven't seen her anywhere lately."

"She's doing okay, however her eyes are troubling her so and she is losing her hearing. We pop in and see her when we can. Reverend Ahlmann visits her on a weekly basis."

"I should pay her a visit."

"She'd like that Betty."

Alice Miller nearly lost her balance when she was reaching for her casserole dish across the table. Immediately Betty came to her side to help her. "Alice, sit down we can help get that for you."

Alice was wiping her forehead with a napkin as she sat down on a chair. "It's been so hot this summer."

Irma asked, "When is the baby coming?"

Alice rested her feet on another chair. "Doc Parker said in about three more weeks. That's not soon enough for me." She closed her eyes while fanning herself with a plate.

The churchyard was big enough to have a baseball diamond. Home plate was in front of the women and the tables. The rest of the field would face the county road so the ball would not hit the church or the parked cars. Cultivator disks were bases and the families brought their own balls, bats and gloves. The children were gathering in the churchyard for a game. Isabelle had decided to play, only because Sara was. She did not like to play outdoor games much. Maggie was good at hitting the ball and wanted to join in. "Mark, are you going to play baseball? It looks like they're picking teams."

Mark answered Maggie, "Yeah, I can smack a baseball pretty good." Mark and Maggie put their plates on the table and headed over to play baseball. They arrived late to the picking of the teams; therefore, they were on opposite sides. Mark would be the pitcher for one team; John White, the other eighteen-year-old, would be the pitcher for Maggie's team.

Maggie's team was up with a couple of the younger boys batting first. Then it was Maggie's turn to bat. Maggie could hit any ball that Mark pitched to her and he knew it. Isabelle and Sara yelled from the outfield, "Hey, batter, batter, batter!"

Maggie put the bat down on her side and yelled back at them, "If you start that chattering, we're going to do the same to you when you're up to bat!"

Mark turned around scowling, "Knock it off!"

John shouted, "Just pitch the ball, lover boy!"

Mark saw red and pitched a fastball right within Maggie's hitting zone. She took a swing at it and missed. Immediately the other team yelled, "Strike one."

Maggie was upset with herself and was determined to hit the next ball, but the pitch went wild. It was too far outside for Maggie to swing. "That's ball one!" she exclaimed. The next pitch was slightly too low for Maggie. "That's ball two."

"You could've hit that one." Mark complained.

"Just pitch me a good one, right here." Maggie swung the bat in the air to show Mark where to pitch it.

Mark slowed the next pitch down so that he could pitch it in Maggie's hitting zone. She swung the bat, but the ball went behind the catcher and headed for the women. "Heads up!" the players yelled. To everyone's surprise, Irma stood up and caught it.

"Good catch Grandma," Dave yelled from second base. "That's one out."

Maggie and her team argued with him saying that the catcher did not catch the ball; therefore, that makes it a foul. Mark settled the argument and pitched the next ball to Maggie. She swung and smacked the ball toward center field. She started to run for first base, but to her surprise, Mark caught it. "That'll show ya." Mark teased. Maggie treaded back to the home plate and picked up the bat to give to the next batter.

Isabelle yelled, "Way to go Mark. That's one out."

The ballgame continued throughout the afternoon. John hit the ball across the road and it went into the ditch on the other side, resulting in a home run with two teammates on base. Although no one kept score, but the players decided, that John's team won.

The men stopped playing horseshoes and spent the rest of the afternoon watching the baseball game while talking about the grain prices. The women gossiped about what was going on in Cleary and reminisced about their childbirths, while reassuring Alice that she would be fine.

The sun was setting in the west, signaling that it was time to go home. The men carried the tables and chairs back into the church. The women packed up their picnic baskets and boxes and loaded them into their vehicles. They all stood around saying their goodbyes and invited each other over for a meal. Henry told Jerry he would call him to set up a Saturday for corn shelling. They yelled at the children to wrap up the baseball game. The children grumbled as they gathered their balls, bats, and gloves. John picked up the cultivator disks and put them in the back of his dad's old Ford pickup he drove.

Sara and Isabelle were walking back to the parked cars. "Isabelle, just think we're going to be seniors when we go back to school in September."

Isabelle excitedly replied, "Yeah, I can't wait!"

Mark and Maggie were behind them. Mark told Maggie that he would write to her and give her his address when he knew it. Maggie said, "You'll be so busy with new friends and school. You won't think about me or anyone back here."

"That's not true." He protested, but afterwards he thought about what she had said. He realized that Maggie might be right.

CHAPTER THREE

Casey was barking at two pickups that were heading up the Sims' lane. Joe Miller got out of his pickup. He bent down, took Casey's head, and rocked it back and forth. "How are you ol' boy?"

Bill Drake shut the door of his pickup. "Now you've done it. He won't leave you alone all day."

"When Jerry starts up that corn shelling machine, he'll run and hide." Joe said.

Art Canter drove into the yard with his 1948 Ford disaster of a pickup. He wired the tailgate to hold it in place and he removed the front bumper when he ran into a tree last spring. Art parked it close to Bill's pickup. When he cut the engine, the pickup popped and let out a cloud of black smoke.

Joe and Bill laughed at him. Bill waved the smoke away from his face. "Art, when are you going to get rid of that old jalopy you drive?"

Art was a retired farmer of sixty-eight years old. He was never married and always showed up at all of the corn shelling events in the county. The farmers tease him about coming just for a home cooked meal. He slammed the door of the pickup, "Aw shucks, that old jalopy has been with me forever. I just can't part with her."

Bill poked Joe and quietly said, "That's the closest he's ever been to a love affair."

Joe chuckled.

Caroline looked out of the kitchen window and announced that Joe, Bill, and Art had arrived. Henry was putting on his shoes, "Yeah, I heard Art's truck. Make sure you save back enough beef for Art's sandwiches at the end of the day. He can enjoy them tomorrow for dinner."

Caroline smiled and said, "Yes, he enjoys the leftovers. The guys shouldn't tease him."

Henry opened the porch door and yelled, "You guys are early. Jerry isn't here yet. Come on in. Caroline has the coffee pot on."

The three men came into the house. Caroline set some cups on the table with a plate of homemade cake donuts. "Have a seat guys." They all pulled up a chair and sat down around the kitchen table. Art picked up the plate of donuts. He took two of them and passed the plate to Joe.

Casey barked again, as Jerry drove into the yard with his tractor, pulling the corn-shelling machine. Tom Anderson was right behind him in his pickup. A few minutes later, Ed Jones came with his fifteen-year-old son Allen. Ed had a farm near Morgan in Dillard County. Henry and Ed have been friends since they were teenagers. Henry stood up from the table. "Sounds like Jerry's here. Are you guys ready to go to work?"

The men drank another sip of their coffee and headed for the door. Art grabbed another donut as he left the kitchen. He saw Caroline smile at him. "Thanks Caroline, I just love your donuts," as he walked out the door.

Jerry backed the corn-shelling machine up to the corncrib. Henry hollered, "Just about two more feet Jerry. Crank the wheel to the left." Jerry inched back until he got the machine in place. "That's good! " Henry yelled.

The rest of the men went to their pickups to get their corn hooks and shovels. They gathered at the corncrib to set the auger in place, as Jerry started up the machine. The machine made a heck of a noise and the process began. Art stayed back while the rest of the men climbed into the corncrib. The men would use their corn hooks to bring down the corn that packed tight in the corncrib throughout the winter months. The corn would fall into the auger. The auger would carry the corn to the corn-shelling machine and shell them from the corncobs.

Carl Wheeler from the Wheelers Cattle Feeders drove into the yard with a truck. The shelled corn would drop into the box of his truck and he would haul it away to the Farmer's Cooperative. Wheelers Cattle Feeders would pay Henry what the current market value was.

They worked all morning. It became so dusty that Caroline and the girls had to shut the windows in the house. Corn shucks were flying everywhere in the yard. They were collecting on the trees, shrubs, and bushes. Even Casey had one attached to his tail. He finally shook it loose and disappeared into his shed.

Caroline and the girls were preparing dinner for the men. Isabelle cut the apple crisp she made the day before. Maggie was getting more chairs to put around the table. "Mom, how many chairs do we need?" she asked.

Caroline was using her fingers to count. "Let's see. Henry, Art, Bill, Joe, Jerry, Ed, Allen, and Tom, that is eight. We need four more." The corn haulers from Wheelers Cattle Feeders usually did not join the farmers to eat. It was a given that the womenfolk ate after the men went back outside to work. "Maggie, when you're done with that, go down to the basement and get three jars of green beans, a jar of beets, and a jar of pickles."

Maggie set up the extra folding chairs and went to the basement for the canned food Caroline wanted. The jars of food looked so nice lined up on the wooden shelves in boxes. She felt proud that her garden had produced so much. It took her two trips to the basement to bring up all of the vegetables.

Caroline emptied the three jars of green beans into a kettle to warm them. She mashed the potatoes and checked the meat in the oven. "Isabelle, there is a divided dish on the second shelf you can put the pickles and beets on." She instructed. Caroline put a plate of sliced bread on the table and covered it with plastic wrap. The meal was ready for the corn shelling crew. "Maggie, you can go out and tell them that dinner is ready. But don't get in their way," she warned.

Maggie went out to the corncrib. She saw a pile of corncobs already piled high in the back of the yard in front of the grove. Maggie eyed Art leaning on his shovel between the corncrib and the corn-shelling machine. She tapped him on his shoulders to get his attention. Maggie yelled, "Art, dinner is ready." Art bent down to hear what she said. "Dinner is ready." She repeated loudly.

"Okay. When we get Carl's truck full we'll stop," he yelled back at Maggie. "Tell Caroline it'll be about another half hour." Maggie shook her head affirmatively to let Art know she understood what he said. She went back into the house and relayed the message.

The men drifted into the house. Each of them taking turns in the bathroom. As all of the men sat down at the table, Ed said, "As always Caroline, this looks great."

Caroline set the platter of beef on the table and removed the plastic wrap from the bread. "Thank you. The girls help a lot. Joe, how is Alice doing?" she asked.

Joe took the bowl of potatoes from Bill. "She's really close. She has been extremely tired lately. My mom thinks she's having a boy."

Caroline walked around the table filling their glasses with water. "Being tired is one of the signs that she is close," she said with certainty.

The girls kept the bowls filled. Caroline knew to fix plenty of food for the farmers. Wives often helped each other on corn shelling days, but Caroline would refuse their help when they offered. She would always reply, "That's why I have daughters." She felt guilty that she could not return the favor because she always seemed to be working at the hospital when their corn-shelling day came around. When the men finished eating, they complemented Caroline and the girls on the meal as they headed back out to finish corn shelling. Allen Jones was the last one to leave the kitchen. Just before he stepped out the door, he tipped his cap at Maggie. Maggie's face turned red at his flirtation, but she smiled back. She looked at Isabelle and her mother to see if either one of them noticed what Allen did, but they were already getting themselves a clean plate and setting down at the table to eat.

The afternoon went by smoothly without too much trouble until Bill stabbed his corn hook into the corn. Tom yelled, "Whoa, that's my boot you got." Bill pulled the corn hook out of Tom's boot. He was relieved to see that the hook had not gone deep enough to reach Tom's toes. Bill apologized for the mishap. Tom replied, "No worries Bill. Now that boot matches the other one." Robert Schmidt stabbed Tom's boot when they were corn shelling at his place the week before.

The corncrib was getting empty. The mice were scurrying about from the bottom of the corncrib. Bill yelled out, "Here they come! Hey Allen, do you have your jeans tied up on the bottom. They like young flesh." He teased.

Allen screamed when he saw them. He was petrified and asked, "Dad will they really crawl up inside my pant legs? There are so many of them."

Ed reassured his son, "They'll just run around and out of the corncrib. You'll be all right. Bill's just teasing you." Allen turned and

26

frowned at Bill. The men teased the younger boys on corn shelling day, but the truth of the matter was they could climb on the corn pushing it down in the crib much faster than the older men do.

By late afternoon, the corncrib was empty. The dust was settling, the corn shucks finally landed, and the corncob pile had grown like a small mountain in the yard. Dirt covered the men from the hair to their shoes and they were exhausted. Henry thanked each of them for coming to help. Art was the only one that followed Henry into the house after he went to his pickup and changed into a clean shirt. They sat at the kitchen table as Caroline offered a cup of coffee to each of them. Henry and Art sipped their coffee. They were too tired to talk.

Art finished his cup of coffee and rose from the kitchen chair. "I should get home."

Henry stood up and shook Art's hand. "Thanks for your help Art."

"Aw, golly, I didn't do much." He put back on his cap and turned towards Caroline. "Caroline the meal was excellent."

Caroline handed him a paper sack. "Here are a couple of sandwiches for your supper."

"Aw, thanks. You're too kind," he said while bending down and placing a kiss on her cheek out of gratitude.

"You're welcome Art. Don't be a stranger. Come over and have dinner with us some Sunday."

"Aw, thanks. I'll do that," he said and left the house. Art had trouble starting his pickup. When the pickup finally started, it popped again and sent out another cloud of black smoke as he drove out of the lane.

Caroline watched him through the kitchen window feeling sorry for him. She knew he was going home to an empty house, but she realized, that was the life he chose to live. She joined Henry in the living room. "Was the yield really that good?"

"We filled four trucks. Carl Wheeler will give us the number of bushels when he weighs the last one."

Caroline was pleased with the news. She had high hopes that maybe she could buy an automatic clothes washer and a dining room set.

CHAPTER FOUR

It was early August and the summer heat was relentless. The small rain showers that fell were far and few between. Maggie was watering the garden daily for lack of rain. Henry's crops were showing signs of suffering.

. . .

Joe Miller came into the house to refill his water jug. He heard a cry for help coming from his wife Alice in the bathroom. He rushed to the bathroom and saw Alice on the floor. He started to help her up, but the pain for Alice was too much to bear. She fell back on the floor hitting her head on the sink on her way down. Alice shouted, "I need an ambulance!"

Joe quickly agreed and dialed the emergency number for the hospital. The dispatcher on the other end said, "Emergency services."

Joe said in a panic, "This is Joe Miller and I need an ambulance!"

"What is your address?" the dispatcher asked.

"Rural Route 1, my Homestead number is F118. Please hurry. Alice is nine months pregnant."

At the hospital, Caroline heard that they had called an ambulance for Alice Miller. The doctor and the nurses were preparing the delivery room when the ambulance arrived. The ambulance driver wheeled Alice into the hospital on a gurney as she was complaining of pain. They rushed her into the delivery room. Alice was shaking uncontrollably and her head ached from the fall. Doctor Parker was telling her to try to relax the best she could. He was ordering the nurses on what to do, and what supplies he would need.

29

Caroline met Joe in the hallway. She could see by the look on Joe's face that he was worried. "Joe, it'll be alright. What happened?"

Joe sat down in a chair in the waiting room and started talking. "Alice hollered when she was in the bathroom. When I got there, she was sitting on the floor in a pool of liquid. That is when I called for the ambulance. She was complaining of a lot of pain. I am just thankful that I decided to come into the house for some water when I did."

Caroline sat down next to him, "Joe, her water broke. She will be okay. The baby will be alright." She was trying to calm Joe down.

Caroline left the waiting room when Doctor Parker came in. Immediately Joe stood up. "Joe, just relax. It might take a little while. The baby is doing fine. We have Alice walking the halls. I examined the bump on her forehead. We will keep a close eye on that too. Other than that she is doing fine."

Joe went out into the hall looking for Alice. As he approached her, Alice doubled over with a painful contraction. The nurse and Joe helped her into a wheelchair and wheeled her back into the delivery room. The nurse called out for the doctor. Alice screamed again as Doctor Parker rushed into the room. Joe could not stand to see Alice in such pain. He just stood back out of the way feeling helpless. Joe watched as the two professionals worked to get Alice onto the hospital bed. The nurse asked him to return to the waiting room. Reluctantly, Joe obliged. Doctor Parker examined Alice and realized that the birth of her baby may become difficult.

Several painful minutes went by before Alice gave birth to a six pound eight ounce baby boy. Doctor Parker attended to the new born when the nurse noticed that Alice's blood pressure dropped dramatically. She became unconscious and bleeding excessively.

The nurse hollered for Doctor Parker when she saw that Alice was hemorrhaging. Doctor Parker ordered the staff to move Alice out of the recovery room and into the surgery room. He worked quickly to stop her from bleeding and gave her an anesthetic.

Minutes went by, which seemed like hours to Joe. He was wondering why he was not visited by the doctor, or a nurse, to tell him some news about the baby. He decided to walk back to the delivery room to find out for himself. He opened the door to find no one there. Joe rushed down the hall.

Caroline came out of a patient's room. "Joe, what's wrong?"

"Where's Alice? I checked on her in the delivery room and she wasn't there."

Caroline could see that Joe was upset. She led him down the hall to the surgery room. She did not know many details why she was there. "She's in here. You cannot go in. Doctor Parker will be out shortly," was all she could say. Joe was furious and wanted to know what was going on. He could not blame Caroline, but he thought someone should be informing him of the status of his own wife.

Doctor Parker finally came out of the surgery room. Joe angrily stopped him, demanding to know what was happening to Alice. Doctor Parker explained that Alice started to hemorrhage, but he assured Joe that she was being taken care of saying, "Joe, we gave her an anesthetic. She will be waking up from it in a short while."

"What about the baby?"

"Joe you have a healthy son." Doctor Parker led him to the nursery to see him. Joe had a tear stream down his face when he saw his baby son in the crib through the nursery glass window. His hair was black just like his. To Joe he was a perfect baby, but then again, Joe might be just a bit prejudice.

Joe visited Alice and his son every day. He would spend hours looking through the nursery window watching his son move his arms and legs back and forth. In the afternoon of the third day, Caroline saw him in the hall. "Joe, you look like you need some rest."

"I just can't sleep without Alice next to me."

"Why don't you come over for supper tonight?"

"Thanks Caroline. I could use a good home cooked meal. I'm not much of a cook." Caroline smiled.

Alice remained in the hospital five days for recovery. Caroline visited Alice on the morning of her last day. She was sitting in a recliner in the corner of the room, "Caroline, I have something to ask you." Caroline was packing up Alice's belongings to get her ready to go home. "Doctor Parker asked me if there was anyone I could get to help me at home while I recuperate. Could Isabelle stay with us for a while to help me and the baby?"

Caroline turned to face Alice with a wide grin. "Why of course. I think she would be thrilled. Maggie is old enough to be home by herself. I'll bring Isabelle over right after work today."

Alice seemed relieved. "Thank you."

. . .

The telephone rang. Joe rushed to answer it. "Hello."

"Joe, this is Cleary General Hospital. Alice and your baby are being released today."

"Oh, thank you for calling. I'll be right there." He hung up the phone and scrambled to clean the house. He washed the dishes, made the bed, and picked up the clothes he had laying on the floor. He went into the baby's room and opened the shades to let the sunshine in. He moved the crib away from the direct sunlight. When he was satisfied that the house was in order for his wife and baby son to come home, he drove his pickup into town to get them.

Joe walked into the hospital. When he saw his wife in a wheel chair holding his baby, his heart nearly burst with joy. Alice looked up with a big grin on her face. She was beaming from ear to ear. Joe walked up to her and proudly said, "Let's take Gregory Wayne Miller home."

Caroline helped Joe get Alice and Gregory into the pickup. She handed Alice her belongings saying, "I will see you tonight when I bring Isabelle over. We will not stay long. Henry and Maggie can visit when you're feeling up to having company."

"Thanks Caroline, for all you do for us." Caroline shut the door of the pickup and Joe proudly drove his family home.

That evening, Caroline stopped the car in front of Joe and Alice's house. Isabelle turned towards her mother, "I am kind of scared. I have only held a baby one time and she was already three months old."

"You'll be alright. Alice just needs you to help her with her house chores. Besides, babies are not hard to take care of. They let you know when something is wrong." Caroline reassured her.

Isabelle got out of the car slowly. She still was not sure she could do what Alice wanted her to do. Joe greeted them at the door. "Come on in. Alice and Gregory are resting in the living room."

Isabelle was amazed how little Gregory looked asleep in Alice's arms. She was even more petrified than before. Caroline sensed Isabelle's apprehensiveness. Alice opened her eyes and smiled at

Isabelle. "Oh, hello, I didn't hear you come in. Joe, you can take Gregory to his crib."

Immediately Caroline reached for the baby. "I'll take him." Isabelle watched with amazement how comfortable her mother was at handling such a little baby. Caroline stopped in front of Isabelle to let her look at him. "Joe, I think he has your nose."

Joe smiled and brushed Gregory's cheek. "Poor little fella."

Isabelle followed Caroline into Gregory's room. Caroline put him down in his crib and covered him up with a blanket. Isabelle whispered, "Mom, he's so little."

Again, Caroline reassured Isabelle that she would be fine. They returned to the living room. "I'm only a phone call away if you need anything." Caroline kissed Isabelle on the cheek and said, "Goodbye."

Joe helped Alice out of the chair she was sitting in. Alice said, "I think I'll go lie down while the baby is sleeping. Isabelle, if you are hungry there is some roast beef in the refrigerator to make a sandwich with."

"I ate before we came over. Thanks anyway. Is there anything I can do for you?"

"Your evenings are free for whatever you want to do. During the day, I will certainly need your help while Joe is gone. I hope you don't mind sleeping on the sofa."

"Oh, no that's fine." Isabelle put her suitcase in the corner of the living room. The sofa looked comfortable enough to her.

The first night Isabelle did not sleep much at the Miller's house. She was not used to hearing a baby cry in the middle of the night. Isabelle could hear Joe helping Alice to Gregory's room and helping her into a chair. She decided that in the future she would get up during the night so that Joe could get some sleep.

The next morning, Isabelle could hear Joe in the kitchen fixing some breakfast. She carried her clothes into the bathroom and changed. When Isabelle entered the kitchen, Joe was putting slices of bread in the toaster. "I'm sorry if I woke you."

"No, I was awake. How can I help?" Isabelle asked.

"I'll need to go into town today. Alice will need some help getting dressed." Joe studied Isabelle's face to see if she was okay being there helping. "Are you going to be alright with that?"

"Oh, sure," Isabelle tried to sound calm. "Go, I can take care of Alice and Gregory."

"Well, okay then. I won't be gone too long." Joe checked on Alice and Gregory before he left the house. Isabelle fixed some toast for herself. She cleaned the breakfast dishes as quietly as she could and sat down in the living room. Gregory let out a cry from his crib in his room. Isabelle immediately got up and went to him. She nervously picked him up from his crib and held him until Gregory stopped crying. He squirmed in Isabelle's arms enough that she thought she was going to drop him. Isabelle carried him into Alice's room. Alice was awake and slowing getting out of bed.

"Isabelle, can you hold him for a little while until I get settled in the rocking chair?" Alice shuffled her feet to the rocking chair and slowly lowered herself into it. She briefly closed her eyes to relax before Isabelle gave Gregory to her. "Thank you Isabelle."

Isabelle did not know what to do next. "Can I get you anything?" she asked Alice.

"Can you get me a piece a toast with a slice of cheese on it, and a glass of milk?"

Isabelle went into the kitchen to fix Alice her breakfast. She brought the breakfast to Alice and set it on the bedside table. "Isabelle, I am so grateful that you are here to help me. The doctor said that I will be better in a week or so."

"You're welcome. What else can I do for you?"

"After I nurse Gregory, I will need you to help me get dressed."

After a week had gone by, Isabelle became comfortable handling little baby Gregory. She bathed him, changed his diaper, dressed him in a clean sleeper, fed him his bottle, and rocked him to sleep. Alice was getting stronger every day too. She bragged to Caroline how wonderful it was having Isabelle there to help her.

On the fourth day of Isabelle's visit, Joe needed to move some hay from the haystack in the meadow into the barn for the cattle. He drove the tractor to the meadow. Just as he lifted a load of hay and put the tractor in reverse, the tractor jumped. It made a loud noise and then quit. Joe knew immediately that the tractor had broken a belt. He walked back to the house. He took the pickup keys off the dresser and headed out the door. Isabelle came from behind the house with an empty laundry basket. She had just finished hanging out a load of laundry to dry. Joe stopped her. "Isabelle, I have to go into town. I have to get a belt for the tractor. I wish I had known I didn't have an extra one the other day when I was at the tractor supply." He sounded upset.

"Okay." Isabelle replied. She walked into the house and checked on Gregory in his crib. Alice was sitting in her rocking chair in Gregory's room and had dozed off. Isabelle decided not to disturb them. She went into the living room to look at the pile of magazines Alice had on the end table.

When Alice called out for Isabelle, she rushed to her side. "Isabelle, can you help me take a bath? For some reason I sure ache today." Isabelle helped Alice out of her robe. She held Alice's arm while she helped lower her into the bathtub. The water felt good to Alice. She thanked Isabelle and just stayed in the bathtub to soak.

Twenty minutes went by before Alice called for Isabelle to help her out of the bathtub. Isabelle assisted her back to the bedroom and helped her get dressed. "Isabelle, I think I would like to sit in the recliner in the living room for a while." Isabelle helped Alice get into the recliner. She pushed the lever to the reclined position. "Oh, that feels better." Alice said as she relaxed. "I should've told Joe that I was hurting this morning."

"Are you going to be alright?" Isabelle was worried about her.

"I think so. Maybe you should get me one of those pain pills that Doctor Parker gave me. I put them in the diaper bag in Gregory's room." Isabelle found the bottle of pain pills and gave them to Alice with a glass of water. Alice took a two of the pain pills and gave the bottle back to Isabelle. "It seems warm in here. Can you open that window?"

Isabelle opened the drape and leaned over the bureau to open the window. It was a windy day. A whisk of air blew the newspaper off the bureau onto the floor. She picked it up. "Is that too breezy? I can shut it down a little more?"

"No." Alice replied. "It feels good. Thank you. The clothes on the clothesline will dry in no time in this wind."

"I know. I was thinking the same thing."

After Alice nursed Gregory, she dozed off again. Isabelle took Gregory back to his crib. She took the clothesbasket outside to get the clothes off the clothesline. A gust of wind slammed the door shut as Isabelle left the house. The same gust of wind blew the drape in the living room and knocked the lamp off the bureau. The lamp fell on the floor and woke Alice up. She got off the recliner to put it back. When she stood up, she blackened out and fell on the floor.

Isabelle walked back to the house with the basket of clothes, but she could not get the door opened. Isabelle called out for Alice, but there was no answer. She walked around the house to the living room and looked in the window, but Alice was not sitting in the recliner. Isabelle assumed that Alice moved to the rocking chair in Gregory's room. She looked in that window and did not see her in there either. She looked in all of the windows, but could not find her. Isabelle tried the door again. She realized that the door locked when the wind blew it shut. Isabelle panicked. Again, she walked around to look through the window in Gregory's room for Alice. Gregory was crying in his crib. Isabelle did not know what to do. She removed the screen from a window, but could not lift the window to crawl through it. She tried the same thing with the bedroom window, but she could not get the screen off that window.

Isabelle was in tears when Joe came back from Cleary. She rushed to the pickup. "Joe, I can't get back into the house. The door is locked and Gregory is crying." She was trying to talk though her own tears. "I don't know where Alice is either. She doesn't answer the door."

Joe climbed out of the pickup. He tried to open the door, but he could not open it either. Isabelle followed him as he rushed to the shed and got the spare key from the toolbox. She calmed down when she saw the key he had in his hand. "We should have told you there was a spare key in here. I'm sorry about that."

Joe opened the door and heard Gregory crying. He rushed to his crib and picked him up. Gregory whimpered then stopped crying. Isabelle went into the living room. She found Alice lying on the floor. "Joe, come quick!"

Joe put Gregory on the floor and touched Alice on the chest. "Alice!"

Alice opened her eyes and saw Joe and Isabelle hovering over her. She was confused. "Where am I?" Joe told her she was on the living room floor. Then Alice remembered that she got dizzy when she got up off the recliner to put the lamp back. Joe and Isabelle helped Alice up and sat her back into the recliner. Joe called Doctor

Parker. He returned to the living room and told Alice that the doctor thought it would be best to bring Alice in to see him.

Isabelle helped Joe get Alice into the pickup. She handed Gregory to her. "I am so sorry I wasn't with you when you fainted." She started to cry again.

Alice touched her cheek, "I'll be okay. It's not your fault that the door locked in the wind."

Isabelle walked back into the house and saw the key laying on the kitchen table. She put the key in her pocket and went outside to put the screen back on the window. She got the basket of clothes, brought them into the house, and put them away.

Joe and Alice returned home from seeing Doctor Parker. Alice handed Gregory to Isabelle. "The doctor said that Gregory gained weight and was doing great. He also said that I was healing well. He said that the pain pills that he gave me made were too strong. They made me dizzy. He changed my prescription." Isabelle smiled at the good news and laid Gregory in his crib for his nap. She turned to face Alice and apologized again for not being there when she needed her. "Oh. Isabelle." She reached out to give Isabelle a hug. "It's not your fault. Everything is alright."

Two weeks had gone by. Alice was finally getting to feeling back to her own self. She did not need help with her daily routine as she did a week ago. After Isabelle cleared the breakfast table, she joined Alice in the living room. Alice pulled Isabelle close to her to give her a hug. "Isabelle, we can't tell you enough how much we appreciated your help. I don't know what we would have done without you these last couple of weeks."

"Thank you, Alice."

Alice invited Isabelle's family for dinner on Friday. Isabelle helped Alice in the kitchen while Joe rocked Gregory. Alice was sad to know that Isabelle would not be there tomorrow morning to help her. Alice's pains had subsided and she could move about much better. The last couple of days when she bent down to pick up Gregory from his crib she felt something pull, but even that had gotten better.

On Friday Henry, Caroline, and Maggie arrived. Joe got up from the chair and greeted them with Gregory in his arms. He could not wait until he could show off his son. Caroline took Gregory from him, while Henry shook Joe's hand and congratulated him. Maggie asked if she could hold Gregory. When Caroline handed him over to Maggie, Isabelle immediately gave her instructions on how to hold his head and keep the blanket wrapped around him. She was like a mother hen. Caroline smiled. Alice informed her that Isabelle had become quite the mother's helper.

After the meal, Isabelle finished packing her belongings in the suitcase to leave. To her surprise, Joe handed her an envelope while saying, "Isabelle, this is for you. Alice and I would like to thank you. You can open it when you get home."

Isabelle did not know what to say other than, "Thank you."

Alice gave her a hug. "We might call you to babysit sometime in the future."

Isabelle nodded and replied, "Sure, I would love to."

When Isabelle got home, she walked upstairs to unpack her suitcase. She finally opened the envelope that Joe gave her. She was surprised to find $15.00 in it. She hurried downstairs to show her parents. "Mom, Dad, look what Joe and Alice gave me! I never expected that!" She was so excited she immediately went to the telephone to thank them for the money.

CHAPTER FIVE

Henry got up from his chair after supper and turned on the radio in the kitchen to hear the weather report. The radio announcer said, "Finally there will be a break from the heat the next couple of days. Tomorrow's high will be in the high 70's. Rain is in the forecast for tomorrow evening through Friday. The rain will break up for sunny weather again on Saturday."

Henry shut the radio off and announced, "Oh I hope the weatherman is right. We need the rain."

Caroline helped the girls clear the table. "If it gets that cool tomorrow, I want you two to do some baking. You can bake a cake and some of those sugar cookies your dad likes so well." Henry smiled.

The next morning the girls did their baking. The last tray of cookies was baking in the oven when Maggie took a couple of cooled cookies and went into the living room. Isabelle washed the baking pans and cleaned up the kitchen. She frowned at Maggie, but did not complain. She was used to Maggie's laziness. Henry walked into the house from doing the chores, "How would you girls like to go into town with me this afternoon? I thought we would buy a washing machine."

Maggie came from the living room with a book in her hand, "That'd be great. Mom would be so surprised. Maybe we can go to the dime store and buy some of their caramel popcorn too." Maggie begged.

Henry grabbed a couple of the cookies, "Mm, these are good." He went to change his clothes. When he came out of the bedroom, he had on a clean shirt and pants. He looked like he was going to church. He looked different when he was not wearing his overalls. The girls went upstairs to change their clothes and get the money they found at the river. Henry tossed a rope into the back of the pickup to secure the clothes washer with and the three of them got into the truck and headed for Cleary.

The Sims walked into the appliance store. The girls were amazed at what the new washing machines looked like. The salesclerk explained to Henry the features that were on the different machines. While they were in the appliance store, the girls asked their dad if they could go across the street to the dime store. "I don't care. I will not be much longer. You two stay in the dime store until I'm done. Then I'll treat each of you to a box of their caramel popcorn you wanted."

Isabelle and Maggie took off for the dime store to spend the $10.00 they found at the river. Isabelle still had the $15.00 that Joe and Alice gave her. She thought she would save that towards a car of her own someday.

Henry turned towards the salesclerk pointing to the machine he wanted and said, "I think I'll take that one. I have a pickup parked out front." The salesclerk told him to drive to the back and he would help him load it.

In the dime store, Maggie went to the shelf where the transistor radios were. She was disappointed to find out that they were worth more than five dollars. She settled for some books and a bracelet instead. Isabelle bought a teen magazine, nail polish, and some makeup.

Maggie finished paying the salesclerk. "Isabelle, how are we going to get home with this stuff without Dad asking us where we got the money?"

"If he asks we'll tell him that Mom gave us some for helping her so much this summer." That really was not much of a lie. Their mother would give the girls money now and then.

Henry entered the store and saw the two girls waiting at the door. He purchased three boxes of caramel popcorn. He did not say anything to the girls about the purchases they had. They figured he did not even notice, because he was concentrating on the washing machine and getting it home. Henry put the pickup in gear. "Remember, girls, don't spill the beans about the washing machine to your mother when we get home. I'm going to keep it in the shed until our anniversary in September."

"What if she sees it?" Maggie asked.

"I'll use Casey's old rug and cover it up."

Isabelle looked at her Dad, "Boy, won't Mom be surprised?"

That evening at the supper table, Henry had another surprise. He looked straight at Isabelle and announced, "Isabelle, I spoke with Charlie Weber the other day. He has an old Pontiac that he wants to sell. I gave him an offer for it and he took it."

Isabelle was so thrilled; she shot off her chair and hugged her father. "Really? Will I have it in time for my birthday on September 8th?"

"Yes, but the car comes with rules. You can drive it to school with Maggie, but you must come home right afterward. You are not to go to any of your friend's houses or the Drive-in Diner. When it is bad weather, I will still drive you to school. This is a huge responsibility Isabelle," Henry warned.

Isabelle could barely contain her excitement. She did not hear any of her father's rules. She was already dreaming about driving her car to school. "When do I get the car? I already have my driver's license." Last winter, Henry taught Isabelle how to drive. Just in case, she would need to take Henry's pickup into Cleary for an emergency.

"I told Charlie we would come by this Saturday."

"Oh Dad, thank you!" Isabelle was almost in tears. She had wanted her own car for so long.

Maggie turned toward Henry with a smile on her face. "This has been quite a day, hasn't it?"

Caroline looked somewhat confused by that remark, but did not say anything. After the dishes were cleaned and put away, Isabelle phoned Sara to tell her the news about the car.

. . .

Isabelle was right about Maggie's hair growing back. Maggie combed it back the way she liked it with the part on the right side and some curls down around her neck. She came downstairs excited for her first day of high school. Isabelle was nervous as she drove her and Maggie out of the lane to go to school.

Sara came up to Isabelle in the hall with a smile on her face. "What's it like driving to school?"

Isabelle put the keys in her book bag, "Oh I like it. Dad gave strict orders that I couldn't go anywhere but straight home after school, or he'll take the keys away."

Sara was jealous, "Well at least you get to drive. I will never, I live too close to the school."

All of the students drifted into the gymnasium for the orientation assembly. Isabelle told Maggie that the freshman class sat on the left of the gymnasium, then the sophomores, juniors, with the seniors sitting on the far right.

Maggie sat next to a girl with long brown hair. The girl slid over slightly on the bleacher to make room for Maggie. She looked as unsure about everything as Maggie was. Maggie said, "Hi."

The girl smiled at Maggie and said, "Hello."

Maggie introduced herself. "My name is Maggie Sims. What's yours?"

"Susan Johnson. I came from the country school in District 12. How about you?"

Maggie answered her telling her that she came from a country school too. "Mine was District 10. I have a sister. She's a senior. She's sitting over there with a blue skirt and white blouse next to the girl with a pink dress and a ribbon in her hair."

Susan leaned over to see around Maggie. "Oh, she's pretty. What's her name?"

"Isabelle." Maggie replied. "Do you have any sisters or brothers?" she asked.

"I don't have any sisters, but I have two brothers. They are still going to the country school. Scott's in the 7th grade and Nathan's in the 3rd grade. We call him Nate."

"I don't have any brothers." Maggie said.

Isabelle and Sara scanned the seniors on the bleachers. Sara said, "Well, it looks like all the same kids from last year are here."

"Yes." Isabelle agreed. She looked up at the boys and said, "However, that boy in the red shirt is new. Do you know him?"

Sara looked up. "Oh, no I don't. He's dreamy!"

Isabelle frowned at Sara. "Oh, Sara."

Isabelle looked back up to see him again. He looked back at her and smiled. Isabelle blushed and turned her head back towards the front.

Principal Jackson came to the podium that was in the middle of the gymnasium. "Good morning everyone. Welcome to Cleary High School." The noise died down to hear what he had to say. He gave a speech about how he expected young ladies and gentlemen to conduct themselves, and introduced the teachers and the classes that they taught. When the assembly was over the students went to their homeroom to get their locker assignments.

At the end of the day, Maggie met Isabelle in the parking lot to go home. Maggie talked about the friends she had made and told her about Susan. Isabelle talked about the new boy she had in the senior class. She did not know what his name was yet or where he came from.

Isabelle's birthday was on Friday, September 8. It was the same day as the first football game for Cleary High School. At the supper table, Isabelle waited for the right moment to ask, "Dad, Friday is my birthday. Can I take my car to the football game? It is the first football game of the year. We're playing Morgan High School." Morgan was a town rival to Cleary. Henry pondered the question for a moment. Isabelle looked straight into Henry's eyes pleading, "I'll come straight home right after. I promise."

Caroline looked at Henry. He gave a slight affirmative nod. Henry said, "It is okay with us," but added, "You can take Maggie with you." Isabelle did not protest. She was just glad to be able to take her car to a Friday night football game.

On Friday night, Isabelle and Maggie came downstairs to go to the game. Isabelle saw Henry reading the newspaper in his chair in the living room. "Bye Dad!" she yelled as they were going out of the door.

Henry dropped the newspaper into his lap. "Wait a minute." He yelled back. The girls stopped. "Remember to come straight home right after the game. Isabelle you are responsible for Maggie tonight." He reached for his billfold and pulled out five dollars. He handed the money to Isabelle, "Here, you share this with Maggie."

Isabelle looked at her sister and smiled. "Gee, thanks Dad." The girls left the house.

Isabelle found a parking place next to the school bus from Morgan High School. The bus driver was the only one in the bus. He said, "Hello." to Isabelle and Maggie when they walked in front of the opened door of the bus. Isabelle and Maggie replied with a "Hello", and continued to walk to the football field.

As Isabelle and Maggie sat down on the football field bleachers, the announcer was introducing the football players for the Cleary High School football team. The announcer called out on the loud speaker, "Number forty six, Matt Carson."

Isabelle turned toward Maggie. "That's the new boy I was telling you about."

Just then, Sara came up to the bleachers looking for Isabelle. Isabelle stood up and waved to Sara so that she could see her and Maggie. Sara was going to try out for the cheerleading team, but she could not do cartwheels. "Hi, happy birthday, Isabelle! Hi Maggie," she said while sitting down next to Isabelle. "Did I miss anything?" Sara asked.

"Not really." Isabelle replied. "They just announced the football players. Matt Carson is number forty-six. Jim is still number twelve." Sara dated Jim Perry a couple of times over the summer.

During half time, the three girls went to the concession stand. They each bought a box of popcorn and a soda. On the way back to the bleachers, they stopped to talk to Hannah Cotter and Heidi Bowman, a couple of girls from the junior class. Maggie felt like she was in the way and proceeded to go back to the bleachers by herself. When halftime was over, all four girls came and sat down by Maggie.

On the first snap of the football game after halftime, Matt took a good hit while defending the quarterback. His helmet flew off. Matt stayed on the ground for a few minutes before Coach Kasper and Jim helped him up. The crowd cheered when they saw Matt walking by his own power to the sidelines.

Isabelle said to Sara, "I hope he's not hurt."

Sara responded, "They'll patch him up and he'll be right back out there. Just wait and see." Sara was right. Matt was back into the game a couple plays later.

When the game was over, the crowd congratulated the football players for their win just before they headed for the locker room. Sara caught Jim's attention by shouting at him as he walked by. Matt noticed Isabelle on the sidelines and waived at her.

"Did you see that?" Sara asked Isabelle. "Matt Carson waived at you." Isabelle did not reply to Sara's remark. Sara asked Isabelle, "Can you stay at my house next Saturday night?"

Isabelle thought for a moment then remembered, "Oh, I'm sorry, not next weekend. That's Mom and Dad's anniversary. We'll be going to Grandma's."

Sara looked disappointed. "Well, we'll make it another time. Good night, Isabelle. See ya Maggie."

"Good night Sara." Isabelle said. "See you on Monday." Maggie waved goodbye.

Isabelle and Maggie drove home listening to a rock station on the radio. They talked about what it would be like to live in town.

CHAPTER SIX

On Saturday, Henry came into the house with a grin on his face. The girls were upstairs getting ready to go to Grandmother Marie's for their parent's special anniversary dinner. Caroline was in the kitchen wrapping up the cake Isabelle baked earlier that morning to take to Marie's house. She looked up at Henry standing in the doorway. "What are you grinning at?"

Without answering Caroline, Henry walked to the bottom of the stairs steps and hollered up, "Are you girls ready to go?"

Isabelle and Maggie came downstairs with their Sunday clothes on. Henry looked at the girls. "You two look nice." He winked at them and opened the kitchen door to the porch. He opened it wide enough for Caroline to see the new washing machine sitting there.

Caroline turned. "Oh my gosh!" she gasped. "That's a washing machine!" She came towards Henry and gave him a kiss.

Henry was beaming. "Happy Anniversary!"

Isabelle and Maggie had big smiles on their faces, too. Maggie asked, "Are you surprised?"

"I certainly am." Caroline was almost in tears.

"Where are we going to put it?" Isabelle asked.

Caroline walked towards the machine to get a closer look at it. Henry followed her saying, "It isn't the fanciest one they had, but I thought it was one that would suit our needs."

"Oh Honey, it's perfect!" Caroline exclaimed. She turned around. "Isabelle I think it'll fit in the bathroom behind the door if we take out the linen cabinet." She already had measured the space some time ago. She turned back to Henry, "When did you buy it?"

The girls were laughing and said in unison, "A month ago."

Isabelle added, "Dad hid it in the shed."

Henry proudly opened the door of the machine. "Look inside."

47

Caroline leaned over the machine and pulled out a large box of laundry detergent. "You thought of everything." She gave Henry another kiss. Henry did not manage to surprise his wife often, but when he did, he was so pleased with himself. Caroline had a smile on her face all the way to Marie's house.

Marie lived in a small ranch style two-bedroom home on a corner lot. The unique thing about her house was the lime green sink in the corner of her kitchen. Above it was a corner window with a great view of the back yard through the one window and the street through the other. The stove and refrigerator matched the green sink. Marie made a pot roast for the family. She was hard of hearing and she had trouble seeing sometimes, but she managed to take care of herself. Henry wrapped on the door twice before Marie finally opened it. She gave the girls hugs while they were telling her about the new washing machine.

Henry walked into the kitchen sniffing his nose in the air. "Mom, something sure smells good."

Marie took the towel that she had laying on her shoulder and chased him out of the kitchen with it. "Henry, the dinner isn't quite ready yet." Henry went into the living room. He took a book off the bookshelf and sat down on the couch to read it.

Caroline lifted the lid off the kettle Marie had on the stove. She took a fork and poked one of the potatoes. "I think your potatoes are done. Do you want me to mash them?" She did not wait for Marie to answer. Caroline drained the potatoes in the sink and added milk and butter. She handed the potato masher to Isabelle to finish them. Caroline opened the oven door, took out the roaster, and set it on a carving board on the counter. She sliced the roast with a knife. "Marie, your roast is done too." She took a deep breath to take in the wonderful aroma of the roast beef.

Marie sat down on one of the chairs by the kitchen table to rest. "I got up early this morning." She said so proudly. "Isabelle, there is a salad in the refrigerator that Louise brought over yesterday." Louise Thompson was a neighbor that lived next door. She lost her husband several years ago and lived alone. Louise and Marie had become good friends.

Maggie set the table and filled the glasses with water for everyone. Caroline set the platter of beef on the table. "How is Louise? She could have come over today too." Caroline turned towards Marie when she did not get an answer. She saw that Marie had her eyes closed. Caroline did not repeat the question.

Henry came into the kitchen and sat down at the table. He saw that Marie had fallen asleep. He tapped her on the shoulder. "Mom, we are ready to say grace."

Marie opened her eyes. "I'm sorry. I'm just a little tired."

The family ate the dinner that was prepared. The girls helped Caroline put the food away and clean the dishes. Henry helped Marie to her rocking chair in front of the window. It was not long before Marie had fallen asleep again.

Henry rested on the couch until Caroline and the girls came into the living room. He sat up. "That was a fine dinner. I think it made Mom tired."

Caroline sat down on the couch next to him. "I wrapped up a piece of cake for her. She sure didn't eat much." She looked at Marie slumped over in the rocking chair that became very still. "Shall we wake her to see if she would like to take a nap in her bed?"

Henry walked over to Marie and tapped her on her shoulder. "Mom, would you like us to help you to your bedroom to take a nap?"

Marie opened her eyes and saw Henry in front of her. "Oh I'm fine Henry. I'm just a little tired." She got up from her rocker and hugged him. She hugged Caroline and the girls, too.

Henry put the book back on the bookshelf. "Mom we are going now."

"Okay." Marie replied. "Happy Anniversary to you both."

Caroline gave Marie a kiss on the cheek, "Thank you Marie for a delicious dinner. I'll stop by on my way home from work on Wednesday."

On the way back to the farm, the family talked about how Marie seemed more tired than usual. Caroline announced that she would call Louise and thank her for the salad she brought over to Marie's house.

After church on Sunday, Henry spent the day installing the washing machine. After he took out the linen closet from the corner behind the door, it did fit in the bathroom.

CHAPTER SEVEN

Isabelle was sitting at a table in the school library before her next class. Matt Carson came in and randomly grabbed a book off a shelf and approached her. "Hi!" he said.

Isabelle lifted her head from what she was reading. "Hi!"

"I'm Matt Carson." Matt sat down next to Isabelle.

"I know. You are the only new senior this year. Everybody knows who you are." Isabelle teased.

"Oh. I suppose you're right."

Isabelle smiled. "I'm Isabelle Sims. I saw you play football at our home game."

"Yeah, I was surprised I got to play the first game." Matt slid closer to Isabelle. "I think my coach from Lincoln High School must have talked to Coach Kasper."

"I was wondering what school you came from." Isabelle felt uneasy that Matt was sitting so close to her, but she did not move. "What brings you to Cleary?" she asked.

"My parents bought the grocery store and the bakery here. I feel out of place, but I am making new friends. This school is smaller than what I was used to." Matt smiled at Isabelle.

Isabelle knew that he was flirting with her, but for some reason she did not seem to mind it. "Do you like it so far?"

"Well, it just got better." Matt looked at Isabelle with a flirtatious grin.

Isabelle's face turned red and she looked back down at the book she was reading. "Thanks."

The bell rang. Isabelle rose from her chair and packed up her books. Matt stood up and placed the book he grabbed on the end of the shelf. He opened the door for Isabelle. "Maybe we could go out sometime."

Isabelle did not know what to say back to Matt. She had never been on a date before. She only went to the movies once with a group. You could hardly call that a real date. Isabelle only gave Matt a smile. Matt took that gesture as a yes.

Matt entered the boy's locker room. Jim was taking his clothes out of his locker and said, "Hello."

"Hi! I met Isabelle Sims in the library." Matt said. "I asked her out."

"How'd that conversation go?" Jim tried to take Isabelle out a couple times but she turned him down both times. He never asked her again.

"Well, she didn't turn me down, but she didn't say yes either."

That remark surprised Jim. "I went out a couple of times with Sara. She's Isabelle's best friend. Maybe we can make it a foursome."

"Yeah, that might work."

Sara and Isabelle were sitting at a table in the cafeteria eating their lunch. Jim nudged Matt. "There's our opportunity." The two boys went over to the table where the girls were and sat across from them. Jim looked at Sara, "We're wondering if you two can go to the movies with us on Saturday."

Sara replied, "You mean a double date? Sure I can." She turned towards Isabelle. "Do you think you can?"

Isabelle did not know what her parents would say. "I don't know. I'll have to ask my parents." She felt so immature to have to get her parent's permission, although the remark did not bother Matt.

Isabelle met Sara in the hall after school. "Can I stay at your house on Friday night?"

"Sure."

Isabelle opened the door to exit the school. "Well, I was just thinking; then the boys wouldn't have to drive out to my house to pick me up and drive back into town for the movies."

"No problem. I'm sure it'll be okay with my Mom."

"Thanks."

When Isabelle and Maggie came home from school, Caroline was in the bedroom. Isabelle joined her. "Mom, I've got to ask you something."

"Sure honey. What is it?"

"Sara has invited me to stay at her house this weekend."

"That's okay. We don't have any plans."

"Well that's not all." Caroline looked up at Isabelle with an inquisitive face. "There's this boy in my class that has asked me for a date. His name is Matt Carson. Jim and Sara will be going too."

"Oh I see." Caroline turned around to face her daughter. "Is this boy a senior too?"

"Yes." Caroline did not say anything back to Isabelle.

At the supper table, Isabelle approached Henry, "Dad, I have something to tell you." Henry put his glass on the table and fixed his eyes on Isabelle. "Sara has asked me to stay over her house this weekend." She continued, "I've been asked to go on a date on Saturday. Jim and Sara will be going too."

"Who's the boy you're going with?"

"His name is Matt Carson."

Henry frowned. "Carson." He was searching his mind. "That name doesn't sound familiar."

"He's new. His family moved here from Lincoln. His parents bought the Cleary grocery store and the bakery."

"I haven't met them yet." He pondered over Isabelle's wishes. He trusted his daughter and liked Sara. "I'll drive you to school on Friday. We can take you home with us after church on Sunday."

Isabelle was surprised that the conversation dropped without them asking any more questions. She was sure they would ask more about Matt. It was a good thing they did not ask, because she really did not know much about him. She only knew that she liked him. She was pleased and excited at the same time.

On Thursday night, Isabelle packed her clothes for Sara's house. She picked out her favorite dress. It was lavender with purple lilacs on the collar. Isabelle packed a ribbon that matched the dress for her hair. She added makeup and the lipstick she bought at the dime store.

Maggie was watching her. "Isabelle, how are you going to wear your hair on the date?'

"I think I'll wear it down with a ribbon." She was looking in the mirror. "Sara can help me curl it at her house."

"Are you going to kiss him?"

"Sure." Isabelle smiled at Maggie.

"Have you ever kissed a boy before?" Maggie was a typical curious fourteen-year old.

"I have only once. It was last year behind the school."

"Who was it?"

"Carl Spencer."

"I don't know who that is."

"Believe me, you're not missing much. He is arrogant. I don't like him." Isabelle closed the suitcase and snapped the buckles shut. "Matt is different. He's a lot kinder."

"When you come home on Sunday, you'll have to tell me all about it."

"Oh, I will. I'm sure Mom and Dad will ask questions too."

"How much are you going to tell them?"

"It'll be alright. They trust me." Isabelle left it at that. She did not want to let Maggie know that she was nervous for her first date.

When the bell rang on Friday, Sara and Isabelle walked to Sara's house. The Parker's house was a large Victorian style home. It had green shutters and was set back from the street. The front lawn was large with several trees. A large oak tree had a seating bench built around it. The Parkers' had a long driveway on the west side leading up to a garage. The house had a porch that spanned the entire front of the house with a porch swing on the one end of it.

Sara led Isabelle through the back door that went into the kitchen. Betty was putting a casserole into the oven. "Hi girls! How was your day?"

Isabelle said, "Hello Mrs. Parker."

"It's nice to see you Isabelle. How are your parents?"

"The day went so slow," Sara interrupted. "I thought it would never end."

Betty smiled. "That's the way days go when you're excited about something, dear."

Sara nudged Isabelle. "Come on, let's go upstairs. I got a new record."

Isabelle followed Sara through the kitchen. The living room was spacious with burgundy flowered drapes. The sofa matched the drapes and there were two burgundy chairs on the opposite side. The girls crossed the living room to the staircase. At the top of the stairs, Isabelle noticed Mark's room. The door was open, so she glanced in. "How is Mark? Does he like going to the university?" she asked.

"He called last Sunday." Sara replied. "His roommate is from Kansas. He said it was hard to stay focused on classes when there was so much to do in Lincoln."

"Has he mentioned any girlfriends yet?"

Sara led Isabelle into her room at the end of the hall. Sara dropped her books on the desk in the corner. Sara's room had yellow flowered drapes with a yellow quilt on her bed. She sat on her vanity bench and brushed her hair. "No. He did say there were not many girls in the Mathematics Department. He mainly complained about how the professors expected so much from the students in every class." Sara dropped the brush on the vanity table and walked over to the record player. She picked out a phonograph record to play. Sara turned the volume down when it started playing.

Isabelle sat on Sara's bed and started tapping her foot to the music. "I don't want to go to college."

"I am." Sara turned towards Isabelle. "My parents want me to go to nursing college. Dad said that I have to keep my grades up to go."

"Is that what you want?"

"Oh, sure, I've always wanted to be a nurse. A while ago, I went to the hospital with Dad. He showed me the emergency room and some of the instruments. He thought it would freak me out, but I was impressed. He showed Mark too, but he didn't like being there."

"Where do you have to go for nursing college?"

Sara got up from the bench and took out a book from her dresser. "Here," she handed it to Isabelle. "This is the school we're looking at. It's in Des Moines, Iowa."

"Des Moines, Iowa, but, that's so far away! I'll never get to see you." Isabelle complained.

"I can call or write. Besides, how do you know where you'll be after graduation?"

"Well, that's true." Isabelle flipped though the college book. "Who knows, I might leave Cleary after I graduate too."

"Exactly!" Sara took the book from Isabelle and placed it back into the dresser drawer. The record finished playing. Sara gave the stack of records she had to Isabelle. "Here! Which one do you want to hear next?"

"That one we just heard was good. I'd like to hear this one now." She handed Sara one she liked.

Sara put the record on the turntable. "What did you bring to wear on the date tomorrow night?"

Isabelle opened her suitcase and pulled out the lavender dress. "This is my favorite."

"That's pretty. I have never seen you wear that before, not even to church."

"I wanted to keep it nice. Mom got it for me when we took Grandma to Omaha for her eyes. What are you wearing?"

Sara opened her closet and looked at her wardrobe. She looked disappointed. She did not have anything new to wear. "I don't know."

Isabelle looked through the skirts and dresses with her. She pulled out a pink dress. "I think you look great in this one."

"My mom made that one for me." Sara said proudly. She held the dress in front of her and looked in the mirror. Her face changed with disappointment. "But I wore that one the first day of school."

"I don't think that matters. It's really pretty."

"I guess that'll be okay. I only wore it the one time. Jim gave me a compliment when he saw me that day."

Isabelle looked at Sara, "I think he really likes you, Sara." She walked over to the vanity. "Will you help me with my hair tomorrow night? I'd like to curl it and wear a ribbon." She pulled out the lavender ribbon from the suitcase.

"Sure. You can help me with mine too."

The girls dug through Sara's jewelry and makeup to find what they wanted to wear on Saturday night. Betty came upstairs and rapped on Sara's door. "Supper is ready." Doctor Parker was already sitting at the table when the girls came into the dining room. Betty set a tuna casserole and a salad on the table. "Isabelle I hope you like tuna."

Isabelle sat down across the table from Sara. She imagined that was where Mark always sat. "I don't think I've ever tasted it before."

Betty sat down on the end of the table. "If you don't like it, I can get you something else."

Sara took a generous helping for her plate. "It's my favorite. You'll like it."

Isabelle smiled at Sara's enthusiasm and took a small helping of the casserole. She passed the casserole dish back to Betty. Isabelle took a bite of it with her fork. "That's good. You'll have to give me the recipe for Mom."

Betty smiled. "Thank you." She handed the casserole dish back to Isabelle. Isabelle took a bigger helping of it and passed the casserole dish to Doctor Parker.

Doctor Parker set the casserole dish down after helping himself with a generous amount. "Caroline told me that Henry got a good price for his corn last month."

Isabelle placed her napkin in her lap. "Yeah, he said the timing was right to sell it. He pays a lot of attention to those grain reports on the radio and in the newspaper."

"He's a smart man."

Betty rose from the table and walked into the kitchen. She returned with a cherry cobbler she made for dessert. She dished up some for Isabelle. "How's Maggie getting along in high school?"

"Thank you." Isabelle took the dessert from her. "She's making friends. She met a girl that came from another country school. Her name is Susan Johnson."

"It would be intimidating the first time you set foot in that high school." Betty set the dessert on the table in front of her. "I'm glad she found a friend."

Sara finished her dessert in a rather hurried fashion. "Can we be excused?" Sara's dad nodded yes.

Isabelle quickly finished her dessert and rose from her chair. "Thank you for supper. It was really good."

Betty smiled. "I'm glad you liked it." The girls left the table and went back upstairs.

Sara had a stack of teen magazines on her end table. Isabelle took one of them and started flipping through the pages. She stopped to look at an article on hairstyles. "Look Sara." Isabelle turned the magazine around her to show Sara what she was looking at. "That one in the corner looks just like Miss Walker." Miss Walker was a young Home Economics teacher.

Sara took the magazine from Isabelle. "She does. Look at that one on the bottom. I think that one looks like Mrs. Reed." Sara said sarcastically. Mrs. Reed was an elderly English teacher that wore glasses down to the end of her nose. The magazine picture was a girl with long blonde hair pulled to one side with a big red bow on the other. Isabelle took the magazine back from her and looked at the picture. They both laughed at Sara's sarcasm. The girls talked and played records well into the night. They finally fell asleep in the wee hours of the morning.

Isabelle and Sara awoke when they heard Betty rap on the door. "Girls, it's nearly nine o'clock. Do you want any breakfast?"

Sara stretched. "Isabelle, are you awake?"

Isabelle sat up and yawned. "Yeah."

"We're getting up." Sara yelled back.

Betty left to go back downstairs. Isabelle and Sara dressed, rolled up the bottoms of their jeans, and walked downstairs into the kitchen. There were two glasses of orange juice and some muffins in a basket on the counter. The two girls each took a muffin and a glass of orange juice. They sat by the kitchen table.

Betty was in a room at the back of the house. Isabelle could hear a sewing machine running. "Sara, I think your mom is sewing."

"Yeah, that's her favorite thing. She sews all the time. She even makes quilts. She made the yellow one that is on my bed. Come on, I'll show you her sewing room." Sara led Isabelle to a back room through the kitchen.

Betty was sewing some blue and green squares together. She had stacks of different shades of blue and green squares in front of her on a table. Betty stopped the sewing machine when the girls came through the door. Isabelle picked up one of the stacks of fabric. "How did you get these cut so perfect?"

Betty opened the drawer on the side of her sewing table and pulled out a piece of cardboard the size of the squares. "I use this as a template."

"This quilt will be beautiful." Isabelle was impressed.

"I am making it for Mark's dorm room." Betty said.

Sara interrupted them and asked, "Mom can we go uptown to the dime store?"

"What do you need?" Betty inquired.

Sara stewed about her answer. "Well, I was going to wear the pink dress you made for me tonight, but I wanted some pink lipstick to go with it. All I have is red."

"That'll be alright. You girls come home for lunch though. Do you have money Sara?"

"Could I have a couple dollars?"

"Lipstick doesn't cost that much."

"I know."

Betty looked at Sara's puppy dog eyes and could not deny her the money. "There's money in my handbag. Only take two dollars Sara."

"Thanks Mom."

Isabelle waited for Sara in the living room while she went into her parent's bedroom to get the money. When the girls walked out of the house, Isabelle stopped and asked Sara, "What did you really want at the dime store?"

"Oh, nothing, I just wanted to leave the house."

Isabelle just raised her eyebrows. The two girls walked four blocks to the dime store. They looked through the records. Sara found one that she wanted. "Isabelle, I think I'm going to buy this one."

"But I thought you wanted pink lipstick?"

"I already have some." Sara looked at Isabelle's disapproving face. "My Mom knows I buy records. She doesn't like the music I pick out though."

That seemed dishonest to Isabelle, but she did not say anything to Sara. The girls came back to Sara's house and immediately went upstairs. Sara put the record she purchased on the stack with the rest of them. The girls went to the kitchen where they found Betty fixing some sandwiches for lunch. "I didn't hear you two come home."

Doctor Parker came into the kitchen through the back door. He was in the garage working on the car. "I'm going have to take the car back to Charlie's to get it fixed. It still doesn't run right." He went to the bathroom to wash. They all sat down at the kitchen table to eat lunch.

59

Sara put down her sandwich on her plate. "Mom, can we borrow the perfume Dad gave you for Christmas? It smells so nice."

The perfume was an expensive bottle Doctor Parker ordered from a pharmacy in Omaha for Betty. Doctor Parker grinned with pride. "Okay. Just make sure you put it back." Betty answered.

"I will."

Early afternoon, Sara came into her room wearing a bathrobe. She told Isabelle, "You can use the shower in the bathroom down the hall to the left." Sara bent over to shake her hair with a towel. "I laid out some fresh towels on the sink for you."

Isabelle took a long nightshirt out of her suitcase. "Thanks." She opened the door to the upstairs bathroom. It was a big bathroom with a long mirror above the sink. There were two white towels folded on the edge of it. When Isabelle finished her shower, she hung the wet towel next to Sara's towel on the towel rack. She wrapped her hair up into the other white towel. She put on her nightshirt and folded up her dirty clothes to go back to Sara's room.

Sara had the new record she bought at the dime store blaring away on the turntable. "Did I leave you enough warm water? Mark always complained about that."

"The water was just right." Isabelle bent over and shook out her hair with the towel just as Sara did.

The girls spent hours fixing their hair and getting ready. Isabelle was getting more nervous as the evening drew closer for the boys to pick them up for the date. She had not had the dating experience Sara had. She really did not know what to expect.

Sara heard Jim's car pull into the driveway. "They're here," she announced. "Oh wait." She pumped some of her Mom's perfume on her neck and wrist. "Here you can have some too." She handed the bottle to Isabelle. Isabelle put some on her wrists and neck too, and then handed it back to Sara, after she sniffed her wrist to smell it. Sara put the bottle on her vanity. "Remind me to give this back to Mom."

Isabelle opened Sara's door to walk downstairs. Sara pulled her back. "Wait. I always let my parents answer the door. I make Jim wait a few minutes before I go downstairs." Isabelle realized that she had a lot to learn about dating. They both studied themselves in the mirror. They primped their hair and checked every detail of their makeup.

Jim and Matt stood in the doorway when Doctor Parker opened the door. Jim spoke first. "Hello Mr. Parker."

Doctor Parker stepped to the side. "Come on in boys." Jim introduced Matt. Doctor Parker extended his hand for a handshake. "Hello. Welcome. I met your dad at the grocery store."

Betty came into the room. "Have a seat, boys. The girls must not be ready yet."

Jim looked at Matt and rolled his eyes thinking to himself, 'this is the way it always was with Sara. He turned toward Betty. "Hi, Mrs. Parker, this is Matt Carson."

Betty walked over to Matt and extended her hand for a handshake. "Glad to meet you Matt." She motioned for them to sit down. Jim and Matt sat on opposite ends of the sofa. When Sara and Isabelle came down the staircase, the boys stood up. They both had big smiles on their faces.

Doctor Parker stood up from his chair and smiled, admiring his daughter. "Where are all of you going tonight?" he asked.

"We have plans to go to the Drive-in Diner for a bite to eat. Then go the movies, Sir." Jim responded.

Sara frowned at her Dad. He always had too many questions. After all she was not sixteen anymore. "Shall we get going?"

"Um, sure." Jim said. He held out his arm for Sara and led her out the door. Matt did the same for Isabelle.

Jim opened the passenger door in the front seat for Sara. She climbed into the car and slid closer to the steering wheel. Matt held the back door open for Isabelle. She slid over to make room for Matt. Matt sat next to Isabelle and put his arm around her shoulders. Jim put the car in reverse and backed out of the driveway. When he reached the street, he lifted his arm and put it around Sara.

The Drive-in Diner was full of teenagers. Jim was worried they would not get a table. He did not want the four of them to have to eat in the car. Jim found a parking place a couple blocks from the diner. "Looks like we'll have to walk from here, they're pretty busy." He parked the car and all four of them walked into the Drive-in Diner. The crowd turned to look at who was coming in the door.

Bob Malcom from Cleary High School was sitting next to a girl in a booth. He lifted his hand and waved. "Hey guys. Come on over." Jim, Sara, Matt and Isabelle walked over to the booth. Bob and his date slid over for Jim. Isabelle, Matt, and Sara slid into the other side. He introduced his date to everyone sitting in the booth. "Jean, this is Sara, Jim, Isabelle, and Matt. "This is Jean Mason. She's from Morgan. She is a senior at Morgan High School." They all exchanged hellos.

Jim did not like sitting on the other side of Sara, but he did not have a choice. He looked around the room, "Sure is crowded in here tonight."

"Yeah, we just walked in and grabbed this table." Bob added, "The couple that was here just left."

The waitress came to take their orders. Bob asked Jean, "What would you like?"

Jean replied, "I'll just have a strawberry milk shake."

Bob looked at the menu. "I'll have a double hamburger and a coke." He handed the menu to Jim.

Jim just handed the menu to Matt without looking at it and said, "I'll have the same, double hamburger and a coke. Sara, what about you?"

"I not very hungry I'll just have a cherry coke?"

Matt ordered, "I'll take a hamburger, fries, and a coke."

The waitress waited for Isabelle to tell her what she wanted. Isabelle was not sure what to order. She copied Sara, "I'll just have a cherry coke too."

The waitress took the menu. "Will this be on separate tickets?"

Matt answered, "If it's not a hassle."

"No problem. We do it all the time."

Sara smiled at Jean. "Glad to meet you," and added. "I love your hair."

Jean had straight red hair cut to her shoulder with a flip on the ends. She wore a blue hair band that matched her blouse. "Thanks."

Bob asked, "Are all of you going to the movies? There playing a good one tonight."

Jim replied. "Yeah."

The waitress came to the booth with the food. She put three tickets in the middle of the table. The waitress had worked there long enough to figure out who was with whom. Bob asked Jim, "Did you get what Mr. Hickson was talking about in Math class yesterday? I didn't follow that."

Jim replied, "Don't worry, he'll explain it on Monday. "

Sara chimed in, "Yeah, he always does that. He brings up something new on Friday, and then he thinks we will spend the weekend trying to figure it out. Everybody knows his tricks." They all laughed. "Isabelle, what did you think of Miss Walker's outfit yesterday?"

Miss Walker wore a flared skirt that was black and white checked with a black sweater. She wore a wide red belt with red high heel shoes. Isabelle replied, "I liked it. I thought it looked nice. But I wonder what the other teachers thought about it."

"I think the other teacher's wardrobes need a little updating." Sara expressed.

Jean asked, "What was she wearing?"

Sara explained the outfit to Jean and added, "Yeah, and the sweater had a low scooped neckline." She used her hands to show how low the neckline was.

The boys smiled at the comment. Jim said, "What's wrong with that?"

Sara tapped Jim's arm and flirtatiously said, "Yeah, you would like it."

Isabelle looked at Matt. He smiled back at Isabelle and raised his eyebrows. Isabelle smiled back at him.

The minutes flew by while the teenagers talked. They asked Jean about her school in Morgan. Bob asked Matt what it was like going to a big high school like Lincoln. Sara looked up at the clock on the wall. "We need to get going. The movie will start in twenty minutes."

The six teenagers slid out of the booth. Matt picked through the tickets and found the one that matched Isabelle and his order. Jim did the same and handed the last one to Bob.

The boys paid for their tickets and they all left the Drive-In Diner. Bob put his arm around Jean's neck. "We'll see you guys later." They started to walk in the opposite direction.

Jim stopped them and asked, "Aren't you going to the movies too?"

"No, we have other plans."

Jean's face turned red. "It's been nice meeting all of you." Bob and Jean turned to walk down the street to Bob's car.

Jim whispered to Matt, "I wonder what they're going to do?" Matt snickered back at Jim as they walked to the movie theatre and stood in line.

Matt said, "I hope there are four seats left." The boys paid for the movie tickets. The cashier handed them four ticket stubs as they walked into the movie theatre. They could not find four seats together. There were two seats in the back corner on the right side. Jim and Sara headed for those. Matt and Isabelle found two seats nearer to the front on the left side.

Sara sat down in the seat. Jim leaned over and gave her a kiss. "Finally we're alone."

"I know Jim. Sorry about the seating arrangement at the Drive-In."

"Oh, that's okay. I just wanted to sit next to you, but it didn't work out that way."

Sara said, "Well I think Isabelle appreciates us going with her. She told me she hasn't dated much."

"She'll be alright. Matt is a nice guy."

"They seem to hit it off."

"So do we." Jim lifted Sara's chin with his hand and kissed her more intensely than the last kiss.

Matt sat down and put his arm around Isabelle. "I'm glad you agreed to go out with us tonight."

Isabelle smiled. "Thanks for asking me."

"You sure look nice." She turned to him and smiled. Matt leaned over to her closer. "Mm, you smell nice too."

Isabelle put her head on Matt's shoulder while watching the movie.

When the movie ended, Jim and Sara waited in the lobby for Matt and Isabelle. Jim said, "Did you want to do anything else?"

Sara looked at Isabelle. "No, I think we'll call it a night. Is that alright?"

Jim looked disappointed, "Okay, I'll drive you home."

Jim shut off the car in front of Sara's house. Matt got out and held the door open for Isabelle. He walked her to the door. Jim and Sara stayed in the car. Isabelle looked back and saw Jim easing Sara down in the front seat.

Matt and Isabelle reached the front door of Sara's house. Matt leaned over and asked her permission to kiss her. Isabelle did not speak any words, but leaned into him and closed her eyes. He raised his arms and drew her closer to him. Matt kissed her softly on the lips. He released her and sincerely said, "Isabelle, I would like to go out with you again."

"I would like that too."

Isabelle opened the door. "Thank you Matt. I had a good time."

"Good night." Matt walked back to Jim's car. He bounced on the trunk to get Sara and Jim's attention. Jim opened his car door and walked to the other side to open the door for Sara to let her out. Sara got out of the car and straightened her dress. Jim gave her another quick kiss. "Good night Sara."

Sara said, "Good night Jim. Thanks for a great evening." She turned towards Matt. "Good night Matt. See ya at school on Monday."

Matt waved and said, "Goodnight Sara.", as he climbed in the front seat of Jim's car.

While Jim backed out of the driveway, he asked Matt, "Well how was the good night kiss?"

Matt gave an affirmative nod and replied, "Oh, yeah!" That is all Matt needed to say. Jim knew exactly what he meant.

Sara came into the house. She did not ask Isabelle about her goodnight kiss from Matt. She was going to wait until Isabelle decided to talk about it. Sara whispered to Isabelle, "Are you hungry?"

"A little," Isabelle whispered back.

The girls tiptoed quietly into the kitchen. Sara opened the cupboard and pulled out the basket of muffins. "Do you want one of these?"

"Sure."

Sara opened the refrigerator and whispered, "Do you want some juice too?"

"That'd be great."

The girls sat at the kitchen table. When they finished with their snacks, they tiptoed upstairs. Betty came out of her bedroom and whispered, "Good night girls."

Sara abruptly turned around. "You scared us."

Betty put her finger to her mouth and whispered. "SH! Your dad is sleeping. I will get you two up at eight o'clock. Will that give you enough time to be ready for church by nine thirty?"

Sara looked at Isabelle. Isabelle nodded. Sara whispered, "That'll be fine. Good night Mom."

Sara followed Isabelle into her room and shut the door behind her. She could not stand the suspense any longer. "Well, what do you think of Matt Carson?" Sara asked.

Isabelle sheepishly answered, "I think he's nice."

"Would you go out with him again?" She probed.

"If he asks me I will."

Isabelle climbed under the covers. "I thought Jean was nice."

Sara shut off the lamp. "Yeah, I thought so too, but I think she's too pretty for Bob."

"You don't like Bob, do you?"

"It isn't that really. It's just that he has been in the same grade as me ever since kindergarten. Back then, he had a crush on me. One day in the fifth grade, he tried to kiss me. I let him have it with a slap on the face."

Isabelle laughed, "Good for you. Well good night Sara."

Sara rolled over and said, "Good night."

. . .

Sara got up and opened the shades of her window. "Isabelle, are you awake? It looks like it's going to rain."

Isabelle sat up and stretched. "Dad was hoping he could start picking corn this week."

Betty knocked on Sara's door. "Girls, are you up? It's already a quarter past eight."

"We're up Mom." Sara saw the perfume that she borrowed from her mom sitting on her vanity. "I forgot to give this back to Mom." She walked out of the room and handed the perfume to Betty. "Here, Mom. I forgot to give this back to you."

"Did you have a good time with your friends last night?" Betty probed.

"Yeah, we went to the Drive-in Diner for supper. It was crowded. We saw Bob and his date there, so we sat with them."

"Who was Bob with?"

"We didn't know her. She was from Morgan." Sara walked back to her room.

Isabelle was packing her things into her suitcase. She folded her lavender dress and put it on top. "I think I have everything." She searched Sara's room for anything that belonged to her.

Sara and Isabelle walked down stairs. Doctor Parker was sitting at the kitchen table reading. "Good morning ladies."

"Hi Dad." Sara popped some bread into the toaster. "Isabelle what do you want for breakfast?"

"Toast is fine. I'll have a glass of milk if you have some."

"Sure we do." Doctor Parker said. "I'm glad to see teenagers drink milk."

"Oh Dad, I like milk. It's just that I like orange juice better." Sara poured a glass of milk for Isabelle. She put the milk back into the refrigerator and took out the orange juice for herself.

Betty came into the kitchen wearing a dark blue suit. Isabelle put her glass of milk on the table. "You sure look nice Mrs. Parker."

"Thank you."

Isabelle could smell the same perfume that she was wearing that the girls borrowed the night before. Doctor Parker smiled at her with adoration. "We need to get going or we'll be late," he announced.

They climbed into the car. As Doctor Parker backed the car out of the driveway, Betty turned towards the back seat stating, "Sara, Mark called last night. He said he was coming home Thursday. He doesn't have classes on Friday."

Sara did not sound too excited to see her brother. She asked, "Why doesn't he have school on Friday?"

"He said that it was the end of the quarter. He's planning on coming home on Thursday after exams."

Isabelle spoke with a little more excitement than Sara did. "Maybe we'll see him in church next Sunday."

Sara did not comment. Growing up with Mark was not easy. There were only eighteen months between them in age. They had their squabbles when they were growing up. She did not like playing with trains and trucks and he did not like playing with dolls. Occasionally they would play a card game or a board game together, but that would not last long before they would get into an argument over some rule.

Isabelle and the Parkers walked into Tranquility Lutheran Church. Isabelle looked around for her family. She did not see them. She sat down in the pew next to Sara. The organist started playing the first hymn. Isabelle looked towards the door wondering why her family was not coming. Reverend Ahlmann started his sermon.

Henry and Caroline walked quietly into the church and sat next to Isabelle. Isabelle looked over to the end of the pew for Maggie, but did not see her. Isabelle frowned and whispered, "Where's Maggie?"

Caroline whispered back, "She wasn't feeling good this morning. She stayed home, that is why we were late for church."

After the sermon was over, the Reverend announced, "Let's close with a prayer for our beloved followers. Barbara Jacobs is recuperating from her surgery; Marie Sims is doing well and Maggie Sims is ill today. In God's name, we pray. Amen."

Henry got up to help usher the people out of the church. Several people of the congregation asked Caroline about Maggie. She replied that she did not feel good today and wanted to stay home. Doctor Parker was concerned and wanted to know more details. Caroline told him that she had a toothache and did not want any breakfast. He was satisfied with her explanation and extended his well wishes for her.

In the parking lot, Doctor Parker handed Isabelle her suitcase out of the trunk. Isabelle thanked Betty and him for letting her stay with them. She told Sara goodbye and said she would see her in school.

Henry drove the car out of the church parking lot. Caroline turned around towards Isabelle and asked, "how was your date last night?'

Isabelle smiled, thinking to herself, 'it took less than five minutes before one of her parents would ask about last night'. "It was fun." Isabelle tried to cut the conversation short.

Caroline was not about to let the conversation end. She wanted to know more details. "What did you do?"

"We went to eat and then to the movies."

Henry was inquisitive too and a bit more presumptuous. He asked, "Did you like Matt Carson?"

"Yeah, he's nice." Isabelle was wondering when they were going to get to the point and ask if he kissed her. To her surprise, they did not ask. Caroline let the conversation drop. She figured Isabelle would tell her if something dreadful happened.

Isabelle carried her suitcase up the steps. She saw that Maggie was asleep. She quietly unpacked her suitcase and changed into a pair of jeans. Isabelle tiptoed down the steps and left Maggie sleep.

Caroline was in the kitchen preparing some dinner. "How's Maggie?"

"She's sleeping. Shall I wake her?"

"No, let her sleep."

Henry, Caroline, and Isabelle were sitting around the table when Maggie came downstairs. She was holding her right cheek with her hand. "Mom, my mouth really hurts." She was whispering and her speech was barely understandable.

Caroline saw that Maggie was pale and her face looked swollen. "Today is Sunday. I don't think I can call Doctor Henderson." Doctor Henderson was the dentist in Cleary.

Henry handed Maggie a glass of milk. "Here, honey. You probably don't want to eat anything, but you should at least drink some milk."

Maggie took the glass of milk from him and took a small sip. She could barely get her mouth open far enough to drink it. It was hard for Caroline to see her daughter in such pain. "First thing tomorrow morning I'll call Doctor Henderson and make an appointment."

Maggie shook her head and whispered, "Okay." She took another sip and set the glass down on the table. She stood up from her chair and went back upstairs.

Caroline turned toward Henry. "I'll call Doctor Henderson from the hospital tomorrow."

Henry replied, "Just let me know when the appointment is. Did you want me to call the school or are you?"

"I can call the school."

Monday morning Isabelle came downstairs to go to school. Henry was at the table fixing some toast and coffee. "Good morning, honey."

"Hi, Dad."

"How is Maggie this morning?"

"I don't think she's any better. I heard her moan in the middle of the night."

"I'll make sure she gets up in a little while." The telephone rang as Isabelle walked out the door to go to school. Henry answered the phone. "Hello."

"Henry, it's Caroline. I called Doctor Henderson. He said you can bring Maggie in at nine thirty this morning."

"Okay I'll get her there. Bye."

Henry walked part way up the stairs and stopped to listen. He did not hear Maggie stirring. He stopped in the doorway, "Maggie, are you awake?"

Maggie rolled over and saw her dad in the doorway, "Hi Dad. When do I go to the dentist?" She said in a whisper.

"Your appointment is at nine thirty."

Maggie opened her eyes and looked at the alarm clock. "I'll get up."

Henry walked downstairs and waited for Maggie to get ready. She came into the living room holding her cheek again with her hand. Henry did not bother to ask if she wanted anything to eat. Maggie climbed into Henry's pickup wincing with pain.

At the dentist's office, Doctor Henderson asked Maggie to open her mouth. He used a tongue depressor and studied her teeth. "Maggie, you have an obsessed molar and it needs to be removed. We should do it right away this morning." Maggie looked at her Dad with wide eyes. Doctor Henderson saw her concern. "Don't worry we will put you under during the operation, you won't feel a thing. You won't be going to school for a couple days until it heals." Maggie still did not look any more relieved. "That usually puts a smile on my teenage patient's face, knowing they don't have to go to school." He tried to cheer up Maggie, but she was not amused.

Henry used the telephone and called Caroline. Caroline informed the hospital about Maggie's operation and excused herself.

Henry and Caroline waited in the waiting room during Maggie's operation. Doctor Henderson walked into the waiting room saying, "We have the molar out. Maggie will be in recovery a little longer. When the anesthetic wears off, she will be in pain. Here is a prescription to help her through it. I will need to see her again in two days."

"Can she eat or drink anything?" Caroline asked.

"There is a piece of gauze in her mouth. She can remove it in fifteen minutes or so. Then she should not have anything too cold or too hot. She should stay with soft foods for a couple days, too."

Caroline turned to Henry, "I should go back to work." She checked on Maggie before she left the dental clinic.

Henry helped Maggie into the pickup. "Maggie, are you going to be alright for a few minutes? We should stop at the grocery store and get you some cans of soup. You will have to eat something with the pain pills Doc Henderson gave you."

Maggie nodded and whispered, "I'm okay Dad. I'm just tired."

Henry put the paper sack of groceries into the pickup. Maggie was leaning against the door with her eyes closed. He tried to drive slow going home, so the pickup would not jar too much.

Maggie went upstairs to go to sleep. Henry was concerned about her. He stopped her and asked, "Don't you want anything to eat first?" Maggie shook her head no and continued up the stairs.

Isabelle came home from school. She did not see anyone in the house. She went upstairs to change out or her school clothes. Maggie was sitting in a chair, doing a crossword puzzle while listening to the radio. "How are you feeling Maggie?"

"I still hurt, but it's tolerable."

Isabelle saw that Maggie had a swollen cheek, "What did the dentist do?"

"I had to get a molar removed. Did anyone miss me at school?"

"Susan asked where you were. Sara did too."

Caroline walked into the house. She took off her shoes and walked upstairs to check on Maggie. Caroline was pleased to see that Maggie was sitting up. "How do you feel now?"

"I still hurt, but it's tolerable." Maggie repeated to Caroline.

"Dad said you haven't eaten anything."

"No, I'm afraid to eat. Dad stopped at the store and bought me some soup. I might try that later."

"Okay honey." Caroline left the room and went back downstairs. Isabelle followed her.

Maggie could hear her family eating supper. She went downstairs to join them. Caroline asked, "Are you feeling any better?"

"I feel the pain, but I'm hungry."

Caroline opened a can of soup and put it into a kettle to warm it. She poured a cup of milk into another kettle to warm for her too. "After you eat, you should take one of those pain pills Doctor Henderson gave you. That might help you feel better."

Isabelle asked, "How long will Maggie be out of school?"

Caroline set the bowl of soup and a glass of warm milk in front of Maggie. "She has another appointment with the dentist on Thursday. She'll probably go back to school then."

Maggie took a sip of the milk and a spoon full of the soup. She was hungry, but it hurt too much to eat. She decided to drink the milk. She swallowed a pain pill and headed back upstairs.

Caroline cleared the table. "I don't work tomorrow. I'll keep an eye on how she feels."

Tuesday, Maggie stayed in her room, reading a little or trying to rest. By Wednesday morning, Maggie came downstairs feeling better. She heard the washing machine going and saw Caroline in the bedroom changing the linens. "Hi, honey. You look much better. The swelling is down."

"I'm hungry, but I don't know what to eat."

"Did you want some oatmeal?"

"Okay." Maggie was certain she could eat that. Caroline set the oatmeal in front of her. Maggie devoured the oatmeal it in record time. Caroline wondered if she should have made her more.

Maggie poured herself a glass of milk and drank that too. "I think I can probably go to school tomorrow after I see the dentist."

"I bet you can too. We'll see what Doctor Henderson says."

Maggie washed her dishes. "Can I help you do anything?"

"No, you just rest."

"I'll go and read my book then." Maggie went back upstairs and picked up her book she was reading. She was sure she would have plenty of homework to do when she went back to school.

Isabelle came home from school and immediately asked how Maggie was. Caroline informed her that she was much better. Maggie was upstairs brushing her hair when Isabelle came into the room. Isabelle dropped her books on her bed. "You're not going to believe what happened at school today!"

Maggie put the brush down and turned to face Isabelle. "What?"

"You know that blonde girl in the junior class? Her name is Heidi Bowman."

"Yeah, I think I do. Was that the girl you and Sara were talking to at the home football game?"

"Yeah, that's her."

Maggie, glued to her sister's face with curiosity, asked, "Why? What happened to her?"

"Well rumor has it, she's pregnant."

"Whoa. You're kidding."

"That's what everyone was talking about. She was not in school today either. I asked Sara if she knew anything about it. She said she didn't, but I have a feeling that she just wasn't supposed to say."

"What do mean? She wasn't supposed to say about what?"

"Well get this. The boy she got pregnant with is a college student and is going to the university in Lincoln."

Maggie's jaw dropped. "It's not Mark's is it?"

"No one knows. I tried to talk to Sara again after school, but I couldn't find her. She left the school without talking to me. I have a feeling she was avoiding me."

At the supper table, neither Isabelle nor Maggie talked about what Isabelle learned in school that day.

Thursday morning, Maggie came downstairs to join Henry and Caroline at the breakfast table. Caroline had made her some oatmeal. "You look much better today Maggie."

"I feel much better too. When do I go back to the dentist?"

"Your appointment is at nine o'clock."

Maggie looked at the clock of the wall. She had one hour before she had to go. "I'll get dressed in my school clothes after I eat."

Henry and Caroline were wondering why Maggie was so anxious to go back to school. Henry smiled, "You miss your friends that much?"

Maggie did not want to let out that she wanted to know more about what Isabelle told her. "I am just bored at home. I probably have lots of homework to catch up on."

At the dentist's office, Doctor Henderson looked into Maggie's mouth. "Looks like you've healed pretty well where that molar was. Do you feel much pain anymore?"

"Not much, just when I forget and chew on that side."

Doctor Henderson smiled at her comment and tossed the tongue depressor into the trashcan. "Well young lady, I think you are back in school." He saw the delight on Maggie's face. "I just don't get it. You act as if you want to go back to school. You got a boyfriend you want to see?" He teased.

Maggie frowned. "No, I don't have a boyfriend."

Caroline laughed at her. "I think she was bored at home."

Caroline dropped her off at the entrance of the school. "Remember Maggie, you aren't supposed to go to Phys-Ed today."

"Yeah I know." Maggie shut the car door. She went to the office with Doctor Henderson's note, and the pain pill she was supposed to give the school nurse. She had to wait in the nurse's office until the bell rang for the next class.

The lunchroom was buzzing. The comments about a doctor's son getting a seventeen-year-old girl pregnant upset Maggie, especially when no one really knew for sure. She sat down at a table next to Susan. "Hi Susan."

"Hey, Maggie. How are you? Isabelle said you had surgery on your teeth."

"Yeah, I had to have a molar removed. What do you know about Heidi Bowman?"

"Everyone is saying that she is pregnant with Mark Parker's baby."

"Does anyone know for sure?"

"No, not even the seniors. Apparently, Sara isn't saying anything. She's been avoiding the questions."

Isabelle came into the lunchroom and saw Sara surrounded by teenagers. She broke through the mob and heard Sara complaining to everyone to leave her alone and that she did not know anything. Isabelle took Sara's hand and led her out into the playground area of the school. Neither one of them said anything. The air was cold and they did not have their coats with them. Isabelle finally broke the silence, "Sara, there isn't much time left before the next class. We can stay out here until the bell rings." She was shivering.

Sara sat down on a swing. She saw Isabelle shiver and rubbing her arms. "I don't care about being cold. I don't want to go back into the lunch room." Isabelle sat down on a swing next to her. The girls sat in silence until they heard the bell ring. They both walked back into the school and went to class.

Isabelle waited by the lockers for Sara after the bell sounded at the end of the school day, but Sara left the school without going to her locker first. Maggie did not want to talk about the situation either. She sat in the car waiting for Isabelle.

At the supper table, Henry and Caroline sensed that something was wrong. Caroline broke the silence and asked, "Maggie, were you in much pain today?"

Maggie looked down at her plate and answered, "Not much. The nurse kept the one pain pill I gave her in case I would need it tomorrow."

"Doctor Henderson said it could take a couple days for the pain to completely go away."

Maggie stood up from her chair and excused herself from the table. Henry was concerned, "Does your mouth still hurt?"

"A little," Maggie lied. She went upstairs and cuddled with a pillow on her bed.

Isabelle went upstairs after supper was over. She saw Maggie just lying on her bed staring up at the ceiling. She saw the pile of schoolbooks on the floor. It was not like Maggie to ignore her schoolwork. "What's wrong with you?" Maggie did not respond to her question. She just rolled over and faced the window. Maggie's silence confused Isabelle. She was not sure if her teeth was really bothering her or if she was upset with the news about Mark. "Maggie, are you alright?"

"Just leave me alone!"

Isabelle did not understand why Maggie was feeling this way. She knew that Maggie liked Mark, but did she really think Mark was going to wait for her to grow up and graduate from high school? That is absurd. She did not pressure Maggie about how silly that was. Isabelle picked up her History book and started to do her own homework.

Sara was not at school on Friday. Isabelle remembered that Mark was supposed to come home on Thursday after classes in Lincoln. She decided not to call her. She thought she would wait until Sunday at church to talk to her.

The Parker's were not in church on Sunday. It was hard for Isabelle not to call Sara all day. She would just have to wait until Monday to find out more information.

Late Sunday afternoon the phone rang. Caroline hollered upstairs that the phone was for Isabelle. Isabelle ran downstairs. "Hello?"

"Isabelle, this is Sara. I want to apologize for ignoring you after school on Thursday."

"That's alright. There is no need for an apology."

"Well I wanted to tell you that the rumors are true about Mark."

"Is everyone okay at your house?"

"Heidi and her parents were here today. The day was stressful. I can't talk long. I just wanted to ask if you could bring a lunch tomorrow to school. We will eat outside during lunch, so I won't have to talk to everybody."

"Sure, we'll bring our coats this time."

Sara snickered. "You are the greatest friend ever, Isabelle."

Isabelle hung up the telephone. She walked into the living room and sat down on the couch. She told Henry and Caroline the news about Mark and Heidi. She thought the conversation would stun her parents, but Caroline had heard about it at the hospital on Friday. She had already told Henry. Isabelle stood up from the couch. "Boy, news sure travels fast in this town." Isabelle went back upstairs.

Maggie was finishing up on some of her homework. "Who was that on the telephone?"

"It was Sara." Isabelle did not know how Maggie would take the news that the rumors in school were true.

Maggie looked up from her math paper. "Is it true about Mark?"

"Yes. Sara wants me to take a sack lunch to school tomorrow and eat outside. We'll talk more about it then."

"Oh." Maggie looked back down on her math paper. She was getting over the shock of the news about Mark. She realized that her affection for Mark was just a 'school-girl' crush. Deep down Maggie knew that Mark was not truly in love with a fourteen-year old girl. He was just being nice.

Isabelle let the conversation drop.

. . .

The bell rang for the lunch period. Isabelle and Sara exited the school before anyone could corner Sara and probe her with more questions. They went out to the playground area. Isabelle waited for Sara to speak first.

Sara put her sandwich down on her lap and broke the silence. "Did you know that Heidi is already eighteen years old?"

Isabelle looked bewildered. "Why isn't she a senior?"

76

"She came from a small country school in Iowa. Apparently, the school officials in Cleary thought she should repeat the eleventh grade."

"I thought she was really smart. Everybody in the junior class says so."

"I know. I heard that too."

"Sara, are you okay with all of this?"

"Oh, I'm alright. I just don't like all of the comments made about Heidi. She's a nice girl."

"I think so too. She's really pretty too."

"I know. I wish I was blonde, but I don't have a blonde hair on my head."

Isabelle smiled. She was pleased that Sara could make a joke. She hated to see Sara so down. It just was not like her. "Everything is going to work out Sara. You'll see."

"Yesterday they made plans to get married in November."

"Wow, that's great!"

"Dad wanted Mark to continue with his studies at the University. Cleary school is advancing Heidi. They determined that she had enough credits to get her high school diploma. They are letting her go through the graduation ceremony with us in May."

"When is her baby due?"

Sara's face lit up. "In April. Just think I am going to be an aunt."

"I can see it now. If the baby is a girl, you'll have lipstick and jewelry on her before she's ten." Isabelle teased.

Sara laughed. "What if the baby is a boy?"

"Then you'll be teaching him how to flirt with the girls before he's twelve."

The girls laughed. The bell sounded for the classes to begin. Sara wrapped up the rest of her sack lunch. "You're so funny Isabelle."

CHAPTER EIGHT

The leaves were turning their golden color and beginning to fall to the earth below. The apple trees were shedding their fruit until the next summer. One of the apple trees in the grove had one apple left on a top branch. The lonely apple was swaying in the breeze begging for the tree to let go of its hold on it. Finally, the tree bid the apple goodbye while the apple plummeted to the ground below. A sign that autumn was here.

Late September, harvest was in full swing. Henry would take the tractor out to the field with the corn picker. The corn picker would pick the ears of corn and drop them into a wagon he pulled behind it. When the wagon was full, he would unhook the corn picker from the tractor and hitch up the wagon. Henry would haul the wagon full of corn to the corncrib in the yard, where he already had the elevator set up to the corncrib. He would lift the gate of the wagon and let the corn drop into the elevator. The tractor ran belts that would operate the elevator to take the corn to the top of the corncrib and drop the corn into it.

The harvest was going smoothly until the corn plugged the top of the corncrib. Henry stopped the tractor and climbed up the elevator to unplug the corn. He carried his corn hook with him. Most of the time the problem was a few longer ears that would plug the opening of the corncrib. Henry moved a long ear from the entrance of the crib with his corn hook. The corn dropped down into the corncrib so quickly that Henry slipped and almost went down with it. He caught himself with the corn hook on a sideboard of the corncrib and pulled himself back to his feet onto the elevator. He sat and rested for a moment before he climbed back down. He thanked God for his safety.

79

When the wagon was unloaded, he hauled the wagon back out to the field and repeated the process. Harvest would take Henry several days to finish. He would pray for no rain. Some years it would be cold enough to snow during harvest. This year was a beautiful fall. The frost at night would make the corn snap off the corn stalks easily. The warmer temperatures during the day would allow Henry to work all day. Henry finished the harvest in just four days.

Henry and Caroline received a wedding invitation for Mark and Heidi's wedding, set for November 18. Everyone at the high school finally stopped talking about the situation and left Sara alone.

. . .

Matt secretly passed a note to Isabelle in Math class before he took his seat in front of her. Isabelle held it close to her while she read it so that no one else could see it. The note read, 'What are you doing Saturday night? I'll catch you after school today'. Isabelle folded the note and stuffed in her math book.

The last bell rang for the day, Isabelle waited by the water fountain for Matt. Matt came towards her with a grin on his face and asked, "Do you want to go roller skating with me Saturday night? I hear there is roller rink in Morgan."

"I'm not very good on roller skates. I have only roller skated once, but I would still like to go."

"Well then, it's a date. I can come and pick you up, but you'll have to tell me how to get to your house."

Isabelle had to think of something fast. She just was not ready for her parents to meet Matt yet. "I told Grandma that I would come visit her on Saturday. You can pick me up there." Isabelle did not feel good about herself for making up the story.

That evening at the supper table, she told Henry and Caroline that she was going to visit Marie on Saturday before going roller-skating with a bunch of her friends. Again, she told another lie. All of a sudden dating became difficult. The scheme worked, as they did not ask any questions. Maggie did not even ask to go with her.

Late Saturday afternoon Isabelle took $3.00 from the money that Joe and Alice gave her. She put them in her purse. She stopped at the flower shop and bought a small bouquet of yellow sunflowers for Marie. Isabelle really did not know why she bought the flowers. Maybe she felt guilty for telling a lie.

Isabelle knocked on Marie's door. Marie finally answered it after the third time. Isabelle gave her a hug and handed her the bouquet of flowers. Marie thanked her for the flowers, but wondered why Isabelle gave them to her. Isabelle saw how puzzled Marie looked. She bent down and gave Marie a kiss on the cheek saying, "I just love you Grandma." Marie put them in a vase and set it on the end table next to her rocker so that she can see them every day. Isabelle was watching the clock in the kitchen. The minutes were not going by fast enough. She tried to make conversation with Marie, but she had become so hard of hearing. Isabelle finally gave up. She sat and read a book from Marie's bookshelf instead. Isabelle heard a knock on the door. She was sure it was Matt. She turned toward Marie to see if she heard it. Marie did not stop rocking in her rocking chair. Isabelle gave her a hug and told her that it was time for her to leave. She knew it was rude of her to not let Matt in the house and introduce him to her grandmother, but that could ruin her scheme. When Matt asked about Marie, Isabelle told him that she had fallen asleep and they should not disturb her. Oh, the tangled web she weaved for this date!

At Alot-A-Fun Roller Rink, Matt and Isabelle rented their roller skates. Isabelle was not sure how she would skate on them. She held onto Matt while he took her out onto the rink. "Matt I don't know if I can do this," she complained.

Matt was laughing at her, "Well, hang onto me." They managed to skate a half way around the rink before Isabelle took a tumble, taking Matt down with her. "Maybe you're right," he said as he regained his footage and helped Isabelle up. He escorted her to the side bench. They watched the other skaters for a while before they moved to one of the booths. Matt roller-skated to the concession stand. He came back to the booth with two hot dogs and two cokes. He sat across from Isabelle and they talked the rest of the evening. Isabelle told Matt about living on the farm and some things she did as a child. She talked about how Maggie could be so annoying. She even talked about Casey.

Matt told her that his Grandmother Helen was living in a nursing home in Lincoln. He also told her he had grandparents who live by the airport there. He also talked about the grocery store his parents still owned in Lincoln. He expressed how much bigger and busier it was than the one in Cleary. Matt talked about the high school he attended before coming to Cleary. He told her about his friend Kevin Davis, whom he still talks to sometimes.

They talked for hours, not caring much about roller-skating. The emcee in the music room announced the last song for the evening. Isabelle and Matt took off their roller skates and returned them. Isabelle was worried that Matt did not get to skate much, but he did not seem to mind.

Matt pulled his car out of the parking lot of the roller rink as he tuned the radio to a rock station. Isabelle started to sing along to one of the songs. Matt kept silent while listening to her sing. He complemented on her singing and confessed that he could not sing a note. He was on the curve of the highway that led into Cleary. "Which way do you live from here?" He asked.

Isabelle told him that she lived on F road to the south, which was just about another half a mile. Matt saw the road marker and made the turn. It was a good thing Matt could not see Isabelle's face, as it was beet red. "You can't go see my family. It's too late!"

"It is only ten thirty," he answered back.

"Matt, we just can't!" Isabelle scolded.

Matt was confused and thought Isabelle was ashamed of him until Isabelle confessed to the lies that she told to her parents about roller-skating with a group. She admitted to Matt that she used her grandmother as a decoy for the date. She felt so guilty; she started to cry. Through her tears, Isabelle assured Matt that he was not the reason why he had never met her parents. She assured him that the she was the problem. She just was not ready. Matt pulled over onto the side of the road. He stopped the car and turned to kiss her. "That's what I love about you Isabelle. You are just so honest. We won't go into the lane. We'll just drive by. Then I will know where you live. Just in case you might want to tell them about me," he smiled. "Then I can come and pick you up on date like I am supposed to do." He teased.

Isabelle was stunned. He said the word 'love'. Of all the words he said, Isabelle only heard the word 'love'. In the moonlight, Matt could see Isabelle staring at him. He interrupted her thoughts, "Isabelle did you hear what I said? I would like to know where you live and pick you up on our next date." He repeated.

If Matt knew what she was thinking, he would probably put the car in gear and rush her back to her grandmother's house as fast as the speed limit would allow. Isabelle came back to reality and said, "Okay." She instructed Matt to drive a little further. Isabelle pointed to the house. Matt continued past the house and took Isabelle back to Marie's house. He opened the car door for Isabelle and gave her a 'goodbye kiss'. Isabelle said goodbye to Matt and promised herself that she was going to tell her family about him the first chance she got.

Linda Jensen

CHAPTER NINE

Sara could not talk enough about Mark and Heidi's up-coming wedding to her closest friends. Betty was making a bridesmaid dress for her. They made several trips into Lincoln to pick out flowers and decorations. Betty ordered the cake and mints from Carson Bakery in Cleary.

The day finally arrived. Isabelle came downstairs at her house wearing the lavender dress that she liked so well. Maggie chose to wear a blue dress that she got in Omaha when Isabelle got hers.

Red roses and ribbon adorned the Tranquility Lutheran Church pews. Pink carnations surrounded the altar candles. Everyone was ushered into the church as the organist played a hymn. Maggie whispered to Caroline in the pew, "The church is beautiful."

Everyone stood up when Sara came down the aisle. She was gorgeous in the pink tea length gown that Betty had made for her. She was carrying a single red rose with a red ribbon tied to it. Heidi's brother was the best man. He was only thirteen, but stood up at the alter waiting for the ceremony to begin like an adult. Mark stood next to him waiting for his young bride. The organist played the wedding march while the flower girl dropped red flower petals down the aisle before Heidi and her dad walked in.

Heidi's bouquet was full of red roses with a strand of white beads weaved between them. Her white wedding dress was floor length and flared at the waist. Matt beamed with joy when he saw Heidi. Maggie studied his face. She was content when she saw how in love he looked. The young couple exchanges wedding vows before they kissed and faced the guests. They walked arm in arm down the aisle beaming with joy.

Henry and Caroline said their congratulations in the reception line. Isabelle gave Sara a hug and commented on how beautiful she was in her pink gown. She gave Heidi a hug and said, "Heidi, you are so pretty. Congratulations!"

Maggie was right behind Isabelle giving Sara a hug. She approached Mark and Heidi. Maggie extended her hand for Mark, but he decided to give her a hug instead. Maggie was somewhat taken aback by the gesture. When he let go of her he said, "Maggie, you look very pretty today." He gave her a wink and turned towards Heidi saying, "Heidi, this is Maggie Sims. She's been a good friend of mine."

"Yes, I already know Maggie." Heidi gave her a hug. "I agree with Mark. You are very pretty." Maggie left the reception line smiling and feeling a sense of pride. She knew that Mark's words were sincere.

CHAPTER TEN

Henry was sitting in the living room reading the weekly newspaper. Caroline came and sat down in her chair, "Are you thinking about butchering soon? We're just about out of meat in the freezer."

Henry put down his newspaper, "When do you want to butcher?"

"It's already the end of November. I was thinking next month sometime."

We'll have to do it the first two weeks in December; the Cleary meat locker closes the last two weeks in December for the holidays."

"I could ask Janet at the hospital to switch days off with me. I could take off a week that way."

"I'll call the butcher and see if they can schedule us in right after Thanksgiving."

Caroline reluctantly continued, "I really would like to make some sausage and canned meat this year. We haven't had any for a couple years."

"That wouldn't leave much for roasts, steaks, and hamburger."

"Well I was hoping we could butcher two cows."

"When I call the butcher I'll have to ask if they would have time and space for that much."

Caroline was pleased. She went into the basement to count the empty jars. She counted thirty-eight quart jars and fourteen-pint jars. She was sure that would be enough. She came back into the living room with some notepaper and a pen. She listed on the paper that she wanted sixty pounds of beef in a chunk for canned meat; thirty pounds of bulk hamburger for the sausage; sixty pounds of

87

packaged hamburger; and the rest in roasts and steaks. She handed the list to Henry, "Do you think this sounds right?"

Henry looked at her list, "I'll ask the butcher to make a few of the roasts and hamburger into smaller packages for Mom."

"Oh that would be fine. We'll need thirty pounds of ground pork for the sausage too." Caroline added.

Henry jotted down 'pork' on the list and put it in his pocket, "They should have that on hand this time of year."

On Friday, December 1, Henry answered the phone in the kitchen, "Hello?"

"Henry, this is George from the Cleary Locker. Your meat will be ready to be picked up by Monday."

"Okay. Can you keep the bulk hamburger and pork until Thursday? Caroline and I won't be ready for it until then."

"Oh, sure, that's no problem. We will have it ready for you whenever you want it. You mentioned that you are making sausage. Do you need casings?"

"Yeah, I forgot to order them. Do you have them in stock?"

"I figured you would need them, so I took the liberty and placed the order for you."

"Thanks. I'll see you first thing on Monday."

"Sure thing, Mr. Sims. Good-bye."

After the girls left for school on Monday morning, Henry got into his pickup and drove to town to get the meat. Caroline did not even take out time to comb her hair. She slipped an apron over her head and tied it around her waist. Then Caroline went right to work washing the jars and sharpening the meat cleaver.

Henry came into the house carrying a box of meat. Caroline stacked the roasts and steaks to one side of the freezer. Henry carried in the second box containing packages of hamburger. Caroline sorted out some of the smaller packages for Marie. She stacked the hamburger on the other side of the roasts and steaks in the freezer, "How many more boxes are there?" she asked.

Henry came in carrying the third box, "There's just one smaller one. The rest is the two thirty pound beef chunks for canned meat. Will it all fit?"

"I think so. This pile I sorted out is for Marie." Caroline shut the door of the freezer, "When you go to town to give Marie her meat, will you stop at the store and get some canning salt? I won't have enough."

"Do you need anything else?" Henry asked.

"You might as well get a can of pepper, table salt, and garlic powder for the sausage. We're out of bread too."

Henry jotted down the list of what he needed from the store on a piece of paper. He knew after the visit with his mother, he would forget something by then. He brought the beef chunks and laid them on the kitchen table for Caroline to cut up. He carried the small box of beef for Marie out the door and drove back to town.

Caroline went right to work. She cut up the beef into small pieces to fit into the quart jars, but had to wait for Henry to come back with the canning salt to finish them. She was nearly finished with the first chunk of beef when she heard a vehicle come into the yard. Casey was throwing a fit barking, but she did not pay much attention to it, thinking it was Henry coming back. Then she heard a knock at the door. She thought it was Henry needing help opening it. She hollered out, "Coming Henry." With the meat cleaver in her hand, her hair mangled, and blood from the beef all over her apron, Caroline opened the door. She faced a nice looking man in a suit.

The man looked at Caroline, without uttering a single word; he ran back to his car and sped out of the driveway. In his haste, he nearly collided with Henry coming up the lane.

Henry walked up to Caroline carrying his sack from the grocery store, "Who was that?"

"I don't know. When I answered the door, he didn't say anything. He just left."

Henry looked at Caroline and laughed, "Well if I was greeted at the door looking the way you do with that meat cleaver in your hand, I guess I'd run away too."

Caroline looked down at her bloody apron and smiled, "I guess so." She laughed at herself. "I still wonder what he wanted. He was very well dressed."

"Maybe he was selling life insurance." They both laughed at the thought of the man wanting to sell life insurance to a woman looking the way Caroline did with a meat cleaver in her hand dripping with blood.

Henry and Caroline worked together to get the first chunk of beef into the pressure canner. They processed two batches.

Caroline wrapped the second chunk of beef and left it on the porch for the night. They were tired and would can that one the next day.

During supper, they told Isabelle and Maggie about the visitor they had that day. The girls thought it was hilarious. They asked Caroline to repeat the story. They knew that the story would be passed from one generation to the next on how Caroline Sims chased away a life insurance salesman.

The next morning Henry helped Caroline with the second chunk of beef. Caroline was pleased that she was able to get thirty quarts and ten pints of canned meat.

On Wednesday, Henry went to Cleary Locker to get the ground beef, ground pork, and the casings for the sausage. Caroline stayed home and washed out the sausage stuffer. She prepared the casings. When Henry returned, he put half of the beef and half of the pork on the kitchen table. Caroline measured out the salt, pepper, and garlic powder. Together they mixed the spices into the meat. Henry and Caroline's hands were red raw by the time they got the meat mixed. Henry scooped some of the mixture into the sausage maker. Caroline slid the casings over the spout while Henry turned the crank. They worked all day until they had all of the meat made into sausage rings with twisted ends.

When Isabelle and Maggie returned home from school, they helped Henry fill the pit in the smoke house with corncobs from the pile after corn shelling. Caroline helped Henry string the sausage rings on the rods in the smoke house. Henry lit the corncobs on fire in the pit and closed the door. The sausage hung over the rods while being smoked for a couple of days to cure. In the middle of the night, he filled the pit with more corncobs as they burned down. It was a cold night, and Henry could hear the north wind howling.

Henry returned to the house and just rested on the couch so as not to disturb Caroline. He would need to fill the pit again before daylight. He woke up when he heard Casey barking. Casey was making such a racket Henry wondered what his problem was. When he looked out the window, he saw the flames coming out of the smoke house. He yelled at Caroline, "Get up! The smoke house is on fire!" Henry rushed out the door. Caroline hurried to get warm clothes on and headed out of the door too. A blast of frigid north wind greeted her as she wrapped her scarf around her face and hurried out to the smoke house. The smoke house was too far in flames for Henry and Caroline to save it. The chicken coop had started to catch on fire as well. Henry hollered at Caroline, "Call the fire department, we won't get it contained!"

Caroline ran into the house. Isabelle and Maggie were downstairs wondering what all of the commotion was about. Caroline picked up the phone and dialed the number.

"Emergency services."

"This is Henry Sims farm. We need the fire department. We are Homestead number F827."

By the time the fire department came to the farm, the smoke house had burned down and the wall of the chicken coop was partially gone. Caroline was devastated. The fire destroyed the sausage that they worked so hard to process. Casey was able to scrounge around in the burnt mess and found some meat that was edible. He worked at it for a couple of days until Henry cleaned up the remains. Henry felt lucky that the fire department put out the fire before he lost his flock of chickens, too. He rebuilt the end wall of the chicken coop with some old lumber he had laying in the barn.

Henry's parents had made sausage this way for years. Henry never remembered the smoke house ever catching on fire. He did not know what went wrong this time. The fire department determined that the flames started at the north end of the smoke house. The north wind was strong enough to blow the flames toward the south wall of the smoke house and set it on fire. Henry and Caroline did not think they would ever rebuild the smoke house. That part of the family history was gone forever.

CHAPTER ELEVEN

Christmas had arrived. Santa's of all sizes decorated the storefront windows in Cleary. The department store had a life-sized one in their window, with a mechanical arm waving to shoppers passing by. Salvation Army bell ringers were outside the front doors of stores waiting for donations.

The Sunday before Christmas, Tranquility Lutheran Church members planned a get together to go caroling around town with a potluck supper afterwards. Caroline removed her beef casserole from the oven and wrapped a towel around the dish to keep it warm. She put the cake that Isabelle made in the basket along with a jar of pickled beets. Isabelle and Maggie came downstairs with their jeans and heavy coats on. There was snow on the ground and the wind was chilly. Henry came in the house from checking on Casey. He reminded the girls to get their scarves and gloves. Henry loaded the basket of food in the trunk of the car. He waited for his family in the car, before he drove to church.

The church was crowded with carolers when the Sims' family arrived. Sara was wearing a new coat that Isabelle had not seen before. Isabelle complimented Sara on how nice it looked. "Oh, thanks." Sara replied, "I begged Mom for it when we were in Lincoln visiting Mark and Heidi."

"How is Heidi?"

"She's doing okay. She says the baby kicks a lot and wakes her up at night."

"Well, wait until the baby is born. I remember when Gregory would wake up sometimes twice in the middle of the night."

"That would be good for Mark. That'll teach him." Sara said with a wide grin.

Reverend Ahlmann and his wife were serving coffee and hot chocolate. They passed out hymnals while everyone gathered at the door. Caroline, Alice, and Irma stayed behind to watch the younger children. They had games planned for them to play.

The carolers headed down the street singing 'Away in the Manger' as their first song. Everyone could sing it without opening the hymnals. Maggie picked the next song. 'Hark, the Herald Angles Sing'. It was her favorite. Down the street they went, singing one song after another. They went past Marie's house. She was sitting in her rocker in front of the window. The group stopped when she opened her door. She handed a bag of chocolates to Maggie, telling her to share them with the carolers. Everyone thanked her and said their goodbyes singing 'We Three Kings' as they walked away.

By the time they arrived back at the church, the evening air was settling in. The carolers were cold and hungry. Caroline, Alice, and Irma had the tables set up. They were removing the casseroles from the ovens and set out the rest of the food that everyone had brought. Reverend Ahlmann said grace before they sat down to eat.

Joe heard about the fire at the Sims' place. He expressed his sympathy to Henry. Henry made light of the situation and said, "Casey got fat during the ordeal."

George got up from his chair and put a sausage link on Henry's plate. "Here Henry, try this. I made some at the locker. It's not as good as yours and Caroline's though. I can cut you a good deal on some, if you like it."

Henry took a bite off the link, "That's good George. I just might be in to get some."

Henry and Caroline told their story about how Caroline answered the door with a meat cleaver in her hand. They told everybody that she chased off a life insurance salesman. Henry added that his wife saved him money that day. Everybody chuckled at the story.

. . .

Just before the Christmas Eve church service, Caroline came out of the bedroom wearing a dark green suit. She had a Christmas scarf draped around her neck and wore a broach pin on the scarf that matched her earrings. Henry stood and admired her while he helped her with her coat. He smiled at her and bent down to give her a kiss. He released her and whispered, "Merry Christmas." The girls watched their parents from the rear of the kitchen with smiles on their faces.

A light snow was coming down, covering the ground. The Sims climbed into the car except for Maggie. She stood still for a minute and looked up at the yard light. The air was so calm that the snow was falling straight down. She caught a snowflake on her tongue, but it quickly melted. She looked around her and saw how clean the yard looked. Snow was accumulating on the bare branches of the trees. She wished she could just stand there for a while and enjoy the peace. Henry honked the horn to get her attention. It startled her. Then Maggie climbed into the car.

Isabelle was annoyed. "Quit your day dreaming. We're going to be late."

Henry pulled up into Marie's driveway. Marie was already at the door with her coat on when Henry rang the doorbell. "Merry Christmas, Mom." Marie did not hear him. He gripped her arm and said in a loud voice, "Be careful. It's a little slippery."

Maggie slid over closer to Isabelle while Henry helped Marie into the car. Maggie leaned over and gave Marie a kiss on her cheek. "Merry Christmas, Grandma."

Marie answered her by telling everyone, "Merry Christmas."

Vehicles filled the parking lot at Tranquility Lutheran Church. Members of the congregation had extra family attending the service. As more people were coming into the church, the ushers were asking everyone to slide together in the pews to make room. The church was overflowing for the Christmas Eve service. Isabelle turned to look behind her and saw that there were several people standing in the back.

The organist started playing the first hymn. Reverend Ahlmann approached the pulpit during the last verse. He got everyone's attention when he started to speak. Marie was sitting between Henry and Isabelle. It did not take long before she was asleep. Isabelle nudged her once, but Henry shook his head at Isabelle to leave her alone. Isabelle let Marie rest on her shoulder after that.

After the service was over, members of Tranquility Lutheran Church wished each other a blessed Christmas. Marie was overwhelmed with all of the members around her wishing her a Merry Christmas and expressing how nice it was to see her. The

Sims' family was the last to leave the church after speaking to Reverend and Mrs. Ahlmann.

Christmas morning, the girls came down to the kitchen. Caroline had sweet rolls in the oven. She had ham and eggs in a skillet ready to serve. Henry was sipping coffee at the table. It was a tradition to have breakfast before they would go into the living room to open the presents. Maggie tried to peak around the corner into the living room to see how many presents were under the tree, but Caroline had put them out of sight in the corner behind the couch.

After breakfast, the girls cleared the breakfast table and wrapped up the leftover sweet rolls. The family retired to the living room to open presents. The Christmas tree was an artificial aluminum foil tree. There was a colored lamp set on the floor that rotated to make the foil branches change colors. The glass ornaments on the tree would take on the colors as it turned making them even more beautiful. There was a shiny gold star on the top.

The first present was a large box labeled for both Isabelle and Maggie. Maggie tore into it and discovered a record player. Isabelle was so surprised. The girls thanked them for the gift. Caroline got up from her easy chair and disappeared into the bedroom. She came out of it holding two packages. The girls could tell by the shape of the packages that they were records. They wondered what kind of music their mother would have picked out from the record store. Isabelle opened hers first. To her surprise, it was rock and roll music. Maggie's records were the same kind of music. Caroline saw their happy faces and teased them that she was not the old 'fuddy-duddy' they thought she was. The girls laughed and could not wait to play them.

Henry handed Caroline an envelope from his pocket. Caroline took the envelope with a puzzled face. "What is this?" she asked. Inside the envelope was a picture of the dining room set Caroline has been eying in the furniture store. Along with the picture was a note in Henry's handwriting, 'this dining room set is already paid for and it will be delivered on December 28th'. Caroline was at a loss for words. It always put a smile on Henry's face when he surprises his wife.

Caroline gave Henry a watch. There were clothes for the girls in the next packages they opened. When there were no more presents to unwrap, both of the girls picked up the empty boxes and wrapping paper from the floor before they went upstairs to play their records. Henry and Caroline stayed in the living room listening to the music that drifted downstairs from Isabelle and Maggie's record player.

In the evening, they went into Cleary to spend some time with Marie. Marie had a pot of potato soup on the stove when they arrived. Caroline brought the rest of the sweet rolls from breakfast. After the family ate, they sat in the living room and exchanged gifts. Marie opened the top drawer of the buffet in the living room and pulled out two silver wrapped boxes from it. She handed one to each of the girls with a smile on her face. Inside each of the girls' box was a heart necklace and bracelet set. Marie told the girls to make sure they looked inside the lid of their boxes. To their surprise, Marie had taped a ten-dollar bill in the lid for each of them. Maggie exclaimed, "Wow, Grandma. Thank you."

Isabelle thanked her Grandmother too and added how beautiful the jewelry was. She put the bracelet on her wrist.

"Merry Christmas, Isabelle and Maggie," Marie said with a smile.

Caroline handed a wrapped package to Marie for her to open. Marie hesitated before she took it from her saying, "You shouldn't have. You and Henry already gave me beef."

"I know, but this is something special that I thought you could use." Caroline replied.

Marie gingerly opened the package to savor the moment. She carefully pulled the tape to keep the wrapping paper intact. She folded the paper and set it on the floor beside her before she opened the box to see what was inside it. When she opened the box, she saw a mantle clock. "Oh, I need one of these to put on my buffet!" she exclaimed.

Henry got up from the sofa to help Marie take it out of its package. He plugged into the wall and set it to the correct time. He placed the clock on the buffet so that Marie could see it from her rocking chair. "Is that where you want it?" he asked. Marie leaned forward to try to hear what Henry had said. He asked loudly, "How's that?"

Marie nodded and said, "I love it. Thank you."

It was time to go home. The family was getting their coats on. The girls each kissed Marie and said goodnight. Caroline shut off the light in the kitchen before she leaned down to give Marie a hug and a kiss. She tenderly said, "Merry Christmas, Marie." Henry stayed back behind Caroline for a moment. He pierced his eyes on Marie's face and realized how old she looked to him. He could not help wondering if this could possibly be their last Christmas together with her.

That night, the girls played their records until Caroline hollered up the stairs to tell them it was time to shut the record player off and go to bed. Maggie turned down the volume, but Isabelle got up from her bed and shut it off.

Christmas school vacation went by slowly for Isabelle until she received a phone call from Matt. She nearly knocked over the lamp in the living room when Maggie told her who it was. "Hi Matt. How was your Christmas?" Isabelle tried not to sound so anxious.

"It was pretty good. We went to Lincoln on Christmas day to see my grandparents." Matt relaxed as he spoke. "How was yours?"

"We went to Grandma's on Christmas day too."

"Did you get anything exciting for Christmas?"

"We got a record player, jewelry, clothes, and some money. I'll probably spend the money on records."

Matt chuckled, "I got records too. I'll let you borrow them if you'd like." There was silence for a moment. Matt finally said, "I miss not seeing you. I can't wait until we go back to school."

Isabelle did not know how to reply. She had a lump in her throat. She finally managed to say, "I miss you too, Matt."

Matt felt the change in her voice. He figured she was in a room with open ears listening. He thought he should cut the conversation short. "See you then."

"Bye Matt. Thanks for calling." Isabelle pushed the telephone receiver down, but held onto the mouthpiece for some time before she put it back onto its cradle on the wall.

CHAPTER TWELVE

Isabelle approached her parents, "There is a dance at the Cleary High School Friday night. Can Maggie and I go?"

Caroline put down her darning, "Is that the annual Snow Ball dance?"

"Yes."

Henry put his glass of tea down on the end table, "You should call your Grandma. Maybe the two of you can stay in town after school and have supper with her before you go to the dance."

Isabelle dialed Marie's number on the telephone, "Hi Grandma. This is Isabelle." She was practically shouting. "Maggie and I are coming for supper on Friday night. Is that alright?" Marie did not get all that she said so she repeated it. Finally, Marie understood Isabelle and then asked her to bring her a loaf of bread and a quart of milk from the grocery store. Isabelle kept the conversation short and told her grandmother goodbye. After she hung up the telephone, Isabelle told her dad that she was supposed to take Marie some groceries from the grocery store when she went on Friday.

Henry said, "I'll give you some money before you go to school."

. . .

Matt noticed a flyer in the main hall of the school above the water fountain. It read:

Cleary High School
Snow Ball Dance
Friday, January 5th
7:00 p.m. – 10:00 p.m.
Featuring: Harry and his Hoppers

Isabelle bent down and got a drink of water. "Hi Matt."

"Hi." Matt pointed towards the flyer. "Are you planning on going?"

"I was planning on it. Maggie and I are going to Grandma's to eat supper first."

"Well then, I'll see you there." He walked with her to the next class.

. . .

The school bell rang on Friday at 3:30 p.m. Maggie saw Isabelle coming down the hall. She waited for her at the exit door of the school. Maggie reminded Isabelle that they needed to go to the grocery store for Marie.

The girls walked through the bakery aisle of Cleary Grocery Store and picked up a loaf of bread. When they reached the cooler for the quart of milk, Matt was stocking it. Isabelle was disappointed to see him working. "Hi Matt! I thought you could go to the dance tonight."

"Oh I can. Dad's letting me off at six thirty."

She let out a sigh of relief and smiled. "Oh that's good. I was worried that you could not go. I'll see you tonight."

Maggie teased Isabelle about being in 'love'. Isabelle's face turned red and left the aisle so that Matt could not see her. In the car, she scolded Maggie about her rudeness.

Isabelle parked the car in front of Marie's house and took the bag they had in the back seat that contained a change of clothes. Maggie took the sack of groceries and walked with Isabelle to the door. Isabelle knocked on the door, but there was no answer. She pounded on the door again, "I think Grandma's hearing is getting worse."

Marie finally came to the door after Isabelle pounded for the third time. "Hi girls!"

Isabelle gave Marie a kiss on the cheek. "Hi Grandma! I wrapped on the door three times." Marie ignored Isabelle's remark.

Maggie gave her a kiss too and said, "hi Grandma," while she showed her the groceries in the bag from the store.

"Thank you for the bread and milk. I was completely out." Marie was pleased.

Isabelle took off her coat, put the change of clothes on the sofa, and hollered, "Doesn't Louise come by anymore?"

Marie followed Maggie into the kitchen. She took the loaf of bread out of the paper sack and put it in the metal breadbox. "She doesn't venture out when it's cold. I made some beef stew for supper."

Isabelle came into the kitchen and took a big whiff, "Mm! It smells good. I'm hungry." She went to the cupboard and took out three bowls, "The school lunch wasn't very good today. They served spaghetti, but by the time we got it the spaghetti was pasty."

Marie sat on a kitchen chair and let the girls set the table. "Did you say the spaghetti was nasty?"

Isabelle glanced at Maggie, "Yes Grandma, it was nasty."

Marie ate part of her stew and pushed the bowl away. Isabelle asked Marie if she was feeling all right. Marie assured her she was fine, just not feeling hungry. The girls cleared the table. They washed the dishes and put them away. Isabelle got out the broom and dustpan from the closet. She swept Marie's kitchen floor. She talked loudly, "Is there anything else we could do for you?"

Marie shook her head, "No, but I thank you for sweeping and doing the dishes."

Maggie was in the living room straightening the bookshelf. "Grandma, do you read anymore?"

Marie came nearer to her and leaned her head toward Maggie, "What Maggie?"

Isabelle came from the kitchen, "Maggie you'll have to talk louder. She can't hear you."

Maggie repeated loudly, "Grandma, do you read anymore?"

Marie stepped back, "Not much." Maggie wondered what she did to fill up her days. "Reverend Ahlmann and Louise come by and visits." Marie stated, sensing that Maggie might be worried about her being lonely.

Isabelle took the bag off the sofa and shouted, "Grandma, can we use your bedroom to change our clothes?"

Marie nodded her head, "Yes, that's okay."

Isabelle and Maggie went into the bedroom to get ready for the dance. Maggie shut the door behind her, "I wonder how Grandma keeps busy if she doesn't even read anymore."

Isabelle checked herself in the mirror. She applied some lipstick to her lips and combed her hair. "I wonder that too. She's not eating much either."

The girls returned to the living room. Marie was sitting in her rocker looking out the window. The girls stood a distance away and watched her. Marie seemed to be in a daze just rocking back and forth. She did not hear the girls come into the living room. Maggie put her hand on Marie's shoulders to let her know that they were there. It startled her. She turned to look at the two girls. "You both look nice."

Isabelle gave Marie a kiss on the cheek, "Thank you for supper Grandma. We are going now, okay. There's a dance at school."

Marie stayed in her rocker, "I hope you have a good time." Marie said. Maggie bent down to give Marie a kiss. Marie added, "Good bye. Thanks for visiting me." She turned her head to look back out of the window and started rocking again.

The girls left Marie's house. As Isabelle opened the car door she said, "I think Grandma spends her days staring out that window."

Maggie looked back and could see that Marie was still rocking in the rocking chair. "I bet you're right."

There was a light snow coming down and the darkness of the evening was settling in. Isabelle started the car, "Dad didn't say anything about the weather changing."

Cars filled the parking lot at Cleary High School. Isabelle parked the car near the flagpole and the girls dashed into the school gymnasium for the dance. Matt was in the lobby waiting for Isabelle. He helped her with her coat, "Hi. I was hoping you would still come. I was concerned about the snow."

"I didn't know it was supposed to snow. Matt, this is my sister, Maggie," she said while straightening her dress and fluffing her hair.

Matt took Maggie's coat and hung it up for her too while saying, "Hello."

"Hi." Maggie replied. She faced Isabelle, "I'll see you guys later." She took off to find her friends from the freshman class. Maggie searched for Susan, but she could not find her. She came up to a classmate, "Hi Megan. Have you seen Susan?"

"No." Megan replied. "I wonder if she's not coming." The band was playing a twist. "The band is good, don't you think?" Two boys approached the two girls and asked them to dance. The girls agreed. The four of them took off for the dance floor.

Matt and Isabelle sat on the bottom of the bleachers and waited for the band to play a slow song. Matt spotted Maggie dancing. He leaned over towards Isabelle, "I think Maggie is having a good time."

"She was looking forward to this dance. It is her first one. We didn't have any music in the country school. I told her she would have a good time."

Jim and Sara walked up to Matt and Isabelle. Sara did the twist in front of them saying, "Hi guys. What are you sitting here for? It's time to shake."

Matt laughed at her and replied, "We're waiting for a slower song, but you guys go ahead. We'll watch you shake," he teased. Jim and Sara went out on the dance floor.

The bandleader got on the microphone to announce that the next song will be the snowball dance. He asked two seniors to volunteer to lead the dance. Jim and Sara raised their hands. The rest of the dancers left the gymnasium floor as the band started playing another song. A few moments later, he announced for them to split off and find partners. Jim and Sara immediately went to get Matt and Isabelle. Partway through the song, the bandleader announced again, "Change partners." Matt took Maggie out on the dance floor. Isabelle took the boy that Maggie was dancing with earlier. It only took two songs of the Snow Ball Dance before there was no one sitting on the bleachers.

Everyone stayed on the dance floor for the following song. Matt found Isabelle again and they danced the slow song they were waiting for. When the song ended, he led her out into the lobby. He leaned over and gave her a quick kiss. Isabelle immediately looked around to see if anyone was watching. She protested, "Matt. Principal Jackson is keeping his eyes on everybody."

"That's why I made it just a quick one," he teased. "What are you doing next Saturday night?"

"I'm not sure."

"Does that mean you can't go out?" Matt was disappointed to be turned down.

"Well, not necessarily."

"It's a date then?"

"I'm sure it'll be okay." Isabelle hated it that she always had to ask her parents if she could go out. She just did not know how to handle that. Matt and Isabelle went back into the gymnasium. Isabelle found Sara and whispered, "Come to the restroom with me."

Sara flirtatiously rotated her body so her skirt would flare out. She giggled and said, "Excuse us boys."

Sara was primping herself in the mirror in the bathroom, "What's up?"

"Matt just asked me out next Saturday night."

"He really likes you Isabelle. Jim told me so. Did you say yes?"

"I told him I thought it would be okay. I hate that I feel I have to ask my parents. How do you get around that?"

Sara smacked her lips together as if she was kissing her image in the mirror. "I'll accept the date, and then I tell my parents that I am going out."

"Does that work?"

"Yeah it does. Although, they do ask who I'm going out with."

"What if they say you can't?"

"I don't know. It has never happened. I suppose they know everyone I've been out with."

"But my parents have never met Matt."

"Well, when he shows up at your house you can introduce him." She turned and left the restroom. Isabelle followed her out and thought about how Sara handled the dating scene. She made up her mind that it was time Matt met her parents.

The girls returned to the gymnasium. The boys were talking to some of the other football players. Matt and Jim left the crowd to dance with Isabelle and Sara.

Principal Jackson announced on the microphone, "We are going to need to cut the evening short." The crowd moaned at his announcement. He continued, "The snow is coming down pretty heavily. I want everyone to get home safely."

Matt helped Isabelle with her coat, "I'm going to follow you home."

"That's not necessary." Isabelle protested. "I'll be fine."

"Just the same I still want to follow you."

Maggie put on her coat and followed Matt and Isabelle out to the parking lot. Large flakes of snow were coming down and accumulating on the windshield. Matt brushed it off with the sleeve of his jacket. "Really Matt, I'll be okay." Isabelle reassured him.

"I won't take no for an answer. It's going to be worse out in the country." He said sternly.

Isabelle was impressed at Matt's concern. She pulled out of the parking lot to go home with Matt following behind her. He was right about the weather being worse outside of town. The wind was blowing the snow around and it was hard for Isabelle to see. She drove cautiously; an eighteen-year-old was not experienced in driving in this kind of weather. She was relieved when she reached the familiar lane with Matt following her into the yard. After Isabelle and Maggie got out of the car, Isabelle went up to Matt, "You were right. It was hard to see the road in the country. Thank you for following me."

Maggie yelled out at Matt, "Goodnight," Then she went into the house.

Henry was in the kitchen waiting for the girls to come home. "I didn't realize the weather was going to be this bad."

Maggie took off her coat, "I know. It was hard for Isabelle to see."

"Where is she? And who followed her home?"

"Matt Carson followed us home to make sure we got here okay. He's out there saying good-bye."

"You can invite him in to warm up." Henry could see that his daughter had become fond of this boy and he wanted to meet him.

Just then, Matt and Isabelle came up the cement steps. Matt kissed Isabelle. "Matt do you want to come inside to say hello?" she asked.

"Okay. I would like to warm up anyway before I head back to town."

Isabelle and Matt came into the kitchen. Henry extended his hand, "Hello I'm Henry."

"Hello Sir. I'm glad to meet you."

Caroline entered the kitchen, "Hello. I'm Caroline." She extended her hand for Matt. "I was worried about Isabelle on the road in such weather." She turned towards Isabelle, "We called Grandma. We thought you would just go there and stay the night."

"The snow didn't look so bad when we left the school."

Caroline hugged her daughter, "Well we're glad you're home. Matt, we are thankful for you to see that the girls got home okay."

Matt answered, "You're welcome."

105

Henry looked out the window, "Looks like the snow is really coming down. You are welcome to stay here until morning."

Matt zipped up his jacket, "No, I'll be okay, but thanks for the offer."

Henry shook Matt's hand again, "You drive careful and I appreciate you following Isabelle home."

"You're welcome Sir. Good-bye." Matt winked at Isabelle and left the house. He drove out of the lane and noticed the snow was already drifting. It was more difficult for Matt to see out of the windshield than before. He cautiously turned onto the county road. The windshield wipers were having a hard time keeping the windshield clean for Matt to see through it. He leaned forward as if that would help him see through the snow. Matt was hoping that the highway would be better. He stopped at the intersection of the county road and the highway. He saw that the highway was snow packed. Matt could not see very far, but took the chance that no other vehicles were coming as he merged onto the highway. The car skidded. He tried to straighten the car out, but it was too far over. The car slid into the ditch and rolled onto its side. Matt slammed into the door and smacked his head on the side window. He was stunned for a moment. Matt shut off the car engine. When he lifted his hand to his aching head, he felt something moist. He realized that it was blood streaming down his face. He laid there for a while until he started to shiver from the cold. Matt thought he could get out of the car and walk to town. His body ached from the crash and his head hurt. He maneuvered out from behind the steering wheel and climbed up to try to get the passenger door open. It took all of his strength, but he could not push it open far enough to get through it. His head was aching. He put his head in his hands and rested before he tried it again. This time he pushed the door open with his feet, but he wondered how he was going to keep it open while he climbed up to get out of it. He let go of the door with his feet. Gravity slammed the door down shut. Matt searched the car for anything that he could use as a wedge. He remembered there was a shovel in the trunk, but realized that would not do him any good. He knew he had nothing in the car. By this time his head was pounding. Again, he put his head in his hands, laid back against the door, and rested. When Matt opened his eyes and looked up at the passenger door above him, he saw the window crank and smiled at his own ignorance. Matt rolled down the window and climbed out of the car onto the highway. He wished he were dressed for winter conditions, as he needed boots instead of his dress shoes, and the wind cut through his dress slacks as if he was naked. Feeling confused and disoriented, Matt looked left, then right, and could not remember which way he needed to go. His head was pounding with pain. He decided to walk right hoping he was going in the correct direction towards Cleary.

The wind was blowing the snow in Matt's face. He put his head down and walked, using the highway as a guide. He lifted his head and peered through the snow to see if he was getting closer to town, but he could not see much of anything through the blowing snow. Matt put his head down again and kept walking. Again, he lifted his head to see how far he had gone. The snow seemed to be coming down harder and the wind was stronger. He searched for a farmhouse he could go to get some help, but he could only see a few feet in front of him. The pain in his head was excruciating. He did not know how much longer he would be able to walk. He thought if only the snow would let up enough for him to see something through it. With his hands on his head, he walked faster.

Matt looked up and saw a curve in the highway. It dawned on him that the highway curved as you were going out of Cleary. He was going in the wrong direction. He stopped and turned around to walk back. Matt was cold and his legs were almost numb. Ignoring the pain in his head, he put his hands in his pockets. It was easier to walk with the wind on his back.

Matt saw something in the ditch ahead, but he could not quite make out what it was. As he came closer to it, he realized that it was his own car. He just went past it and kept walking. He lifted his head again and saw a faint light in the distance. He was not sure, but he thought it was a vehicle coming towards him. When the vehicle came closer to him, Matt put up his hand to flag the car down. The car pulled over onto the shoulder of the highway. Matt saw the logo on the car that read, 'County Patrol'. Matt said aloud to himself, "Thank you Lord".

The officer in the car rolled down his window, "What are you doing out here walking in weather like this?" He scolded, as he shined his flashlight on Matt. He saw blood frozen to his face. "Son you're hurt."

Matt could not say anything. Suddenly he did not feel anything either. He collapsed and fell to the ground. The officer got out of his patrol car, picked Matt up off the highway, and put him in the back seat. The officer returned to the front seat and radioed into the county Sherriff's office, "This is Officer Downs. I picked up a young man. Please notify the hospital that I will be bringing him in."

Officer Downs drove to the next intersection and turned the car around. He headed for Cleary General Hospital.

. . .

Matt's dad, Alfred Carson, dialed the telephone, "Is this Jim Perry?"

"Yes, this is Jim Perry."

"This is Alfred Carson. Matt has not come home yet. I was wondering if he was with you."

"No the dance ended hours ago because of the weather. You say he's not home yet?"

"No!"

"Well the last thing I knew, he was going to follow Isabelle and Maggie Sims home."

"Where does she live?"

"She lives about six miles out of town. Maybe Matt is there waiting out the weather."

"Do you have her phone number?"

"No, I don't. I can call Sara Parker. She would know what it is."

"Well, I can get the phone number from information. What's her dad's name?"

"Henry."

"Okay, thanks." Alfred hung up and called information to get the phone number for Henry Sims. Alfred thanked the operator and immediately dialed the number.

"Hello."

"Is this Henry Sims?"

"Yes it is. Can I help you?"

"This is Alfred Carson, Matt Carson's dad. We're wondering if Matt is at your house."

"No, he left here nearly an hour ago. Hasn't he come home yet?"

"No! Something must be wrong."

"Oh my, I thought he should have stayed here until morning."

"I'm going out to look for him. Which roads would he be taking to get back to town?"

"You take the highway three miles east then south on F road. We live three and a half miles south. I will get into my pickup and look for him too. I couldn't see what he is driving in the dark."

"He drives a white 1952 Ford with a black stripe on the side. Thanks Henry. I'll head out too."

Caroline was standing in the doorway of the kitchen, "Who was that?"

Henry was putting on his coat, "That was Alfred Carson. Matt didn't get home yet."

Isabelle heard the phone ring and came downstairs, "What's going on?"

Henry knew that Isabelle heard what he told Caroline, "I'm going out to help find Matt."

"What happened?" Isabelle said in a panic.

Henry tried to calm Isabelle, "We don't know anything. He just hasn't come home yet." Henry walked out into the porch and put on his overshoes.

Caroline followed him, "You be careful out there."

Henry drove his pickup out of the lane through the snowdrifts. The county road going north was not bad to drive on, but he was worried about the highway going east and west. It had been snowing for several hours and the drifts were piling up. Henry pulled out onto the highway. He went through a snowdrift and saw something in the ditch. He eased up to it and saw the overturned car. Henry stopped the pickup and got out to investigate the car. He saw that it was a white Ford car with a black stripe on its side. He yelled, "Matt?" There was no answer. He noticed that the front side window was open. Henry was not sure, if Matt was able to escape the crash on his own, or if someone came to his aid. Either way, Matt was not at the scene. Henry saw a vehicle coming down the highway from the west. The car stopped.

Alfred pulled off the road and ran out to the car. "Matt?" He yelled.

"He's not in the car. He must have gotten some help." Henry said.

"Are you Henry Sims?"

"Yes."

Alfred scanned the countryside, "There aren't any houses close by."

"If he tried to walk back to town, Art Canter's place is up the road about a half a mile. Maybe he went there for help."

"I came from that direction. There is a big drift right there because of the trees. I barely got through it."

"My pickup might sit up higher. I think we could get through the drifts easier." Alfred agreed with Henry and the two men got into Henry's pickup.

Henry pulled into Art's yard and walked up to the door of the farmhouse. Art opened the door and was surprised to see Henry. "Henry what are you doing out here in such weather?"

"Hi Art. We are looking for an eighteen-year-old boy. His name is Matt Carson. He had an accident about a half a mile from here. We thought he might have walked to your place for help."

"Um no, nobody came here. How long ago?"

"It's been an hour by now."

Henry turned towards Alfred, "Let's go into town. Maybe he got home."

"Thanks Art."

"I hope the boy is okay. I wish you luck. Drive careful." Art said and shut the door.

Henry and Alfred drove back onto the highway. The snow let up and it was easier to see. They got to the edge of town. Alfred pointed, "You can turn left here and go three blocks then turn right. We live in the second house."

Just as soon as Henry parked the pickup in front of the house, Bonnie Carson came running out panicking, "Cleary General called and said that Matt is in the hospital." Alfred informed Bonnie that he saw Matt's car in the ditch. Bonnie climbed into the pickup and slid over for Alfred. Henry drove as fast as he could to the hospital.

Bonnie and Alfred ran into the hospital and asked a nurse, "Where is Matt Carson? We are Matt's parents." Henry stayed back and waited in the lobby while the nurse led Bonnie and Alfred down the hall. Matt was lying on a bed in one of the rooms. He was wrapped in blankets and sleeping sound.

Doctor Parker came out of the room, "Matt will be okay. He has a deep abrasion above his left eye. I stitched it up and gave him a sedative to calm him down."

Bonnie looked scared. "What do mean, you had to calm him down?'

"Officer Downs found Matt walking back to town. Matt flagged him down, but then he passed out on the highway. Officer Downs brought Matt into the hospital. When Matt woke up, he did not know where he was. He was rather distraught."

Alfred asked, "Does he have any broken bones?"

"I checked him over. The only thing I could see was the abrasion. I treated him for a slight concussion."

Bonnie gasped. "Can we see him?"

"Yes, but he is sleeping."

The doctor led Alfred and Bonnie into the room where Matt was sleeping. Bonnie gasped again when she saw the bandage on her son's face.

Doctor Parker saw her worried look and said, "I put four stitches above his eye. I want to keep him overnight and see how he acts when he wakes up."

Alfred embraced Bonnie and asked the doctor, "Do you want us to stay here?"

"That's up to you. The waiting room chairs are not very comfortable. If you do not want to stay here, the nurse can call you at home as soon as he wakes up. He shouldn't wake up for the rest of the night."

Alfred turned to Bonnie, "I think we should go home and get some rest ourselves. Henry needs to get home too." Bonnie had a hard time leaving her son in the hospital, but she agreed. They joined Henry in the waiting room.

Henry looked concerned. "How is Matt?"

Alfred answered, "He has a cut above his eye. The doctor stitched it up."

"How did he get to the hospital?"

"Officer Downs found him walking on the highway. He said Matt flagged him down. Then he passed out."

"I'll take you guys back to your house to get some rest."

Alfred looked at his pickup, "You're not going to try to drive back to your house in this weather are you?"

"No, my mom lives in town I'll stay with her until morning."

"I feel better knowing that," Alfred said.

Henry drove Alfred and Bonnie back to their house. Before Alfred closed the door of the pickup, he said, "Good night Henry. I deeply thank you for your help tonight. I'll call the sheriff's office and tell them that my car is on the side of the road and Matt's car is in the ditch."

Henry looked at Bonnie. He knew that she would not sleep much until she could see her son again. "You're welcome Mr. Carson. Goodnight to you both." Henry parked his pickup in front of Marie's house. He went to the back of the house and quietly opened the back door. He did not bother to wake Marie. He dialed the telephone to call Caroline.

"Hello?"

"Caroline, this is Henry. I am at mom's house. I'll spend the night here."

"How is Matt? Isabelle is standing right here. She says she wouldn't go back to bed until she heard something about him."

"Matt went into the ditch with his car. He rolled the car on its side." He heard Caroline gasp. Henry continued, "Matt crawled out of the car and tried to walk to town. The county patrol picked him up and took him to the hospital."

"Was he hurt?"

"Well, Matt has a deep cut on the side of his face above his eye. Doc Parker sewed it up. They're keeping him in the hospital overnight."

Caroline moved the phone away from her ear and told Isabelle that it was Henry on the phone. She handed the phone to Isabelle, "Dad, is Matt okay?"

"Yes honey he's okay. Doc Parker will take good care of him."

"What happened to him?"

"He had an accident on the highway, but he's okay Isabelle."

Isabelle was holding back tears. Her voice cracked while she said, okay." She handed the phone back to Caroline and went upstairs.

"Henry, it's Caroline, Isabelle was pretty anxious to hear about Matt. She went back upstairs. We'll see you in the morning."

"Okay. Goodnight." Henry hung up the phone and walked back to the spare bedroom to get some sleep.

The next morning Marie walked out of her bedroom. She was startled to find Henry in her kitchen making coffee. "Henry, what are you doing here?"

"Hi Mom!" Henry said. He told her the story about the night before. He had to retell the story to her because she misunderstood. She thought Henry said Isabelle crashed her car. Marie fixed some eggs and made some toast with the bread that Isabelle and Maggie brought her the night before. They ate breakfast together.

Henry lifted himself off the chair in the kitchen and put his empty plate in the sink. He looked out the window and saw that the snow had stopped. "Mom, thanks for breakfast. I am going to see if I can get home. The snow plows should have been out by now." He bent down and gave her a kiss on the cheek.

"Bye Henry. You drive careful." Marie sat in her rocking chair and saw Henry reach into the back of his pickup and get a shovel. He cleared the snow from Marie's step and sidewalk, but he did not stop there. Henry cleared Louise's sidewalk and stoop before he headed out of town. Marie smiled and thought to herself, 'what a wonderful son she has'.

Henry saw that the snowplows had already been through on the roads. Henry drove past Alfred's car and noticed that the snowplow partially buried it. He approached Matt's car in the ditch. Henry wondered how they would ever get his car out of the ditch, and how much damage it had. He drove past his car too and turned onto F road to go home.

Isabelle came downstairs and dialed the Carson's phone number. There was no answer. Caroline came into the kitchen as Isabelle was hanging up the telephone, "I just tried Matt's number, but no one answered."

"Matt's parents are probably at the hospital."

Henry pulled into the lane. Isabelle ran out of the house asking, "Dad, can you take me to the hospital to see Matt?"

"We better wait until we talk to his parents first." He hated to disappoint her, but he thought it was best to wait until they knew more about Matt.

Isabelle realized that her dad was right. She would have to wait until she received a phone call from Matt. She went into the house and called Sara. "Hi Sara. This is Isabelle. Matt had an accident last night."

"Is he alright?" Sara asked.

Isabelle replied, "I don't know much. Dad said that Matt had a cut by his eye."

"Jim called me last night. He said Matt's dad called him wanting your phone number. He was looking for him. He thought he was with you."

"No, after he followed Maggie and I home, he went back to town. What did your dad say about Matt when he came home from the hospital?"

"I don't know anything. Dad didn't come home from the hospital last night. What happened?"

Isabelle told her everything she knew and ended the conversation with, "I have Matt's phone number. I'll call later when I know more details."

"Call me back Isabelle."

"I will. Bye."

Isabelle's day was agonizing. She could not stand it. She tried Matt's phone number again, but there was no answer. After she ate dinner, Isabelle tried Matt's number again. There still was no answer. She was getting more worried as the day went on.

Just before supper, the phone rang. Isabelle wasted no time answering the phone. "Hello?"

A voice on the other end said, "Isabelle, this is Matt."

Isabelle had a tear coming down her cheek, "Oh Matt. Are you okay?" She was hoping Matt could not tell by her voice that she was crying.

"Yes, I'm home."

"What happened to you?"

He told her how he ended up in the ditch and that his car rolled. He told her he did not remember anything after that. He said the next thing he knew he was laying in the hospital.

"Oh Matt, thank heavens you're alright."

"Apparently the county patrol picked me up and took me to the hospital. I sure don't remember that. I don't have any broken bones, but I have a good cut above my left eye. Doc stitched it up." There was a pause. He was waiting for Isabelle to say something. He

114

continued, "I should have taken up your dad's offer and stayed the night at your house. I thought I could get back to town."

Isabelle was in tears, her voice cracked as she talked. "My dad went out to look for you when your dad called here."

Matt sensed that she was crying, "That's what my dad said. That was extremely nice of him to be so concerned. I want to thank him."

Isabelle could not compose herself. She managed to say, "Goodbye Matt. Take care of yourself. I'll see you in school."

"Okay Isabelle. Bye." Matt hung up the phone.

Caroline saw that her daughter was crying, but she decided to say nothing to embarrass her. Isabelle went upstairs, buried her face in her pillow, and wept. She did not understand why she felt this way. She has only known Matt for five months. She stayed upstairs until Caroline hollered up to say that supper was ready.

. . .

Isabelle and Maggie came downstairs for some breakfast. Henry and Caroline were already finished with their breakfast. They let the girls sleep and decided not to go to church. Isabelle was afraid to call Matt on Sunday, especially after the way she acted on the phone to him the day before. Matt did not understand why Isabelle did not call him, but he did not call her either.

Alfred dialed the phone number for Charlie Weber.

"Hello, Charlie speaking."

"This is Alfred Carson. I'm sorry to bother you on a Sunday Mr. Weber, but I need a tow truck."

"Oh that's fine. That is why I am here. What do you need towed?"

"My son's car is in the ditch three miles west of town on Highway 12."

"I know that the snowplows have been already through. They probably buried his car. I will throw in an extra chain. Do you need me to pick you up on my way out?"

"That would be great. I live at 210 Kennedy Avenue."

"It'll take a few minutes."

"Okay, I'll be watching for you."

Alfred rapped on Matt's bedroom door, "Do you feel up to going with me to get your car?"

"Yeah, I'll go." Matt put on his coat and boots. "Who did you call for help?"

"I called Charlie Weber."

Alfred and Matt watched out the window for the tow truck to arrive just as Charlie pulled up to the curb and honked the horn. Matt opened the door of the truck and climbed in first. Alfred climbed in next to Matt. Charlie saw the bandage on the side of Mat's face, "Son, what happened to you?"

"I had an accident last night. My car is in the ditch."

Alfred explained to him what happened with Matt's car. He also explained that his car was still on the side of the road too. He was sure the snowplow buried both of them. Charlie came closer to the cars. "Oh wow son," he exclaimed. "Looks like you were lucky you didn't get hurt more than you did."

Matt defended his driving, "Well I wasn't going that fast. The highway was snow packed. I couldn't get the car straightened out when it started to slide into the ditch."

Charlie pulled the tow truck alongside of Alfred's car. "We'll get your car out first to get it out of the way. Then we can work on your son's car."

Matt looked at his car in shock. He leaned over to Alfred, "Dad, I don't remember any of this. All I remember is the highway being snow packed. It's frightening."

Alfred touched his son's shoulder, "I'm just glad you're alright. It could have been much worse."

All three men got out of the tow truck. Matt climbed through the snow to see if he could get into Alfred's car to steer it. The snow was too deep in front of the driver's door. He climbed through the snow to the other side of the car. Matt positioned himself in front of the steering wheel waiting for Charlie to hook up the car and pull him out.

Charlie pulled the chains out of the back end of the tow truck and attached them to Alfred's car. He told Alfred, "When I get the chain tight, motion to your son to crank the wheel towards the highway."

Alfred saw a truck come towards them. "You better wait until that truck passes." He saw that the truck coming down the highway was Henry Sims.

Charlie rolled down the window of the tow truck. Henry stopped and walked up to the tow truck, "Hi Charlie. I was just going to get Alfred and see if he needed help."

"Well I don't think it will take much to get Alfred's car out, but I don't know about his son's car."

"I'll stand by and help." Henry walked up to where Alfred was standing.

"Good afternoon Alfred. How is Matt doing today?"

"He seems alright. Thanks for coming by to help. How did you know we were out here?"

"I called your house to see if you needed help getting your cars. Bonnie said that was what you were doing."

"Thanks for your concern Henry."

Just then, Charlie pulled the tow truck until the chain pulled tight. Alfred ran to the car and motioned for Matt to crank the wheel towards the highway. The tow truck pulled Alfred's car out with ease.

Henry yelled, "Charlie, that's good! The car is out."

Charlie backed the tow truck slightly to let the chain slack. Then he unhooked it. Matt drove the car onto F road. He parked in on the side of the road.

Charlie backed the tow truck up to Matt's car. He got out of his tow truck and joined the other three men on the side of the highway. The four men stood back to analyze the situation. Charlie said, "The first thing we'll have to do is tip the car back onto the bank of the ditch. Then I can hook the chain to the front of the car. One of you needs to climb into the car and steer it."

Alfred was concerned, "Won't the car roll back over?"

"I will take it slow." Charlie looked at the highway to judge the width of it. "I think the highway is wide enough. I will use the shorter chain. Two of you could help push it once we get it started up and out of the ditch."

Matt started to climb into the car through the open window. Alfred stopped him and asked if he was positive, he wanted to steer the car out of the ditch. "Dad, I'll be fine," he said as he climbed into the car. He had to use his hands to scoop the snow out from behind the steering wheel in order for him to get behind it. When he settled himself behind the steering wheel, he saw the crack on the window where his head smacked it. He just could not believe that he lost all recollection of everything after that. His hands were sweating though his gloves as he took the steering wheel. His nerves started to get the best of him as he gripped the steering wheel tight and closed his eyes.

Charlie hooked the chain onto Matt's car. He put the tow truck in gear and slowly pulled forward until he felt the chain tighten. He yelled out the window, "Is everything still okay?"

Alfred hollered back, "Yeah, just pull it ahead slowly."

Charlie stepped on the gas of the tow truck and inched forward. Matt's car slid further down the ditch. Matt's hands gripped the steering wheel so tight that they started to hurt.

Henry yelled, "Stop!"

Charlie put on the breaks of the tow truck. He got out looking at the situation. "I don't know guys. I don't think we are going to get the car out this way. The ditch is too deep. I'll have to hook up the tow and winch it out."

Matt climbed back out of the window of the car. "What's he going to do?"

Alfred answered, "He's going to winch it out."

Charlie set up the winch and said, "You guys make sure the car stays on its wheels while the winch does its job. If you see the car going back over on the side give me a holler." Charlie pushed the crank to winch out Matt's car. The winch took nearly a half of an hour before the car was out of the ditch.

When Charlie had the car onto the highway, they saw the damage to the car. Alfred eyed the driver's door of the car. "I bet that door won't open without prying it with a crowbar."

"The inside of the car is full of snow." Matt informed his dad.

Charlie put the tow truck in neutral and joined the three men. "I'll go on and tow it to town. We can deal with it tomorrow."

Alfred shook his hand, "Thanks Charlie."

Matt extended his hand to Henry, "Thank you Mr. Sims." He was wondering about Isabelle's reaction towards him on the telephone. "How is Isabelle?" he asked.

"She is better today." Caroline told Henry how Isabelle reacted on the phone with Matt. Without going into any detail, he went on to say, "She was worried about you."

"I could tell. Tell her for me that I'm fine and that I'll talk to her in school tomorrow."

"I'll sure do that." Henry walked back to his pickup thinking that Matt was as nice a boy as anyone that Isabelle could have chosen for a boyfriend.

. . .

On Monday, Isabelle walked down the hall and saw Matt in the middle of a crowd telling everyone his story. She saw the stitches above Matt's eye. Matt noticed her watching him and broke from the crowd. "Good morning Isabelle."

Isabelle looked sheepishly at Matt, "Good morning. How does your head feel?"

"I'll be alright. I gave the school nurse the pain prescription from the doctor. I can ask for it if I have any pain. "She looked into his eyes. "I am so sorry for cutting you off on the phone."

"You said nothing wrong."

"It was rude of me. I apologize."

He looked into her eyes. "Apology accepted. I was thinking I still want that date."

Isabelle smiled and looked right into his eyes and said, "So do I."

They walked together to the next class.

CHAPTER THIRTEEN

January in Nebraska was brutal. Snow seemed to fall every other day. At night, temperatures fell to the zero mark on the thermometers.

Friday night snow started to fall and snowed all day on Saturday. Cleary County was again at a standstill. Henry came into the house and sat down at the breakfast table, "If this keeps up I don't think you'll have school on Monday. The snow is getting deep. We must have nearly ten inches already."

Caroline put the plate of eggs and toast on the table, "It's a good thing I don't work until Tuesday this week."

The school officials cancelled school on Monday. On Tuesday, Henry did not let Isabelle drive to school because of the possible bad road conditions. He drove the girls to school instead.

Maggie found Susan in the school hall. "What did you do yesterday?"

"The boys and I played games. How about you, what did you do?"

Maggie pulled her books out of her locker, "Oh, I just hung out listening to records and read one of my books. Isabelle messed with her hair and tried some new makeup."

The two girls went to Susan's locker. She picked out the books she needed, "Your birthday is Sunday, right?" The two girls walked into their first class.

"Yeah," Maggie said and sat down at her desk.

Susan sat in the desk in front of Maggie and turned whispering, "We have an awesome hill at our house for sledding. Can you stay over this weekend for your birthday?"

"Oh that would be fun," Maggie whispered back. "I don't think dad will let Isabelle drive me to your house though, because of the snow."

"Can you come on Friday after school? My mom picks me up then."

"I'll have to ask if I can stay that long."

Mrs. Reed tapped a ruler on Maggie's desk to hush the girls.

After supper, Maggie approached her parents. "Susan Johnson has invited me over for the weekend for my birthday. Can I go?"

Henry asked, "How are you getting there? I think they live about ten miles west of town."

Maggie said enthusiastically, "I'll go with Susan when her mom picks her up after school on Friday."

Caroline said, "Is it alright with her parents that you stay until Monday?"

"Susan said it was okay." Maggie reached into her pocket and pulled out a piece of paper. She handed it to her mother. "Here is Susan's phone number. Her mom's name is Margaret. Susan said you could call her."

Caroline took the paper from Maggie, "I'll call her tomorrow. It's getting too late tonight."

Henry added to the conversation, "As long as you don't overstay your welcome."

Thursday night Isabelle helped Maggie pack some clothes for Susan's house. Caroline hollered upstairs for the girls to come down. When Maggie came into the living room, she saw a package on the sofa. "Is that for me?" She asked, even though she knew it was. Maggie opened the package and found a transistor radio, batteries, and a book in it.

"Happy Birthday," Caroline said and gave her a hug.

"Gee thanks!" She put the batteries in the radio and turned it to a rock and roll station. "I've wanted one of these for a long time." Isabelle smiled. Maggie realized that Isabelle tipped her parents about her wanting a transistor radio.

Friday morning Henry drove the girls to school, while Maggie held her clothes on her lap for the weekend. She was anxious about staying at Susan's house. Henry parked the pickup and waited in the school parking lot until Margaret Johnson came. Maggie pointed to the Johnson's car, "There she is."

Henry greeted her, "Hello. I am Henry Sims. I know your husband Fred."

Margaret extended her hand for a handshake, "Hello I'm Margaret. I'm glad to meet you."

Henry turned towards his daughter and said, "You have a nice time, but stay out of trouble."

"Oh, Dad," Maggie replied. The three girls entered the school.

All day, Maggie and Susan were watching the clock. To them it seemed like an eternity for school to let out. When the bell finally rang, they both bolted out the door to find Margaret.

Margaret drove up the long lane. Maggie could see their house at the top of the hill. Susan pointed out the left window, "That's the hill we sled down."

Maggie looked at the direction where Susan was pointing, "Oh. That looks like fun!"

Margaret parked the car in front of the house, "Tomorrow will be the first warm day we've had for a week. The weatherman said the temperatures could reach into the 40's."

Susan led Maggie upstairs to her bedroom. She explained that the bedroom on the other side was Scott and Nate's room. Susan told Maggie that Scott and Nate had not been back from their school yet. Her dad, Fred, would pick up the boys from their country school. Susan's room was small, with a closet in the corner next to her bed. She had two dressers along the wall on the opposite side of her bed, where the roof slanted. Susan had a jewelry box on a vanity with a mirror along the other wall.

Maggie walked closer to the drawings Susan had hanging on the wall above her bed. She pointed to them, "Where did you get those?"

"I drew them."

"Gosh Susan, they're good. I didn't know you could draw like that. You're even better than my sister."

Susan pulled out a box from in a drawer of her dresser saying, "I have started to keep some of my favorites."

Maggie sat on Susan's bed and opened the box to scan through them. She was impressed. "Have you shown these to anyone else?"

"No."

"You should. They're great. I bet the Art teacher would like to see these." Maggie handed the box back to Susan.

"Maybe someday I'll show them to her." Susan replaced the box in the dresser drawer.

Scott and Nate were shoving each other as they were racing up the stairs. Susan went to her door, "Boys behave. We have company. Maggie, this is Scott and Nate." They stopped shoving each other and said hello.

Maggie smiled and replied, "Hi."

Susan shut her bedroom door saying, "Sometimes they can be so annoying." Maggie smiled, thinking that is exactly what Isabelle says about her.

Saturday afternoon Susan, Scott, Nate, and Maggie hauled two sleds to the hill. Maggie was excited, "This is a great hill for sledding."

Susan cautioned her saying, "One thing I've got to tell you. Do you see that barbed wire fence down there?"

"Yeah," Maggie replied.

"Before you reach that fence, you have to turn the sled so you won't run into it. It's a long way down; you'll have plenty of time."

Scott put his sled in place, "Watch me. I'll show you." Down he went. It seemed to Maggie that he was going to hit the fence, but just before it, he turned the sled and stopped. He picked up the sled and walked back up the hill. "The snow is melting. You can really go fast," he remarked. Nate was ready with his sled. He did the same thing as Scott, although he turned his sled sooner than Scott did.

Scott handed his sled to Maggie, "Are you ready to try it?"

Maggie put the sled down in the snow, "Sure." Maggie was excited and scared at the same time. She pushed the sled with her hands to get started. When the sled shot off the top of the hill, she grabbed the handles of the sled. She did not realize how fast she would go. Maggie saw the barbed wire fence was fast approaching. She knew she had to turn the sled, but she could not manage it.

Susan, Scott, and Nate were yelling from the top of the hill, "Turn the sled! Turn the sled!"

Maggie was trying, but she was going too fast. Scott yelled, "Bail out! You're going to run into the fence!"

Maggie was heading straight into a post. She leaned over to fall out of the sled. Her backside hit the post and the sled continued to slide under the barbed wire fence down the hill. Susan, Scott, and Nate ran down the hill to find out if Maggie was all right.

Scott helped Maggie up, "Are you okay?"

Maggie stood up, "I guess so. I didn't realize how fast I would go." She was rubbing her buttocks. "My bottom hurts a little, but I want to go again." Susan, Scott, and Nate laughed at her rubbing her buttocks. Scott climbed over the barbed wire fence to get the sled.

Nate said, "I was scared, I thought you were going to hit that fence."

Maggie put her arms around his shoulders saying, "So did I."

They took turns sledding down the hill the rest of the afternoon. Their clothes were soaked, but they did not care. They were having fun. Late afternoon, the air was getting colder. Susan said to Maggie, "One more run, then we should be heading back to the house." Nate complained. Susan let him have one more run too before the four of them walked back to the house talking about how they could go sledding again on Sunday for Maggie's birthday.

They took off their coats and gloves. They draped them on chairs to dry overnight and went upstairs to change into some dry jeans before they ate supper. Scott told their parents about how close Maggie came to the barbed wire fence on her first run. He said, "When she got up from hitting the post, she was rubbing her butt."

Fred was laughing, but Margaret was not amused. "You could have been seriously injured," she said. "I don't think you should go sledding down that hill tomorrow."

Scott and Nate protested and said they would be more careful. Fred added, "Just make sure you don't wait so long before you turn the sled. We don't want Maggie to go back home with broken bones." He smiled at Maggie.

The next morning Margaret fixed everyone pancakes for breakfast. She would not let the children out of the house to go sledding until the afternoon. Susan turned on some music while the four of them played board games and cards. Before long, they were all singing along to the tunes. Maggie was surprised that Nate knew the words too.

After lunch, they put back on their coats and gloves and headed out to the hill again. Scott and Nate went down the hill together. Then Maggie and Susan did. At the top of the hill, Scott and Nate were into a snowball fight. Maggie and Susan joined them when they returned up the hill. The snow was melting and they could pack the snow. Scott through a snowball at Susan had enough it knocked her down. "What did you do, put a rock in that one?" She accused.

Maggie decided to build a snowman. They worked together to put the head on the top. It did not take long before the four of them had a five-foot tall snowman. Susan took off her scarf to put around its neck. Nate found two small stones for the eyes and Scott found two sticks for the arms. Scott bowed to the snowman and asked, "May I have this dance?" They laughed when he took the sticks and pretended to dance with the snowman.

Margaret yelled for them to come in for supper. She set a steaming pot of chicken noodle soup on a trivet in the middle of the table. The children devoured it. Maggie finished her second bowl and thanked Margaret.

Fred rose from his chair and returned with a cake with candles on it. He lit the candles while they sang 'Happy Birthday' to Maggie.

"Thank you." Maggie said. "I don't know what to wish for. I've already had a great birthday." She blew the candles out. Margaret cut the cake and gave Maggie the first piece.

CHAPTER FOURTEEN

Matt came home from the flower shop with a red rose and a heart shaped box of chocolates for Isabelle. He planned a Friday night date with Isabelle to go bowling. Valentine's Day was the following Wednesday.

Isabelle dressed herself in a red plaid skirt with a white blouse. She tied a crimson red scarf around her neck and attached a broach to hold in place. Isabelle applied red lipstick on her lips, pumped some perfume on her neck, and brushed her hair. She was ready for a date with Matt. Maggie just watched her while she sang to the tune on the record that was playing.

Of course, Isabelle kept Matt waiting on the sofa in the living room before she went downstairs. She learned that from Sara. Matt was making small talk with Henry, when Isabelle walked in. Matt rose from the sofa saying, "Wow!" He handed her the rose and candy. He murmured, "Happy Valentine's Day, early."

Isabelle took the rose and held it to her nose. "It smells nice. Thank you Matt." She went to the kitchen cupboard and pulled out a vase, filled it with water, and placed the red rose into it.

Henry stood up from his chair. Matt immediately said, "We have plans to go bowling." Henry did not ask where they were going, but Matt was compelled to tell him.

Caroline rose from her chair and said, "You two have fun tonight."

Isabelle answered, "We will," as Matt helped her with her coat.

Matt held the door open for Isabelle to get into Alfred's car, as he had not yet saved enough money for another one. Isabelle slid over closer to the steering wheel. Matt turned towards Isabelle to give her a kiss before he put the car in gear and drove out of the lane.

The Jamboree Bowling alley was crowded. Matt and Isabelle found a bowling lane on the sidewall that was unoccupied. Isabelle found a blue ball that she thought she could use. It did not seem to be as heavy as the rest of them. Matt picked out a black one and put it in the ball return. Isabelle lifted it saying, "I could never bowl with your ball. It is way too heavy."

"Well then I'll probably win," he teased. He was right. Matt's score on the first game was 180 to Isabelle's score of 74. Matt confessed that Kevin and he bowled on a Teen Bowling League in Lincoln. They bowled every Tuesday night in the wintertime. Isabelle never had a chance to come close to Matt's bowling ability. The second game, Matt came up behind Isabelle and took her by the waist. He moved her hips to align them with the bowling lane. Isabelle just melted and wanted to turn around and take over his body right there in the bowling alley, but she showed restraint. Matt took her arm and lifted the ball into position. He said, "Now take three steps." Isabelle legs were like jelly, but she took the steps and released the ball. She surprised herself by throwing a strike. "See how easy that is?" Matt asked. Isabelle wanted to tell him that she needed more instructions, but kept the thought to herself; after all, they were in a public place. Isabelle was pleased with herself to score 110 on the next game, but Matt more than doubled her score with 212. Matt and Isabelle moved to the upper deck of the bowling alley to where they sold concessions. Isabelle sat down in a booth to watch the other bowlers as Matt ordered each of them a milk shake. A group of two couples took over the bowling lane that Matt and Isabelle just left. The girl bowled first and sent her bowling ball into the gutter. Matt laughed at her saying, "She should have moved to the left a little or put a spin on her ball."

Isabelle did not know that Matt was so serious when it came to bowling. "Do you miss bowling every week?" she asked.

"Yes I do, but I wouldn't have time now. Dad keeps me busy at the store. I am saving my money. Someday I will have enough to buy a car." Isabelle told Matt that she wished she had a job to earn money too. After Matt and Isabelle finished their milkshakes, they left the Jamboree Bowling alley.

Before Matt reached Isabelle's lane he pulled the car over along the road. He shut off the car, leaned over Isabelle's face, and kissed her. He lowered her down on the seat and kissed her neck while Isabelle nibbled on his ear. Matt lifted his head to gaze into her eyes as she tenderly touched his scar above his eye. He kissed her again with such passion it was hard for Isabelle to breathe. This time, Matt had to show restraint. He regained his composure and let Isabelle straighten back up. He put the car back in gear and drove Isabelle home.

Isabelle tiptoed up the stairs to her bedroom, hoping not to wake Maggie.

CHAPTER FIFTEEN

Henry was listening to the radio in the kitchen, "This strange weather pattern for February will continue for a couple more days. Heavy rain will continue through the night, and break up tomorrow noon. Temperatures will be falling in the afternoon tomorrow reaching only a high of twenty degrees. Watch for flooding and ice jams in the low lying areas."

Never in February does it rain in Nebraska. Most of the time, it would just snow. The weatherman was right, for it rained all that day. Isabelle and Maggie went upstairs to go to bed that night, and it was still raining. In the middle of the night, Henry and Caroline were downstairs walking around. Caroline yelled upstairs, "Isabelle and Maggie get some warm clothes on and come downstairs." The girls hurried as fast as they could to get dressed. Isabelle and Maggie did not know what was going on. When they came downstairs, Caroline instructed them to put on their overshoes. Water in the basement was rising. Henry came up from the basement wearing hip waders. He was carrying a box of quart jars of canned meat. Caroline and the girls formed an assembly line from the basement to the living room. First Henry handed a box to Isabelle who would carry it up the basement steps. Maggie would take the box from Isabelle, carry it to the doorway of the kitchen, and pass it to Caroline. Caroline would carry the box and set it down on the living room floor. The first boxes were quarts of canned meat. Maggie was scared that she might drop one of them. Jars of green beans came next. Even though it was February, there were still plenty of jars of food in the basement.

Caroline yelled down to Henry, "How far up is the water now?"

Henry handed Isabelle another box and yelled back, "Nearly two feet or so."

Maggie took the box from Isabelle and handed it to Caroline. She yelled back to Henry, "What is left of the jars down there?"

"I don't know. I still see plenty on the west side. I think those are apples." Henry yelled back.

Caroline could not see Isabelle and was worried about her. She asked, "Isabelle, are you doing okay?"

Isabelle yelled back, "I'm so tired! Can't we stop for a minute?"

Isabelle handed a box of canned apples to Maggie. "Isabelle, don't go so fast! I just about dropped that box!" Maggie scowled.

Isabelle protested, "You're holding us up, Dad is waiting for me."

Caroline interrupted, "Will the two of you quit bickering. Just do the best you can. We'll be done soon."

Boxes just kept coming, one after another. Maggie handed a box of tomatoes to Caroline, "Can't we rest? My feet hurt and my arms ache."

Caroline took the box of tomatoes from her, "Just keep going, you're doing fine." She knew that if the family stopped, the water would be too deep for Henry to get anymore.

Henry yelled from the basement, "Hey Ma! The water is three feet deep. What do you want to save, the rest of the tomatoes or the pickles?"

Caroline asks, "Isabelle what did dad say?"

Isabelle retorted harshly, "Tomatoes or pickles?"

Caroline hollered back. "Just grab the pickles, we have enough tomatoes."

The girls were getting slower and slower, neither one of them cared if they saved the rest of the food. All of a sudden, the lights went out. Henry and Isabelle came up the basement steps, each carrying a box of pickles. Henry could not see to get the rest of the jars and the water was too deep for him to walk around in anyway. They four of them just sat around the table in the kitchen, too exhausted to talk.

It was not raining as hard as it had been, and they could see daylight coming through the windows. Caroline removed the extra blankets stored in the closet. Isabelle and Maggie went upstairs to get the blankets from their beds. The girls fell asleep on the living room floor.

Caroline and Henry went to their bedroom to get some rest.

Hours later, a strange sound outside the bedroom window woke Caroline. In fear, she nudged Henry, "Henry wake up. I think the foundation of the house is breaking!"

Henry hurried out of the bedroom and opened the door of the porch. He could not believe what he saw. There were ice chunks drifting against the side of the house. Henry realized that was what Caroline heard in the bedroom. He walked into the living room and told the girls to get up.

Maggie crawled out from the blankets shivering, "It's cold in here."

Isabelle woke up and listened, "The rain stopped." Henry was putting his hip waders back on and went outside. Isabelle got off the floor to look out of the window. She could not believe what she saw either. "Maggie come look! The house is surrounded by water and there's ice floating on top of it!"

Maggie went to the window and gasped. "I'm scared. What about Casey?" With frightened eyes, she turned to her Mother, "Mom, what happened to Casey?"

Caroline did not know what to say to her daughter, "I don't know. Dad went outside to look for him."

Henry came back into the house and ordered, "Everybody, get on as many warm clothes as you can. The water is only about three feet deep out there, but it is bitterly cold. I am going to get the tractor out. We will go to the Miller's house. The tractor will get through the water as the ground is frozen underneath it." Caroline wanted to protest, but Henry gave her a stern look and continued, "We can't wait for the water to go down. It's too cold and we will freeze in here. I am going to get the tractor pulled up to the steps as close as I can. Be ready to get on it."

Caroline did not say anything to Henry about his decision. She pulled out the boots from the closet and instructed the girls to dress in layers and put on two pairs of socks. She did the same. They folded up the blankets and waited for Henry.

Henry looked in the barn to see if the cattle were still in there. He saw that the cattle had moved to the west hay field where the ground was out of the floodwater. Henry searched but could not see Casey anywhere. He called out for him, but he did not hear anything either. He walked out to the tool shed through the icy water hoping the tractor would start. He climbed onto the seat and gave the starter a tug. The tractor sputtered, but did not turn over. He tried it again, but to no avail. "Oh please God! I need to get my family out of here," He said aloud to himself. Henry tried it again. With an answer to his prayer the tractor started. Henry looked up and said a silent, "Thank you".

Maggie walked past the basement steps. "Look mom. The water is to the very top. Will it get into our house?" she asked with tears in her eyes.

Caroline put her arms around Maggie and drew Isabelle close, "Don't worry about the house. It has stopped raining and the water will not rise any more. The water will only go down." She was hoping she told the girls the truth.

Henry inched up to the cement steps of the house as close as he could with the tractor. Caroline and the girls were waiting in the porch with blankets in their hands. When they heard the tractor at the steps, they opened the north door of the porch. A blast of frigid air rushed in; it took their breath away. Henry put the tractor in neutral. Caroline handed the blankets up to him. He placed them on the seat of the tractor. Isabelle was the first to climb onto the tractor. Henry reached out his hand, "Don't look down Isabelle. Only look at me." Isabelle was so brave she even surprised herself. She stepped onto the step of the tractor and took her dad's hand. "I've got you. Just steady yourself." Henry hoisted her up onto the tractor. She stepped to the other side of the seat, took the blankets, and leaned against the fender of the tractor.

Maggie was more frightened. She turned to face her Mother, "I'm scared I might fall."

Caroline looked into Maggie's eyes, "You can do this Maggie. Just take your time."

As soon as Henry had Maggie's hand, he grabbed her with his other hand. With one big swoop, he lifted her onto the tractor. Maggie was shaking as Isabelle wrapped her up in a blanket.

Caroline was waiting until the girls were safe before she got on the tractor. She looked down and realized that there was another cement step underneath the water. Caroline stepped into the icy water onto the first cement step to get closer to the tractor. The water made her boots slippery. With her right foot, she found the step of the tractor, but she slipped off it. She put her left hand down to catch herself and fell back onto the cement steps.

The girls gasped, "Mom!"

Henry climbed down into the water and grabbed Caroline's arm. She could feel a sharp pain at the shin of her leg and her left hand hurt. Henry helped her up, "Are you all right?" Caroline gave an affirmative nod, but not so convincingly. The pain in her left hand was excruciating. Henry managed to get Caroline onto the tractor. She braced herself against the other fender of the tractor holding her left hand. Isabelle handed Henry a blanket for Caroline. He helped her wrap up in it. Caroline winced with pain. Henry studied her face and saw her worried look as he put the tractor in gear. "Everybody, hang on." The girls were terrified and shivering from the cold. Caroline held on with her right hand while keeping her left hand inside the blanket.

Henry drove the tractor cautiously down the lane, trying to avoid the deep ditches on both sides of it. At the end of the lane was another ditch on the other side of the road. Henry had driven his tractor out of this lane many times, but never had he been so blinded doing it. Henry had to use his instincts to get the tractor safely turned to go north. Caroline, Isabelle, and Maggie held their breath. It seemed to Caroline that Henry was making the turn too wide, but she did not say anything.

Henry was inching his way around the corner so slowly, that the tractor quit. He put on the brake. Maggie fell against Isabelle nearly knocking her off the tractor. The two girls regained their footage. He started the tractor up again. Henry safely finished the turn north onto the road. Finally, Henry straightened the wheel. He slowly drove onward using the fence posts and trees as guides. Ahead of him, he could see the road as the hill was forming out of the floodwater. When the tractor was out of the floodwater, Henry sped up.

The family could feel the brisk wind on their faces and through their blankets and clothes to their bodies. They were going to the Miller's farm up on the hill. The frigid north wind made the three miles seem like ten.

Casey was on everyone's mind. They searched for him, as they drove away from the farm, but there was no sign of him anywhere. They were wondering where a dog could go in such a storm.

When they arrived at the Millers, they were nearly frozen. Joe Miller came out of the house when he heard a tractor come into his yard. He was shocked when he saw the Sims on it, "Are you guys alright?" He helped Isabelle and Maggie down from the tractor. They were shivering and frightened. Joe said, "Go into the house. Alice can fix you something hot and get you warm."

Henry came down off the tractor, "Joe, help me with Caroline. I think she's hurt." Joe and Henry helped Caroline down from the tractor. She cringed with pain from her wrist and shin as they helped her into the house.

Alice immediately gave her a chair to sit on next to the oil burner in the kitchen, "Caroline, are you hurt? What happened?"

Henry was taking off his hip waders, "She slipped off of the tractor and put her hand down on the steps to brace herself."

Caroline broke down in tears, "I think I broke my wrist and my leg is throbbing with pain."

Henry asked, "Can you move your hand at all?"

Caroline could not lift her left hand off her lap, "The pain is to sharp." Alice cut up a bed sheet to make Caroline a sling. She put her left arm into it and tied it around her neck. She put a pillow under her arm for her to rest it on. Caroline's tears were streaming down her face. Henry went to the telephone to call the hospital.

"Cleary General."

"This is Henry Sims. Is Doctor Parker there?"

"Just one moment please."

There was silence on the other end of the telephone. What seemed to take forever, were only a few minutes before Henry heard Doctor Parker say, "Hello, Doctor Parker speaking."

Henry explained what happened with Caroline and the incident with the tractor. Doctor Parker asked if she could move her wrist at all. Then he asked if she could feel her fingers. Caroline nodded affirmatively when Henry relayed the question to her. Henry put his hand over the receiver of the telephone and said, "Joe, Doc Parker is asking if you have anything you can make a brace with. Some pieces of wood perhaps?"

Joe went to the porch and brought back two slats from an egg crate he had and slid it under Caroline's wrist in the sling. Henry relayed the Doctor's instructions back to Joe as did the best he could to follow them. He used tape to hold the two slats in place. The Doctor informed Henry that the main thing was to keep Caroline's wrist from moving as much as possible. He told Henry to keep ice on the wrist as long as Caroline could stand it in order to keep the swelling down. He wanted Henry to bring her into the hospital for x-rays as soon as he could. Henry thanked him and put the telephone back in its cradle.

"Does that feel better?" Joe asked. Caroline nodded and started to calm down.

Henry helped Alice take off Caroline's overshoes. Henry took off her shoes and saw that her sock was red with blood. Alice bent down on her knees with a clean washcloth and a pan of warm water. "Joe, there are some clean diapers in Greg's room." Henry lifted Caroline's leg onto another chair. Joe returned with some cloth diapers for Alice. She wrapped one of them around Caroline's shin.

Maggie picked up Gregory from the floor. She was glad to be distracted, as she could not stand to see her mother in so much pain. When they did everything they could for Caroline, they moved the recliner closer to the oil burner for Caroline to sit in. Alice gave her some pain medicine that she had. Caroline took the medicine and wiped her face with a washcloth. Joe offered her a cup of coffee, but Caroline refused it. He handed it to Henry instead. Henry thanked him and sat down at the kitchen table.

Henry told Joe and Alice about the jars of food they brought up from the basement before it filled up with floodwater. Joe asked about Casey. It saddened everyone when Henry said he could not find him. Maggie picked up one of Gregory's toys to rattle it. She did not want to hear the conversation about Casey. They sensed her diversion and moved on to talk about the weather.

Two day passed before the water receded enough for Henry to take Caroline to the hospital. Joe went outside to get his pickup out of the shed. He helped Henry get Caroline into it and handed him the keys. Henry concentrated on driving slowly through some icy water still lying in the low spots in the road. Caroline was frightened to find out how bad she broke her wrist. Neither one of them spoke as they went to Cleary General Hospital.

The nurse at the hospital set up the x-ray machine while Doctor Parker un-wrapped Caroline's bandage around her shin. He inspected the wound, cleaned it, and applied a fresh dressing. He then carefully removed Caroline's arm from the sheet sling. He removed the tape and the wooden slats that held her wrist in place for the last two days. He put her wrist under the x-ray machine and took the pictures.

Henry and Caroline waited for Doctor Parker to return to the waiting room with the news about Caroline's wrist. He came in holding the pictures from the x-ray machine and sat down in a chair beside Caroline. He pointed out a fracture on the picture. "Caroline, this is where you broke your wrist. It is a clean break and should heal; unfortunately you will need to wear a cast from your thumb to your elbow for six weeks." Caroline broke out in tears. Henry put his arm around her. Doctor Parker continued, "Like I said it is a clean break and should heal one hundred percent. It will just take some time."

Caroline managed to say, "Okay."

Doctor Parker assured Caroline that she did not need to worry about her job at the hospital until she fully recovered. He would make sure that the staff was informed and the office secretary will rearrange the shift schedules to fill in.

Henry and Caroline walked out of the hospital. They welcomed the sunshine. The sun felt warm on Caroline's face as she lifted her head to absorb it.

Henry parked Joe's pickup in front of the Miller's house and helped Caroline out of it. Isabelle and Maggie were surprised when they saw a cast on their mother's forearm. They both wanted to know the details from the doctor. Alice asked about Caroline's shin. Caroline replied that the shin was all right. She just needed to change the dressing on it in a couple days.

Joe said, "You can stay here for as long as you like."

Henry thanked him and added, "Joe, will you go back to the farm with me tomorrow?"

"Of course," Joe answered.

The next day, Henry and Joe headed out of the Miller's driveway to go back to the Sims' farm. They turned onto the lane and saw broken tree limbs all over the yard. A big branch from a cottonwood tree floated in the water and settled in front of the cement steps. To their amazement, Casey was sitting in the sunshine on the top step against the door of the porch. He raised his head, barked, and ran to greet Henry when he got out of the pickup. Henry was so relieved to see him. He bent down to let Casey lick his face. Henry had tears in his eyes when he stood back up.

Joe opened the door of the porch to go into the house. Henry and Casey followed him in. The water was still halfway up the steps of the basement. Henry walked into the living room to get a jar of canned meat. He dumped the entire quart jar into a bowl for Casey. Casey gobbled it up in no time. Henry hugged Casey again "Boy am I glad you are alright." He opened the door of his pickup to let Casey in the front seat beside him. Joe followed Henry down the lane, back to the Miller's place.

Maggie heard the pickups come up the Miller's lane. She put on her coat and headed out the door. When Henry opened the door to let Casey out, Maggie ran towards him. Casey nearly knocked her down when they met.

Through her tears she said, "Casey, you're alright!"

The Sims' family thanked Joe and Alice for their hospitality. Alice hugged Caroline saying, "You take care of that wrist. Take advantage of the situation and let Henry and the girls pamper you for a while."

Henry spoke up and said, "If she lets us." The girls were pleased to see a smile on Caroline's face. He went on to tell Joe that he would come and get the tractor when the weather warms up. Joe and Alice waved good-bye as Henry drove out of the lane.

Caroline was glad to get home. She hobbled to the living room and sat in her easy chair in front of the jars of food. She closed her eyes and thanked God.

CHAPTER SIXTEEN

In March, Alfred Carson came into the house after closing the store. Bonnie handed him his supper plate. "How was your day?"

He took the plate of food from her and sighed. "We could use another cashier at the store and the bakery is getting busier. It's hard for those girls to keep up."

Bonnie asked, "What about Marge Higgins?" Alfred hired Marge to work part time when they bought the store to fill in when needed.

"I asked her if she would like more hours. She said yes, if she could work in the bakery." Alfred had been thinking about his situation for a long time. He wanted the store to stay open later on Friday night, as well as Saturday night. He asked Bonnie, "What do you think about asking Isabelle Sims to take Marge's place at the store and then move Marge to the bakery?"

'I've never met the girl."

"Me either. I know that Matt has become fond of her. Her dad is a kind soul."

Bonnie cleared the table and put Alfred's plate in the sink. She hung the dishtowel on the rack. "I've been thinking about inviting the Sims' family over for Sunday dinner as an appreciation for helping Matt. Maybe we can approach them about Isabelle working at the store then?"

Matt was in his room listening to music when Bonnie rapped on his door. When she opened his door, she saw Matt surrounded by schoolbooks. She saw him sprawled out on his bed pounding on a book with a pencil to the beat of the music. Matt looked up when Bonnie came into his room. "What's up?"

"Your dad and I would like to talk to you." She turned and left Matt, leaving the door open behind her.

Matt was confused about how his parents could have found out that he was failing English. He had a bad grade on his last test. He knew he would have to buckle down and get better grades to pass it. Matt shut off the record player and walked into the living room.

Alfred and Bonnie motioned for Matt to sit down on the couch across from them. Alfred got up and shut off the television set. That is when Matt knew that the conversation was serious. He was uneasy. Maybe the school called them about his grades, or maybe his mother saw the test with a failing mark on it in his room saying that he would have to redo it. Maybe the teacher talked to his dad at the store. Matt was almost in a sweat by the time he reached the couch to sit down. "What do you want?" He said in an agonizing tone.

Bonnie sensed the fret in Matt's voice and Alfred frowned at Matt wondering why he was so nervous. He returned to his easy chair. "We're wondering if you think Isabelle Sims would be interested in working a couple hours at the store on Friday after school and on some Saturdays."

Matt let out a breath of relief. "Oh that's what you wanted to talk to me about." Matt sat back against the couch and relaxed.

Bonnie saw the fright leave Matt's face and probed, "What did you think we wanted to talk to you about?"

Immediately Matt became nervous again. He looked down at the floor. "Well I might as well tell you. I'm having a hard time in a couple of my classes."

Bonnie was concerned, "How bad is it? Are you failing?"

"I just need to redo a couple of assignments and retake a test in English. Mr. Hickson said my grade in math can improve if I get a good score on the test this week."

Alfred knew that Matt was saving his money to buy another car. Matt had his eye on a 1957 Oldsmobile at Weber's Sales and Service. "Matt, maybe you need to go home after school instead of working at the store, until after graduation."

"But Dad, I want to buy that car at Charlie's." He protested.

Bonnie butted into the conversation, "But school comes first. We want you to graduate."

"I'll get my grades taken care of. You'll see." Matt got up from the couch to go back to his room. "I'll ask Isabelle if she is interested in the job."

Bonnie put her hand on Matt's shoulder to stop him from leaving the living room. "I was going to ask Isabelle's family over for Sunday dinner to thank them for helping you with your car."

Matt stopped and turned with a smile on his face. "Okay, I'll ask Isabelle about that too." Matt looked into his mother's eyes, "Mom, don't worry about my grades. I'll work harder at them." Bonnie smiled at Matt and knew that he was sincere about his schoolwork. She also could tell that Matt had great affection for Isabelle.

. . .

Isabelle shoved her books into her locker. She was upset with herself. She received a 'D' on her math test and was not happy about it. She knew she could have done better, but she just could not concentrate on the story problems with Matt sitting in a desk in front of her. Mr. Hickson, her math teacher, even noticed the change in Isabelle. He pulled her aside and asked if she was feeling well. She did not want to tell him that it is 'love'. What was she going to say to her parents when they found out? How could she get her grade back to a 'B', before the semester report cards came out? The more she mulled it over in her mind, the more upset she became. She grabbed her jacket and slammed the locker door so hard that it popped back open. She slammed it shut again and hurried out of the school. Matt saw her and tried to catch up to her. He called out her name, but Isabelle ignored him and walked faster. She was almost in a run. Isabelle opened the back door of her car and threw her books on the seat.

Maggie came up to the car and saw Isabelle slam the car door shut. "What are you so mad about?"

"Don't ask." Isabelle replied and started the car. She put the car in reverse to pull out of the parking stall. When she straightened it back out, she put the car in drive and stepped on the gas to get out of the school parking lot.

Maggie braced herself on the dashboard. "Slow down before you hit something."

Isabelle slowed the car down and pulled out onto the street. She turned up the radio to let Maggie know that she did not want to talk. Maggie got the hint and they went home without speaking to each other.

The two girls went upstairs to change out of their school clothes. Maggie finally asked, "Did you and Matt have a fight?"

Isabelle plopped down on her bed and opened her math book. "No, that's the problem. We need an argument so I can stay focused in math instead of Matt Carson. Now go away!"

Maggie could not help but smile to herself. She left her and walked downstairs to help make supper.

The phone rang. Caroline got up to answer it. "Mrs. Sims, this is Bonnie Carson." She proceeded to ask Caroline if Isabelle mentioned that they would like them to come over on Sunday and have dinner with them. Caroline replied that Isabelle did not say anything, but they would be delighted. Caroline asked if she could bring anything, but Bonnie declined the offer. "No, but thanks anyway. We want to thank Henry for helping with Matt's car."

Isabelle came down stairs and asked who it was on the telephone. She thought it might have been Matt calling her. Caroline explained that it was Mrs. Carson. "She asked us for dinner on Sunday."

Isabelle smiled, "All of us, or just you and Dad?"

"All of us." Caroline replied.

Isabelle had butterflies in her stomach while getting ready for church on Sunday. In some ways, she did not want to go to Matt's, but thought that would be rude. She did not quite know what she would talk about with Matt sitting at the same table as her in front of both sets of parents.

Henry parked the car in front of the Carson's house. Matt came to the door and greeted the Sims' family. "Welcome! Come on in." He opened the door for everyone to enter. Isabelle stepped through the doorway and saw Matt wink at her. She became even more nervous than she was before.

Alfred and Bonnie exchanged handshakes with Henry, Caroline, and Maggie. Alfred extended his hand to Isabelle. He took Isabelle's hand and gave her a hardy handshake. "It is a pleasure to meet you young lady." Isabelle smiled.

Bonnie announced that dinner would be ready in a few minutes and returned to the kitchen. Caroline asked if she could help her do anything. Bonnie replied, "Thank you, but I have everything ready. I just need to set it on the table."

Alfred led everyone into the formal dining room. The table was set beautifully with napkins matching the tablecloth. Bonnie came in with a bowl of mashed potatoes and a platter of pork chops and set them on the table. Caroline complemented on how beautiful the table looked. Henry complemented on how good the food smelled. Matt pulled out a chair for Isabelle to sit down in and did the same for Maggie. Alfred was pleased with how well his son was behaving. After saying grace, Alfred passed the platter of pork chops to Henry. "We want to thank you for helping us with Matt's car."

Henry looked at Matt's scar from the cut above his eye. "You're welcome."

Alfred did not waste any time about what else he wanted to say. "I am also wondering if you would allow Isabelle to work in the grocery store."

Isabelle was surprised. She put her glass down on the table before she dropped it. She immediately set her eyes on her dad wondering how he was going to reply. Isabelle looked at her mother to see if she could tell if she approved. She was saying to herself, 'Please say yes. Please say yes'.

Henry saw his daughter beaming with joy. "It looks like Isabelle would like that."

Alfred went on to tell Isabelle that the job would be for a few hours after school on Friday until the store closed at eight o'clock and six hours on Saturday. She would be a checker at the cash register. "How good are you in Math?"

Maggie almost choked on her food. She had to take a drink of water to clear her throat. Isabelle frowned at her and replied to Alfred, "I'm pretty good. I am sure I can do the job. When would you like me to start?" She was thrilled. Finally, she had a job and could earn some money.

The conversation at the table was buzzing with arrangements for Isabelle working at the store. Isabelle could start on Saturday after Easter so that Marge could train her. On Friday's, Henry would come and get Maggie from school. During inclement weather Isabelle would not work. Alfred reminded Henry that he closed the store if the weather was bad anyway. Alfred mentioned that Matt worked at the store stocking the shelves and made home deliveries.

Alfred said, "At least up until last week." He added, "Unless his grades improve in school."

Matt was embarrassed. He frowned at Alfred and retorted, "Oh Dad, there's no problem."

The Sims' thanked Bonnie for the meal. Before they left, Isabelle extended her hand to Alfred and thanked him for the opportunity to work in his grocery store. She had no idea she was invited to the Carson's house that day for a job interview.

CHAPTER SEVENTEEN

Marie was sitting in her rocking chair slumped over in a deep sleep. She slowly brought herself back to consciousness when she heard her phone ring and rose to answer it. "Hi Mom, its Henry. I was calling you to see if you wanted to come with us to church on Easter and then afterwards come out to the farm for dinner?"

Marie heard Henry invite her for Easter at the farm, but wondered what he said before that. She asked him to repeat it. Marie accepted the invitation and said she would be ready when they came to get her for church service. It had been a long winter; Marie was ready to get out of her house for a day. She surprised Henry by her willingness to join them. He reminded Marie to wear an extra sweater, as their house might be too cold for her. He also confirmed that she did not need to bring anything. He told her that Caroline and the girls would make the Easter dinner.

Easter Sunday, Henry parked the car in front of Marie's house. Caroline got out of the car to help get Marie. Marie came to the door ready for the day. Caroline stared at her for a moment. To her she seemed older than usual in her gray suit. She helped Henry get her into the front seat. Maggie slid over in the back seat for Caroline. Henry drove everyone to church.

The Parker family drove into the church parking lot at the same time as the Sims. Doctor Parker opened the door for Marie to help her out of the car before Caroline and Henry got out. He greeted her saying it was so good to see her. Marie thanked him for the kind words and coughed. Doctor Parker as well as Caroline was alarmed by how deep Marie's cough was, but neither one of them commented on it.

Mark and Heidi drove into the parking lot. Mark parked the car and went around it to help Heidi get out. She was eight months pregnant and it was a struggle for her to get out of the car. Mark shut the car door for her and extended his arm. Everyone smiled at Mark and Heidi as they entered the church. Mark looked proud as he escorted Heidi to the pew that the Parker's always sat in. Sara walked down the aisle, followed by Doctor and Betty Parker. They looked like a proud family.

Reverend Ahlmann greeted everyone after the church service. He was especially pleased to see Marie. Henry and Caroline were holding on to Marie as they exited the church. The cool breeze greeted them as they walked her to their car. Marie put her head down and held her scarf over her face as she walked. The cool breeze made her cough again.

Marie looked out of the car window at the trees in the yard as Henry pulled up into his lane. To her the farm seemed bigger than she remembered it. The last time she was at the farm was last summer. She eyed the corncrib and saw that Henry had a good crop last fall. Casey greeted the family and jumped on Maggie, wanting to play with her. Maggie scolded him to get down. Henry and Caroline helped Marie into the house. She took a deep breath at the aroma coming from the ham in the oven. She saw a loaf of sweet bread and a pie on the counter. "Caroline, it smells wonderful in here."

"Thank you Marie." Marie coughed again while Caroline helped her take off her coat. Caroline was concerned about her. "How long have you had that cough?"

"Not long. It just started a couple days ago. I think it's getting better." Marie sat down on a dining chair and held her hand over her mouth while she coughed a deeper cough than before.

Isabelle and Maggie set the table for the five of them. Henry slipped into the living room to sit in his easy chair until the food was ready. Caroline reminded him that the dinner would not take long before they could eat. Isabelle cut the sweet bread, got the salad out of the refrigerator, and set them both on the table. Caroline finished warming the vegetables. She took the ham and the scalloped potatoes out of the oven and set them on the table. Maggie got out a candle and put it in the center as a centerpiece. Marie was impressed at the efficiency of the Sims' women getting the dinner ready.

Henry put his newspaper down on the end table when Caroline announced that dinner was ready. He joined the family in the dining room. Henry lit the candle and said grace. Just before the end of the prayer he said, "Lord we thank you for letting us enjoy this meal with Mom. Amen." Marie lifted her head and smiled at her son.

Food was passed around the table, as Marie took a little of everything. She just nibbled at the food on her plate. Caroline took notice of her nibbling, but did not say anything. Henry and the girls were devouring their food as if it was to be the last meal on earth.

Henry and Caroline escorted Marie into the living room. They helped her sit down on the sofa. Isabelle and Maggie cleared the table and washed the dishes. They soon joined them in the living room. Isabelle told Marie about getting the job at the Cleary Grocery store. Maggie chimed in and told her that Isabelle had a boyfriend. She also said that his parents bought the grocery store and the bakery in Cleary.

Marie was excited to hear about the boyfriend. She motioned for Isabelle to sit next to her on the sofa. She wanted to hear all about Matt. Between coughs, she asked where the family came from. Isabelle told her that his family came from Lincoln and that he was an only child. Isabelle leaned over and whispered in her grandmother's ear, "Grandma, I love him." She looked around the room wondering if anyone else heard what she said. It appeared that no one did. She looked at Marie's face to see if she had any expression. It appeared to Isabelle that Marie did not hear what she said to her either.

Maggie talked about how she liked going to the high school. She talked about the friends she made and the teachers she had. She was across the room from Marie. Maggie wondered if she heard anything, she was telling her.

Caroline asked in a loud voice, "Marie, have you seen Louise lately?"

Marie responded that she saw her a week ago and that she brought over some chocolate cake. Henry excused himself and went outside to check on Casey. The women just kept on talking. Caroline liked to hear the girls talk about what was going on in their life. She had never heard some of the stories they were telling Marie. She sat back in her chair to listen.

When Henry returned to the living room, he saw that Marie had fallen asleep. Isabelle was reading the newspaper and Maggie was reading one of her books. Caroline had drifted off to sleep too. He tapped Caroline on the shoulder, "Shall we wake up Mom and take her back home?"

Isabelle and Maggie lifted their heads from what they were reading. Caroline replied, "I wonder if she would like any leftovers to take with her."

Henry walked over to Marie and tapped on her shoulder, "Mom."

Marie woke up and apologized for her rudeness about falling asleep. Isabelle said, "No need to apologize. Mom did too." Marie looked at Caroline and smiled. Caroline nodded and said that it was true and smiled back at her.

Caroline went into the kitchen. She made a ham sandwich and wrapped up a slice of the sweet bread for Marie to take home with her. Marie had a vigorous coughing spell and had to stay seated until she got through it. Caroline looked concerned as Henry helped her with her coat. Isabelle and Maggie decided to stay home while their parents drove Marie back to Cleary.

Later in the evening, the phone rang. Isabelle answered it. Matt was on the other end. "Hi! Happy Easter!"

"Hi Matt! Happy Easter to you too!" She exclaimed. Isabelle went on to tell him that they spent the day with her grandmother. "What did you do today?"

"We just got back from Lincoln visiting my grandparents too. I bragged about you."

"Yeah, I talked about you too." Isabelle told Matt that she was excited to work at the grocery store.

"Dad talked to me about that. He said that I need to get my grades up in school if was to continue to work. He asked me if I would be uncomfortable working with you at the store."

"Why would you?" Isabelle did not understand why Alfred thought that would be an issue.

"I think he knows we have strong feelings for each other." Matt was silent waiting for Isabelle to comment on what he just said. When Isabelle did not react right away, Matt was regretting saying it.

Finally, Isabelle just said, "Oh I see." Matt could not see that Isabelle's face was bright red. Caroline walked through the room to the bedroom. "Matt, I'll talk to you in school."

Matt realized that she maybe had someone on the other end listening to her conversation and said, "Sure, I'll talk to you then. Bye." He hung up the telephone.

. . .

Unusually warm days arrived in the week following Easter. Three o'clock in the afternoon, Louise wrapped up the rhubarb pie she had baked earlier in the morning. She walked out her door to visit Marie. Louise pounded on the door until Marie finally opened it. "Hi Louise," she said as she held a handkerchief to her mouth while she coughed. "Come on in."

Louise walked past Marie, "Hi Marie. How are you?" Louise thought that Marie looked stressed.

Marie had a hard time talking through another cough, "Oh I haven't been feeling well." She saw her carrying in the pie. "What did you bring?" and coughed again.

Louise walked into the kitchen. "You still have that cough Marie and I think it has gotten worse." Marie followed her into the kitchen and sat down at the table while Louise uncovered the pie. "I baked a rhubarb pie. I know it's your favorite." She put two plates and forks on the table. She took a knife out of a kitchen drawer and sat down with Marie. Louise served a generous piece of pie to Marie.

Marie took a bite of the pie, "You are so good to me Louise." She coughed again.

"I had some rhubarb in the freezer. I could not eat the pie all by myself. How was your Easter?"

"The girls are so pretty. She has a boyfriend."

Louise was confused, "Who has a boyfriend?"

"Isabelle."

"Oh. She's a senior isn't she?"

"Pete said that she got a job at the grocery store."

Louise frowned. She knew that Pete was Marie's husband that died several years ago. She figured she was talking about Henry and did not correct her. "My daughter and her husband came over with the grandkids. They are sure growing fast." Marie did not respond

151

to the conversation. Louise wandered if she heard what she said. She talked louder, "Have you seen Reverend Ahlmann lately?"

Marie coughed again, "Yesterday." Louise knew that could not be because yesterday was Sunday. She did not ask Marie again. Marie took another bite of the rhubarb pie, "This is good pie Louse. I'd say it is a blue ribbon pie."

Louise smiled, "Thank you." Louise finished her piece and got up to get a plate from Marie's cupboard. "Would you like a couple pieces?"

"Thank you."

Louise put a piece in the freezer and noticed that is was full of the meat that was in there the last time Louise was there. She also noticed the piece of chocolate cake was still in there. Louise put the other piece of pie in the refrigerator. She noticed that Marie had almost a full quart of milk. It had been two weeks since Louise got some groceries for Marie. Louise looked in her breadbox and saw a full loaf of bread in it. "Marie, did Henry get some groceries for you?"

"No. I went to the farm for Easter."

Louise ignored the fact that Marie did not really answer her question. She leaned over and talked in her ear, "What have you been fixing for yourself to eat?"

"Soup," Marie replied.

Louise opened the cupboard with the canned goods. She saw three cans of soup. There were pints of tomatoes, apples, and green beans in there also. Louise figured those came from Caroline. Marie left her partially eaten piece of pie and went to her rocker in the living room. Louise wrapped up Marie's leftover pie and put it in the refrigerator. She washed the pie plates and forks. She touched Marie on her shoulder and talked into her ear. "I'll be going to the store tomorrow, do you need anything?"

Marie turned towards Louise, "No, I don't need anything. Thank you Louise." She coughed deeply and her face turned red.

Louise bent down to give Marie a hug. She noticed that Marie felt hot when she touched her cheek. "Bye Marie. I'll stop by again tomorrow." Louise thought she would make her some homemade chicken noodle soup. When Louise got back to her house, she called Henry.

"Hello?"

"Henry, this is Louise."

"Hello Louise. How are you?"

"I'm fine, thank you. I just left Marie's house. I'm worried about her."

"What's wrong?"

"Have you delivered any groceries to her lately?'

"No. Caroline went through her refrigerator and cupboards when we took her home from Easter. We thought you stocked her up."

"No. I haven't bought her milk or bread for a couple weeks. I don't think she is eating much of anything and I think her cough has gotten worse too. She felt warm when I touched her today."

"We noticed she didn't eat much at our house. Tomorrow Reverend Ahlmann will visit her. I will go into town on Thursday to check on her. We appreciate all that you do for her, Louise."

"You're welcome. I told her I would stop by tomorrow, but maybe I'll wait until Friday."

"That's nice of you Louise. You take care of yourself too."

"Oh I will. Bye Henry."

"Bye Louise and thanks again." Henry hung up the phone. When Caroline retuned from work, Henry told her about the conversation he had with Louise.

. . .

Reverend Ahlmann knocked on Marie's door. There was no answer. He pounded on the door again until Marie opened it. She was still in her robe.

"Hello Reverend." Marie said in a whisper and coughed.

Reverend Ahlmann frowned at her and walked into the house. "Hi Marie. You are not looking well." Marie slowly shuffled her feet back to her rocker and sat down. Reverend Ahlmann went to Marie's telephone and dialed Henry's number.

Caroline answered, "Hello?"

"Caroline, this is Reverend Ahlmann. I am at Marie's house. She is very ill. I think you and Henry should come right away."

"Oh my, we'll be there in a half of an hour."

"I'll stay with her until you come. See you then."

"Thank you Reverend." Caroline hung up the phone and hurried outside to find Henry. He was in the tool shed working with some barbed wire. "Henry, Reverend Ahlmann called from Marie's house. He said that Marie was not feeling good. He says we should come right away."

"Did he say what's wrong?"

"No, he just said that she wasn't feeling good and that he would stay with her until we got there."

"Okay, I'll put this up and be right in." Caroline left to return to the house. Henry came in and changed out of his overalls before him and Caroline went into Cleary to Marie' house.

Henry parked the car in front of Marie's house. They both walked inside without knocking first. Reverend Ahlmann had pulled a chair up to Marie's rocker. He was holding her hand. Marie was slumped over and not moving. Henry and Caroline rushed over to her thinking that she had already passed away, but when they came closer to her, they could hear her burdened breathing. Reverend Ahlmann saw their worried faces and said, "She is sleeping."

Henry touched Marie on her shoulders, "Mom."

Marie woke up and was surprised to see Henry and Caroline in front of her. "What are you doing..." she coughed and could not finish her question.

Henry was worried at the sound of her cough. "Mom, I think we are going to take you to see Doctor Parker."

Marie said nothing to protest. Henry and Reverend Ahlmann helped Marie out of the rocker. They took her into her bedroom and set her on her bed. Caroline opened her chest of drawers and gathered her some clean clothes, as Henry and the Reverend returned to the living room.

Reverend Ahlmann said, "I haven't seen her since Easter. How long has she had that cough?"

Henry replied, "She was coughing then, but not this bad."

Caroline helped Marie get dressed. She had Marie sit on the bed while she helped her into her clothes. Caroline opened the bedroom door, "She is ready. She is very weak."

Reverend Ahlmann and Henry took each of Marie's arms to help her to the car. Reverend Ahlmann said, "I will call you tomorrow and find out how she is."

Caroline opened that back door of the car, "Thank you Reverend for calling us."

When Doctor Parker came into the waiting room, Henry and Caroline got up out of their chairs. "Marie has pneumonia. I am going to put her in the hospital. She is awfully weak."

Caroline said, "We noticed that too. We don't think she's been eating much either."

"We'll keep her in the hospital at least a couple days. Hopefully by then she will regain her strength."

Henry asked, "Does she need anything?"

"No. We will give her some medicine and get her settled into a room. We'll call you if anything changes."

Henry shook Doctor Parker's hand, "Thanks."

Caroline and Henry walked back out to their car. Caroline wanted to go back to Marie's house. She noticed that her bed linens needed changed. Henry decided to go over to tell Louise that Marie was in the hospital. He parked the car in front of Marie's house and walked next door. "Hi. Louise."

"Hello Henry."

"I came to tell you that Marie is in the hospital."

"I was worried about her. I saw Reverend Ahlmann there earlier. How is she?"

"Doc Parker said that she has pneumonia. She will be in the hospital a couple of days. She's very weak."

"Is there anything I can do?"

"Caroline is over there cleaning. We can let you know. Thanks Louise. You are a good friend to my mom."

"Thank you for coming over Henry to let me know how Marie is doing." Louise's husband died two years ago from having pneumonia. She had a sick feeling in the pit of her stomach about Marie. Marie and she had been good friends. They counted on each other. If something were to happen to Marie, Louise would not know what she would do.

"You're welcome." Henry walked back to Marie's house.

Caroline had stripped Marie's bed and had a pile of laundry on the floor. She was cleaning the bathroom when Henry walked in. "What can I do to help?"

"Can you go into the back room to see if she has a laundry basket?"

Henry went to where her clothes washer was, but could not see a basket. He saw a neatly stack of paper sacks from the grocery store. He took two of them and returned to the living room. "I didn't see a basket, but I found these." He put the laundry in the paper sacks. "Is this all of it?"

"Just a minute, I have some towels and wash clothes to add to that." Caroline added the towels to Henry sacks, and then Henry walked out of the house and put them in the car. Caroline walked into the kitchen and went through the food in Marie's refrigerator. She opened the milk. It smelled sour. She poured it down the sink and washed the milk bottle. Henry walked back to the house just as Caroline met him at the door, "Well, I think that is all we need to do." Henry locked the door of Marie's house and headed back to their farm.

Henry parked the car in the yard and went back into the bedroom to change back into his overalls. Caroline started the clothes washer with Marie's laundry.

The girls came home from school. They walked into the house and headed upstairs to put on their jeans. Caroline stopped them, "Grandma is in the hospital."

Maggie stopped on the first step and turned around, "What's wrong with her?"

Isabelle came back down to hear the conversation. "She has pneumonia. Doctor Parker said she would be there a couple of days. I work the rest of the week, so I'll check on her."

. . .

Caroline heard the phone ring and looked at the clock on the nightstand. It was two o'clock in the morning. She rushed out of the bedroom to answer it. "Hello."

"Caroline this is Mary at the hospital. We need you and Henry to come to the hospital immediately. We are concerned about Marie."

"Okay. We'll be there as quick as we can." Caroline walked back into the bedroom.

Henry heard the phone ring and was already getting dressed. He was sure that the phone call was the hospital. With hesitation he asked, "Is she gone?"

"Mary didn't say that, but I could tell by the tone of her voice it didn't sound good. I'll wake the girls." She went upstairs and turned on the lamp next to Isabelle's bed. Isabelle opened her eyes, "Mom, what's wrong?"

"It's about Grandma. Your dad and I are going to the hospital."
Neither one of the girls said anything. She continued, "We don't
know anything for sure. I'll call you before you go to school."
Caroline shut the lamp back off and walked back downstairs.

Maggie rolled over in her bed. Isabelle heard her stir, "Maggie,
are you awake?"

"Yeah, I heard what Mom said." Maggie said in a sad voice.

Isabelle got up and went downstairs with her blanket to lie on
the couch, waiting for the phone to ring.

Caroline and Henry walked into the emergency door of the
hospital. Doctor Parker came up the hall. "Hello. We have Marie in
here." He led them to a room at the end of the hall.

Marie was lying in the bed. Caroline could hear that she was
struggling to breathe. Doctor Parker picked up her wrist and used
his stethoscope to check her heartbeat. "Her heartbeat is not
steady."

"Henry walked closer to his Mom and leaned over to her ear.
"Mom, can you hear me?"

Marie opened her eyes, but closed them again. She tried to
cough, but was too weak to do it. Just then, it seemed that she was
at peace. No one in the room could hear her burdened breathing
and her eyes remained closed. Caroline went closer to Henry. He
put her arms on Caroline's shoulders and pulled her closer to him.

Doctor Parker put his stethoscope on her chest to check her
heartbeat again. "I am sorry." He left the room to let Henry and
Caroline grieve. Caroline put her head on Henry's chest and cried.
Henry stood there without any movement and had tears swell up in
his own eyes, too. He let a tear fall in Caroline's hair. They both
stood still for several minutes without saying a word. No one at the
hospital disturbed them.

Caroline lifted her head off Henry's chest and whispered, "We
should call the girls."

Isabelle woke up with the sound of the telephone ringing.
"Hello," she said.

"Isabelle, this is Mom." She paused to compose herself,
"Honey, Grandma died."

"Oh, mom, when?"

"Just a few minutes ago," Caroline said in a solemn voice.

"What do we do?"

Caroline informed her that she would call the school and let them know. She told her to come to the hospital. Isabelle was silent. "Isabelle, are you okay?"

"Yes, I heard you. I will tell Maggie. Bye Mom."

Henry walked up to Caroline, "Carmen Douglas, the director of nursing, came by. She wants us to wait for the caretaker from the funeral home to come."

Caroline walked back with Henry to the waiting room. Henry sat down on one of the chairs, put his head back against the wall, and closed his eyes. Caroline looked down at his hands and saw strength in them. She looked at his face and saw how weathered it was from working outdoors. To her, Henry seemed to look older today.

Mr. Meyer, from the funeral home, came into the room. Henry opened his eyes and stood up. Mr. Meyer immediately said, "Oh please, stay sitting." He sat down on a chair and opened a notebook.

Henry and Caroline were exhausted by the time Mr. Meyer finally closed his notebook, "Well that is all I need. I will need you to bring one of Marie's dresses to the funeral home."

Caroline spoke, "We will do that right after we leave here."

Mr. Meyer fixed his eyes on Henry, "I am so sorry for your loss." Henry nodded. He added, "I will make sure that Thursday will work for Reverend Ahlmann. I should know by the time you come to the funeral home with Marie's dress." He turned to Henry. "Are there any special family mementoes you would like displayed at the funeral? We can arrange them nicely in the entryway of the church for you. Some pictures, her Bible, heirlooms, perhaps."

Caroline looked at Henry; he seemed distant. She took over the situation. "Okay. Thank you. We can gather some and bring them with us." Mr. Meyer left the waiting room. Caroline took Henry's hands into hers and asked, "Henry, are you okay?"

Henry looked back at Caroline, "Yeah. It is hard to believe that Mom won't be with us anymore."

Isabelle and Maggie walked into the waiting room. Caroline gave them each a hug. They fixed their eyes on their dad. He rose up from the chair and hugged them both. Maggie started to cry when Henry hugged her. "Oh Dad, I am going to miss her."

Henry wiped her tears off her face, "We all will."

Caroline looked up at the clock on the wall. She saw that it was already after six o'clock. She turned to Henry, "I can get us a cup of coffee from the staff lounge if you want one."

"I sure could use one." Again, he took both of his daughters in his arms and hugged them at the same time. He sat back down on the chair, leaned his head back against the wall, and closed his eyes again. Isabelle and Maggie sat down on both sides of him and did not say anything.

Caroline went to the staff lounge. Mary was putting on her coat. "Caroline, I was going to come and say goodbye before I left." She walked over and gave Caroline a hug. "I am so sorry. Is Henry doing okay?"

"I think so, although, he is worn out. We both are. I was going to take him a cup of coffee." It dawned on Caroline that she was supposed to come in to work this morning. "Oh I forgot that I am scheduled to work today. Who is coming to work?"

"Don't worry about that Caroline. We have it covered. Janet is coming to fill in."

"Oh, thank you Mary."

Caroline returned to Henry carrying two cups of coffee. Henry sat up straight and took one of them from her. Caroline watched Henry drink his coffee. It seemed to bring Henry back from where ever his mind took him. "Do you know what I forgot?" she asked. Henry looked at her with a puzzling look. She went on to say, "I forgot that I work today."

"Oh." He was worried that she would have to stay.

"Janet came in to help out. They said that I could take as much time as I needed."

"That's good." Henry finished his cup of coffee and handed the cup back to Caroline. "I needed that. Shall we go and get Mom's dress now?"

Caroline returned the empty cups to the lounge. She called the school to tell them about Marie. She informed the school that Isabelle and Maggie would be late for school today. She explained that they would not be in school on Thursday, as that was the day of the funeral.

. . .

The Sims arrived at the Tranquility Lutheran Church the day of Marie's funeral. Reverend Ahlmann escorted them to the fellowship

159

hall, where they waited for the rest of the family. Caroline's sister Delores and her husband Ron walked in. Their son-in-law Rick and daughter Julie walked in behind them. Julie was carrying their two-year-old daughter Lillian. She had grown so much since they last saw them.

Joe and Alice entered the hall with Gregory. They gave their condolences to the Sims' family and went back to the chapel. Caroline was wishing they would have stayed with her, but they were not family. Louise came into the hall to give her condolences to Henry and the girls, and hugged Caroline. When she turned to leave the hall, Caroline pulled her back, "Louise stay with us. You are one of the family."

People were filing into the church. The ushers were asking people to slide over in the pews to make room. All of the farmers were there that Henry helped with shelling corn. The hospital staff attended to support Caroline. Alfred, Bonnie, and Matt sat in the pew with Doctor Parker, Betty, and Sara. Mark and Heidi came down the aisle. Heidi was trying to pull her coat shut around her, but her abdomen was too big for the coat. Mark helped her into the end of one of the pews. Several of the families that had children from the school arrived, including Fred, Margaret, Susan, Scott, and Nate Johnson, to support Maggie.

It was time for the family to enter the chapel. Henry let Caroline take his arm as they walked down the aisle to the front of the chapel. Isabelle and Maggie followed them. The rest of the family filed behind them, along with Louise. It seemed that everyone from the whole county attended the service for Marie.

During the service, Henry was saddened. His father had a heart attack nearly five years ago, now his mother was gone too. He looked at Isabelle and remembered his sister. She was riding her horse and hurrying home before a rainstorm. The lightening spooked her horse and she fell off it, breaking her leg. She never recovered from the accident. She developed a blood clot that took her life. She was nineteen, just one year older than Isabelle is. Isabelle sensed that her dad was deep in thought while looking at her. She knew the story about Aunt Martha and reached for her dad's hand. He put his other hand on top of hers and gently squeezed.

After the service, they went to the cemetery. Caroline would not let go of Henry's arm, as she needed support at that moment. Henry was having a hard time holding Caroline up to walk to the burial plot. Louise saw him struggle and took Caroline's other arm. When they reached the row of chairs in front of the graveside, Henry and Louise immediately helped Caroline sit down in one of them. Caroline broke down in tears as the Paul bearers carried the casket to the burial plot. Isabelle and Maggie put their hands on Caroline's shoulders as they were wiping their own tears from their cheeks. After the graveside service was over, Revered Ahlmann announced that everyone was invited to a lunch at the fellowship hall at the church. He then plucked a flower from the wreath on top of Marie's casket and handed it to Caroline. She wiped her tears, and managed a small smile. Henry and Louise lifted Caroline from her chair and escorted her back to Henry's car. Isabelle and Maggie plucked a flower from the wreath also, as they left the graveside service.

Everyone returned from the cemetery to the Fellowship hall for a meal. The Sims' family made their way through the tables thanking everyone for attending the funeral. Isabelle finally noticed Matt and his family. She went up to them to thank them for coming. Maggie approached the Johnson family and expressed her gratitude for their support.

The women from the church, who helped prepare and serve the meal, wrapped up the left over sandwiches, salads, and cake. They gave Caroline a large box for her to take home for the family. Caroline thanked them for it. Delores approached her wondering if there was anything, she could do for her. Caroline asked, "When are you all leaving to go back to Kansas City?"

Delores replied, "We will be leaving tomorrow morning. We have a room at the motel in Cleary. Rick and Julie are spending the night there too."

"Why don't you come out to the farm with us? We can visit for a while. It has been a long time since we have seen you. Tell Rick and Julie too."

"We just might do that if you are not too tired."

Henry took the box of food from Caroline to put into the car, "We would love having you."

Mr. Meyer, from the Funeral Home, handed Caroline a folder with all of the sympathy cards. He informed her he would call Henry when he had everything finalized from the funeral. "I give you my sympathies, Caroline. Please relay that to Henry as well." Caroline took the folder from him and thanked him for all of his work he did to help them arrange the funeral.

Caroline wanted to thank Reverend Ahlmann before she walked out of the church, but she could not find him. She decided she would call him later in the week. When Caroline came up to the car, Henry was surrounded by neighbors and friends. Friends from the school surrounded Isabelle and Maggie in front of the church. Everyone finally bid them good-bye.

When Henry pulled into his yard, they saw Ron and Delores' family already there. Julie let Lillian out of the car. Lillian bent down to pick up a stone she saw. Julie took the stone from her and led her into the house. Henry held the house door open for everyone. "I'm sure glad you decided to come over." They went into the living room. Isabelle went upstairs to the attic to find the small box of old toys they kept, to help keep Lillian occupied. Lillian liked the baby doll she found in the box. She put the doll to her chest and hugged it. Julie announced that she was pregnant again and would be due in November. Everyone congratulated her. Ron told Henry that the steel mill industry was booming in Kansas City. The plant he worked in had a hard time keeping up with the demands. Rick talked about how he likes teaching at the high school. He turned towards Isabelle and Maggie saying, "You two would like the high school I teach in. There are over two hundred seniors that will graduate in May."

Maggie gasped, "Really! I wonder what it's like to go there."

Rick went on to say, "Sometimes the students don't know their own classmates."

Lillian fell asleep on the living room floor, still hugging the doll Isabelle gave her to play with. Isabelle covered her up with a blanket. Caroline offered everyone some left over food from the funeral. Isabelle made some lemonade and set the pitcher and glasses on the dining table. They ate and talked throughout the day. Delores looked at the time and announced, "Ron, we should let Henry and Caroline rest."

Lillian woke up. She saw the piece of cake Rick was eating and wanted some too. They sat around the table until she finished her piece of cake. Julie washed her mouth and hands, "It was nice seeing all of you again."

Caroline took Lillian from her and squeezed her. Lillian fussed until she gave her back to Julie. Henry and Caroline walked out with them to their car. They waved as they drove down the lane. Caroline tuned toward Henry and said, "It was good to be with family on a day like this." Henry agreed with her and put his arm on her shoulders as they walked back into the house.

Henry sighed as he sat down in the easy chair in the living room. He closed his eyes and fell asleep. Caroline and the girls did not disturb him.

CHAPTER EIGHTEEN

Early April, at six o'clock in the evening, Matt walked out of the Cleary Grocery store with a grocery order for Mr. and Mrs. Peters on Maple Street. It was a chilly night and the air was already thick with fog. He put the groceries in the back seat of his dad's car.

Matt knocked on the back door that led into Mrs. Peters' kitchen. "Cleary Grocery," he yelled.

"Matt, is that you?" A woman in her elderly years hollered while shuffling through the kitchen in her house slippers.

"Yes, it's me from Cleary Grocery."

"Just come on in. The door is unlocked." Mrs. Peters sat down on one of the chairs at the kitchen table.

Matt entered the kitchen and put the sacks of groceries on the kitchen counter. He greeted Mrs. Peters and saw that she was wearing a jacket. Without noticing that she was wearing slippers he asked, "Are you going somewhere this evening?" He opened the paper sack that contained milk, eggs, butter, and a package of freshly sliced bacon, and put them in the refrigerator. He put the bread in the breadbox on the counter and set the canned goods in a cupboard near the stove. He put packages of chicken, ground beef and a small roast in the freezer. "It's not a very good night to be out. The fog is settling in and it will be hard to see in the dark."

"No, we're not going anywhere. I am just cold."

"Oh, sorry," Matt apologized. "Where is Mr. Peters?"

"He went to bed early with his newspaper."

Matt folded the paper sacks and left them on the counter. "I think that's everything you ordered." He gave Mrs. Peters the bill for the groceries.

Mrs. Peters had her checkbook lying on the table and wrote out a check for the groceries. She handed the check to Matt. "Thank

165

you for delivering the groceries." She took out three dollars from her purse and gave them to Matt. "These are for your trouble."

"Thank you." Matt put the money in his pocket and zipped it shut. "Tell Mr. Peters hello for me." Matt went back to the car. He looked down the street and saw that the streetlights had already come on. It was going to be a dark night with the fog as thick as it was.

At the store, Matt handed Isabelle the check that Mrs. Peters gave him for the groceries saying, "You might want to ask Dad if you could get off early. The fog is getting thick out there. It will be worse in the country."

Isabelle rang the money into the cash register. Alfred heard what Matt said about the weather. He walked up to Isabelle's checkout and put up the sign 'This register is closed' on the counter. "Matt is right. You should go home for the night."

Isabelle did not argue with either of them. She pulled out the cash from her cash register and put it in a moneybag. She totaled the register out, wrote the total on a piece of paper, and stuffed it in the moneybag with the money. She handed the moneybag to Alfred and said, "I'll see you tomorrow then."

Isabelle put her car in drive and headed out of town. She was surprised she needed to turn on her headlights to see so early in the evening. The streetlights gave off a dim glow through the fog. No one was out and the air was still. It was eerie and Isabelle felt a shiver go up her spine. When she passed the last streetlight, she leaned forward. The fog seemed thicker in the dark air. She saw Art Canter's farmyard light. It was barely visible in the fog. She switched her headlights to dim on the car. She recalled her dad did that while he was driving in the fog when she was with him. That seemed to help tone down the glare on the windshield. She trembled when she came upon the place where Matt slid in the ditch. She slowed the speed on the car even more. All she wanted was to get home. Her knuckles were turning white from gripping the steering wheel so tight. She was frightened to the point where she thought about parking the car on the side of the road and walking the rest of the way.

Isabelle was nearly to the corner of F road. She made the corner onto the gravel road. She was glad to be off the highway and relaxed a little. She leaned forward when she thought she could see something in the middle of the road. She could not quite make out what it was. She slammed on the brakes when she saw a deer right in front of her car. The headlights of Isabelle's car seemed to paralyze the deer, as he locked eyes with Isabelle. Isabelle broke the stare by honking the horn to startle the deer. The deer turned back to the ditch and disappeared into the fog. Isabelle felt sick to her stomach. She put the car in park on the side of the road, opened the door, and vomited. She sat back into the seat to rest for a moment, all the while hoping that no other car would come upon her. She regained her composure and put the car back in gear. Isabelle cautiously drove on until she came to the lane that was so familiar. She was thankful to see her dimly lit yard light. She shut off the car, turned off the headlights, put her head down on the steering wheel, and cried. She was so glad to be home.

Caroline saw Isabelle pull into the yard, but wondered why she was not getting out of it. She went out and tapped on the window to get Isabelle's attention. Isabelle was startled and shot her head up from the steering wheel. Caroline saw that she had been crying. She opened the door and helped Isabelle out of it. "Isabelle, what's wrong?"

Isabelle melted into her mother's arms and sobbed. Through her tears, she told her about how she could not see where she was driving through the fog. She told her about all of the bad memories that came back to her when she drove past the spot where Matt wrecked his car. Isabelle told her she got sick when she almost hit a deer. Caroline just held her close and listened to Isabelle tell her the story. "Mom, maybe I shouldn't have taken this job at the grocery store." She sobbed.

Caroline helped her into the house, "It'll be alright in the morning after you get some rest dear."

Isabelle went to the bathroom and washed her face. She went upstairs without any supper, curled up on her bed, and closed her eyes. She went to sleep for the night.

At nine o'clock the next morning, Isabelle took a bath and washed her hair. She ate some breakfast and headed out the door to go to work. Caroline watched Isabelle as she drove out of the lane. All of a sudden, she realized that her daughter had grown up to be a responsible adult.

Isabelle arrived at the store the same time that Matt did. Matt asked her if she got home okay in the fog. Isabelle told him that it frightened her when she came up to the spot where he had his car wreck. She also told him about the deer, but she did not say anything about getting sick.

After Isabelle clocked out from the store, she walked over to the bakery. She bought some cherry turnovers and went home. Isabelle handed Caroline the box of turnovers when she came into the kitchen. Caroline thanked her as Isabelle walked up stairs to change her clothes. There was no need for Isabelle to explain why she made the gesture. Caroline knew that it was Isabelle's way of saying 'thanks for being there for me'.

Later in the evening, Caroline hollered up the stairs, "Isabelle, the phone is for you."

Isabelle rushed down the steps, "That's funny. I didn't even hear it ring." She took the receiver from her mother. "Hello?"

"I'm an aunt!" Sara was so excited she could hardly contain herself.

"Congrats. Did Heidi have a boy or a girl?"

"A girl, she was born this morning. Her name is Ivy. Gotta run, we are going to Lincoln. I just wanted to tell you the good news before we left. See ya on Monday. Bye."

"Okay. Thanks for calling Aunt Sara. Bye." Isabelle heard Sara chuckle before she returned the phone to its cradle. She announced to Caroline that Mark and Heidi had a baby girl and they named her Ivy.

On Monday, Sara was sitting on the steps of the school waiting for Isabelle. She was writing on her tablet Ivy Lynn Parker. She wrote it in cursive, then printed it and filled the page with hearts around the name. Isabelle came up to her, "Hi Sara. What are you writing?"

Sara turned the tablet around to show Isabelle the name. "I just love her name. Don't you?"

"That is a pretty name. I like it too." Both of the girls walked into the school. Sara boasted to everyone she met, saying that she was an aunt.

CHAPTER NINETEEN

Isabelle followed Caroline into the bedroom asking, "Mom, can we go shopping for a prom dress on Saturday? I don't work that day. I thought we could go right away in the morning."

"I think we could do that. Dad will not want to go. It'll just be a shopping trip with us girls," Caroline answered

"Thanks Mom."

On that Saturday, Caroline, Isabelle, and Maggie entered the dress shop in Morgan. Isabelle eyed the rack of prom dresses. There were tea length and floor length gowns. A salesclerk approached them and asked if she could be of any help. Caroline knew from experience that the dresses on the show room floor were the ones that would cost the most. Caroline asked, "Are these the only prom dresses you have?" The salesclerk escorted Caroline and the girls around the corner. Isabelle was amazed at the rack of dresses that spanned the entire length of the wall and of every color imaginable. She pulled out a tea-length ball gown that was birds-egg blue and held it up to her in the mirror. Caroline looked at the price tag attached to the hem. She did not show any emotion when she saw the price. Isabelle was afraid that the prices for any of the dresses would be too expensive. She returned the dress to the rack. Caroline asked her, "Didn't you like that one?"

"I thought it costed too much," Isabelle answered.

Caroline said, "You pick out the one you want. Don't worry about the cost. You will only attend one prom."

Isabelle tried on several more dresses. None of the other dresses she tried on appealed to Isabelle. "Mom, I still like the blue one that I saw first." Caroline was surprised that her daughter made up her mind so quickly. She was even more surprised when Isabelle asked Maggie her opinion. Maggie replied that she liked it too and that it looked good on Isabelle.

Isabelle did not ask her mother for anything else. She knew she had makeup already. She planned to wear the jewelry she got for Christmas. The navy pair of heeled shoes in her closet at home would be just right to wear with the gown.

Caroline treated the girls to a lunch in the boutique next to the dress shop. She asked Isabelle if the shoes she wore for Easter would be okay for prom. Isabelle replied, "I can wear those. They are a navy and would match just fine." She held up her hair above her neck, "I can put up my hair and tie a ribbon in it to match."

Caroline was so proud of her daughter.

. . .

On the night of the prom, Isabelle was checking last minute details in front of the mirror, making sure her reflection was perfect. She pumped some perfume on her neck as Maggie watched her in envy. When Isabelle asked Maggie if her hair was all right in the back, she assured her it was perfect and stared at Isabelle for a moment, feeling jealous, and wished it were she instead that was going to the prom.

Matt drove up into the yard. He straightened his tie and checked his hair in the rear view mirror before he took the corsage from the front seat and walked up to the door.

Caroline answered the door and escorted Matt into the living room. Henry rose from his easy chair. He shook Matt's hand and asked him if he wanted to have a seat. Matt knew that no matter if Isabelle was ready or not, he would have to wait for her.

Matt heard Isabelle's footsteps coming down the stairs. He rose from the couch and exclaimed, "How beautiful you are!" in a whisper. Isabelle smiled and blushed. Matt handed Isabelle the corsage and Caroline immediately offered to help her put it on. Maggie watched to absorb the moment.

Matt and Isabelle walked out of the house. Matt paused before he opened the car door for her and bent down to kiss her. Isabelle protested, "Matt, you know they're watching us."

"I know, but I just couldn't help it. I thought I would give them something to see." He chuckled and repeated, "You are so beautiful, Isabelle."

Isabelle had butterflies in her stomach and a lump in her throat. "Thank you," was all she could manage.

Matt parked the car in the school parking lot and went around it to open the door for Isabelle. Sara and Jim were just about ready to enter the school when Isabelle called out to get their attention. Sara spoke first, "Isabelle your dress is gorgeous."

"Thank you. You sure look beautiful in pink, Sara."

"This is the same dress I wore for Mark's wedding. I agreed with Mom that it was pretty enough to wear it again."

Jim smiled and gave her a kiss on her cheek. "I think she looks magnificent."

Sara took Jim's arm. "Thank you, Jim."

Brightly colored streamers decorated the gymnasium. The art students made a waterfall in the corner of the room out of foil paper and put two Christmas lamps on either side of it. The colors from the Christmas lamps illuminated the foil backdrop as they rotated.

The band was playing a slow song as Matt took Isabelle out on the dance floor. Jim and Sara did the same. The evening was perfect until Sara mentioned to Isabelle that she was sad that Heidi did not get to have a real prom. Isabelle reminded her that Heidi had a beautiful wedding and she was very happy. Isabelle's comment made Sara feel better.

The prom was nearly over when Matt asked Isabelle if she was ready to leave. Isabelle gave Sara a goodbye hug. Jim nodded at Matt and smiled. Matt smiled back and escorted Isabelle out the door. He opened the car door for Isabelle, but this time she slid over closer to him when he started the engine. Matt reached over and put his right arm over her as he drove out of the school parking lot.

Just before the Sims' lane, Matt shut off the car and turned off the lights. Isabelle did not say anything. He turned towards her and kissed her with such passion it made Isabelle feel dizzy. She put her hands around his shoulders and drew him closer to her. He slid her closer to the door, so that he could get out from behind the steering wheel. She slid down to get more comfortable. Again, he kissed her with such intensity it was hard for Isabelle to breathe. He looked into her eyes and said, "Isabelle, I love you."

Isabelle was dreaming about hearing those words. She was teary eyed when she heard them said aloud. "I love you too." She whispered.

Matt brushed a hair from her face and kissed her again. He wanted to continue, but he straightened back up and slid back behind the steering wheel. He started the car, turned back on the lights and drove up the lane. Matt opened her car door. Isabelle got out of the car and straightened her dress. "Matt, do I look okay?"

"You're perfect." He walked her to the porch door and kissed her again. He released her and said, "Good-night."

Isabelle just stood behind the porch door after she closed it with her eyes shut, savoring the moment, not wanting the evening to end. Henry opened the kitchen door and brought her back to reality. "Hi Dad." she said in a startled voice.

Henry held the kitchen door open for Isabelle while she walked passed him. She went up the steps to her bedroom still dreaming what a breathtaking night it was. She finally fell asleep after hearing those three wonderful words 'I love you' repeatedly in her mind.

CHAPTER TWENTY

The school year was ending. The graduating seniors of 1962 were congregating in the Cleary High School gymnasium to practice for the graduation ceremony and chattering about their upcoming graduation. Isabelle and Sara saw Heidi surrounded by the girls of their senor class in the gymnasium. She was passing around pictures of Ivy, bragging about what a beautiful baby she was. Principal Jackson announced that everyone take their seats on the bleachers so they could get started. He had a list in his hand of the graduates and the order in which they would be walking in the ceremony. The seniors got into their positions in the music room. Mrs. Banks, the music teacher, played the graduation march on the piano as the graduates practiced filing into the gymnasium and sat in the seats arranged in the front. Principal Jackson went up to the microphone again. "I have an announcement to make." The crowd hushed to hear what he had to say. "I want to personally congratulate Sara Parker as this year's Valedictorian. She has the highest grade point average of the senior class!"

The class clapped, whistled, and cheered as Sara approached the front and took the microphone from Principal Jackson. "Thank you. I promise to make the speech short and sweet." Everyone applauded. Jim whistled.

Principal Jackson took the microphone back from Sara. "Everyone settle down. I'm sure Sara can prepare a speech that we can all be proud of."

A windy Cleary High School graduation day had arrived. The graduates were to meet in the music room. The girls were admiring each other's dresses and hair. The boys gathered around talking about what they were going to do after graduation. Mrs. Banks entered the music room. She put her finger up to her mouth, "SH!

The guests are arriving and they can hear you." She went on to say quietly, "Remember to rotate your tassel on your caps after Principal Jackson gives you your diplomas. Also, hang onto your caps when you line up outside. The wind is strong." Roger Berle and Mary Taylor from the junior class escorted the seniors to their gymnasium. Mrs. Banks instructed them to start when she gave them the signal.

Alfred and Bonnie Carson met Henry, Caroline, and Maggie in the lobby of the gymnasium and sat together. Caroline had looked around for the Parkers. The Parkers were already seated on two seats up front. Mrs. Banks walked through the gymnasium and took her seat at the piano. Principal Jackson and the school board filed in and took their seats on the stage. He signaled Mrs. Banks to play a song. When she played, the guests found their seats and quieted down. She finished and signaled Roger and Mary to begin the procession. All eyes were on the graduates as they marched into the gymnasium. They sat in the front row seats reserved for them.

Principal Jackson announced Sara as this years' Valedictorian. Everyone clapped as Sara approached the stage microphone. "Thank you." She began her speech. "Good afternoon, everyone. It is an honor to represent the graduating class of 1962. I want to first thank my parents." She paused while they stood up. "I want to give them credit for preparing me for school and beyond. Thank you." Doctor Parker and Betty sat back down. The rest of Sara's speech was so heartfelt; Betty had tears in her eyes. She ended with, "To the graduating class of 1962, I applaud you. You have the ability and the perseverance to be whatever you want to be." Everyone in the gymnasium stood up and clapped when Sara finished. She smiled and said, "Thank you, again," before she left the stage. She was not expecting a standing ovation.

The ceremony ended with Mrs. Banks playing on the piano as the graduates filed out of the gymnasium. She was right when she told them to hang on to their caps when they went outside, as a gust of wind came up and carried several caps with it. By the time the graduates reorganized, the guests started to come out of the school. They congratulated Sara for such a fine speech. Betty invited all of Sara's friends and their families to their house for a party.

Isabelle and Maggie went up to Sara's room to change out of their dresses. Before the girls returned downstairs, their friends were already there. Some brought food and sodas. Jim and his family brought tables and chairs to set up on the lawn.

Alfred and Bonnie Carson said they would come over a little later. They wanted Matt to come home first. Matt was disappointed, and wondered why. Alfred parked the car in front of their garage. Bonnie had a wide grin on her face and told Matt to get out of the car and open the garage door. Alfred followed Matt and took a key out of his pocket. Matt lifted the garage door and saw a 1956 Oldsmobile in it. Alfred put his hand on Matt's shoulder and said, "Son the car is yours." He handed Matt the key. Matt was stunned.

Bonnie touched her son's other shoulder saying, "We decided that you have been working so hard. We thought you deserve. . ." Before Bonnie finished, Matt gave her a hug.

He shook his dad's hand and asked, "Can I drive it to the Parker's house?"

"Of course," Alfred said back to Matt and shook his hand again.

Alfred and Bonnie got back into their car and backed it out of the driveway to let Matt get his car out of the garage. Matt backed it out of the garage and saw his parents drive off down the street. He had an idea. He shifted his car in park. Matt went back into the house and returned with a blanket in his hand. He tossed in the back seat of his car.

Matt honked his horn as he parked it in front of Sara's house. Isabelle was the first to see Matt get out of the car. "Is that yours?"

"Sure is. Isn't it a beaute? I just got it for a graduation present." He leaned over and whispered, "After a while we'll take it out for a spin."

The rest of the friends came over to look at Matt's car. Jim opened the driver's door and looked inside. "Congratulations Matt. It's grand. Just be careful with it in a snow storm."

Matt touched his scar above his eye saying, "Boy, that's for sure."

Sara brought down her record player from her room. She plugged it into an outlet on the porch and turned up the volume. Some of the teenagers danced on the lawn. Betty served sandwiches and lemonade. She cut the decorated cake she bought from the bakery and served Sara the first piece. The families took several pictures of the graduates. Bonnie wanted one with all of the graduates in front of Matt's car.

The party was winding down. Henry and Caroline said their goodbyes and thanked the Parkers for a fun time. Matt approached Henry as they were leaving. "I would like to take Isabelle home."

Henry raised his eyebrows. He turned to look at Isabelle. "See you at home then." Caroline and Maggie climbed into the car. Caroline knew that there was a real relationship brewing between the two of them.

Matt opened the car door of his car for Isabelle. He put the car in drive and headed out of town. Isabelle tuned the radio to a rock and roll station she liked and slid over next to him. Matt drove several miles before he turned onto a gravel road south of town. He drove the car into an alfalfa field and parked it behind a haystack. Matt helped Isabelle out of the car before he reached behind him and took the blanket out from the back seat. Isabelle helped Matt spread the blanket out on the ground. A soft breeze blew Isabelle's hair in her face. Matt reached over and brushed the hair away from her lips before he kissed her. Isabelle drew him closer to her. He held her while he lowered her down onto the blanket. She let his hands roam over her body as he reached under her blouse and cupped her breast. Isabelle drew him closer to her while she searched to loosen his belt.

It started to sprinkle on the two of them, but they were both so oblivious to what was happening, neither one of them noticed the sprinkles. The sound of thunder brought both of them to their senses. Matt lifted himself off Isabelle. "I don't think we should go any farther."

Isabelle sat up, straightened her blouse, and kissed him. "I agree." She whispered, "I love you."

Matt helped her to her feet. "You are the sweetest girl I have ever met. I am so in love with you." Just then, the clouds opened up and the rain poured down on them. Matt scooped up the blanket and took Isabelle's hand while they ran back to the car.

Isabelle looked in the rear view mirror saying, "I'm a mess."

Matt just looked at her and smiled. "I have never seen a prettier mess," he said as he started the car and drove her home.

Isabelle kissed Matt goodbye and ran through the rain into the house. She immediately went upstairs to change her clothes before her parents could stop her and ask questions. Maggie was on her bed listening to records playing on the record player while thumbing through some magazines. She looked up at Isabelle. "What happened to you?"

"We got caught walking in the rain." She did not go into any details and left it at that.

CHAPTER TWENTY-ONE

At the supper table, Alfred leaned back in his chair. He took a drink of his tea, put his glass down, and cleared his throat before he spoke. "Matt, I want to talk to you."

Matt thought to himself, 'Oh no, this is serious. He cleared his throat.' "What's up?" he asked.

"George wants to retire." Matt knew immediately that Alfred was talking about George Gibbs. George was the manager at the Lincoln grocery store that Alfred and Bonnie still owned. He had wanted to retire for over a year now, but Alfred talked him into staying on until he got the store in Cleary more established. Alfred told George he was hoping to keep him on until the assistant manager, Doug Ayker was ready to take it over.

Matt did not understand why his dad was telling him this. "What's that got to do with me?"

"You're mom and I have been talking it over. We would like you to go to work at the store in Lincoln. George is retiring after the first of the year."

"Wow, I wasn't expecting you to say that. What about Doug?"

"Doug will move up into manager when George retires."

"Where will I live?"

Alfred told Matt that he had already checked things out in Lincoln. There was an apartment building not far from the Lincoln store. He told Matt that when he inquired about it, there was an apartment available to rent.

Matt's face lit up until he remembered Isabelle. He had fallen for her and could not bear to leave her in Cleary. "What about Isabelle?"

"I don't understand the question? She still would have a job here for as long as she wants it."

"Dad, I was going to ask her to marry me. I was going to save my money to get an apartment in Cleary for the both of us." Matt studied Alfred's face. To his surprise, he did not show any emotion. Somehow, it seemed that Alfred knew that was what Matt was going to say. Alfred could see the affection Matt had for her when they worked together at the store. Matt looked at his mother. Bonnie did not seem to be surprised either.

Bonnie smiled and said in a soft voice, "Matt, we figured that you two have become very close. We adore her. We do not want this change ruin your relationship with her. After you are in Lincoln and settled, you can make plans to get married. A year is not that far off."

"But, I don't want to wait until next year to get married. That's too long." He continued to protest. "I wanted to get married sometime this fall."

"But son, it's already nearly June. That's rushing things a bit, don't you think?" Without saying another word, Matt got up from the table and went into his room. Bonnie looked at Alfred. "I didn't think I said anything that would upset him that much." She was about to get off her chair to follow him until she heard him return to the kitchen.

Matt was carrying a small box in his hand. He opened it and handed it to Bonnie. "I bought her a wedding ring already."

Bonnie gasped, "That's beautiful! Has Isabelle already seen it? Have you asked her to marry you already?"

"No. She hasn't seen it. Nobody has except for you. And no, I have not asked her to marry me yet."

Bonnie rose from her chair. "We are so proud of you Matt. I think you can get established in Lincoln and marry Isabelle in the spring."

"No mom. I don't want to wait until spring." Matt protested again.

Alfred approached Matt saying, "It is a good future for you son. I think you can work in Lincoln and still make plans on getting married in the fall." He looked at Bonnie and went on to say, "Weddings have been planned in less time." Bonnie surrendered and gave her son a hug.

Matt was beginning to absorb the news. It was a huge change for him. In the back of his mind, he has always known that he would follow his dad's footsteps. He just did not think it was going to be so quickly after graduating from high school. He went back into his room, closed the door, and plopped down on his bed. He laid there with both arms under his head and pondered over his new life. He liked the idea of living on his own in an apartment. He knew that he would have to work hard at the store and learn everything that went on there. The store in Lincoln opened up at 7:00 a.m. and stayed open until 9:00 p.m. every night, for seven days a week. He thought about Isabelle living with him in the apartment after they were married. He wondered how big the apartment was. Was the apartment furnished? Where would he buy furniture? How was he going to pay for the deposit and first month rent? He had so many uncertainties it was hard for him to fall asleep.

Matt finally fell asleep in the wee hours of the morning. He woke up before his alarm went off. Again, he started thinking about moving to Lincoln. He reached over to shut the alarm off. It was Thursday; he knew that Isabelle worked at noon today. He got ready for work and went into the kitchen. Matt was hoping that his dad was still home so he could talk to him some more, but Alfred had already gone to the store. Matt was anxious; going to work had a different meaning to him this morning. He spread peanut butter on a piece of bread for his breakfast. He then left for Cleary Grocery store.

As Matt was parking his car, he saw the delivery truck coming down the alley. Matt went right to the back of the store to help unload it. He saw the driver of the truck hand Alfred the paperwork for the delivery. Matt wanted to read it and find out the costs, but Alfred took the file to the Kathy James, the bookkeeper in the office, before Matt could ask him about it. He could not work fast enough getting the truck unloaded. He loaded the dolly cart with one more box than he should have. Just as soon as Alfred returned to help unload the truck, the top box slipped off the dolly cart and fell to the floor. The box of glass bottles of cooking oil opened when it fell. Two of the bottles tumbled out of the box and broke. Cooking oil quickly spread all over the floor.

"Matt, slow down!" Alfred yelled. "Go get a mop and bucket with a bottle of dish soap to clean this up with."

"I'm sorry, but the box slipped off the dolly." Matt apologized.

"Don't stack them so high next time. Just get it cleaned up! Now!"

Matt was mad at himself. The last thing he wanted was to let his dad down. He cleaned up the cooking oil and carefully put the rest of the cooking oil cases in their place on the shelf. He slowed down his pace and helped unload the rest of the order from the truck.

Matt waited until Isabelle finished checking out a customer's order before he approached her. "Can you go to the movies with me on Friday night? They have a good one playing at the Drive–In Theatre. I'm off at six and I saw that you don't work at all on Friday."

"Sure. I'll be ready by seven." Isabelle smiled and watched Matt walk away, taking an empty box with him from her checkout stand. She was thinking how wonderful and hardworking he was. She wished she had enough money saved to get an apartment and live on her own. Then he could come over any time he wanted to.

A woman interrupted Isabelle's thoughts when she took her groceries out of the cart and placed them on the checkout stand for Isabelle to ring up. Isabelle finished ringing up the woman's order and told her the total. There was a coil pen with a plastic base glued to a podium for all of the check-writing customers. The woman used the coil pen, handed Isabelle her check, and put her checkbook along with the coil pen in her clutch purse. The woman snapped her clutch purse shut and stuffed the clutch purse under her arm. She scooped up her paper sack of groceries and proceeded out of the grocery store. Needless to say: The coil pen was stretching out to its limit. One of two things were going to happen; either the glue on the plastic base was going to give way leaving it dangling underneath the woman's armpit, or it was going to stop her in her tracks.

Isabelle's next customer was a small elderly man. Just as soon as the man asked Isabelle for a pen to write his check, the woman's clutch purse slipped from under her arm. The purse came flying back and hit the man in the back of the head. The woman was so embarrassed. She came back, retrieved her clutch purse, and took the coil pen out of it and handed it to the man. Without uttering a single word, she exited the grocery store.

182

The man just stood there stunned until Isabelle asked him if he was okay. The man replied, "I just came in here to get a jar of peanut butter and a loaf of bread. I get whacked in the head with a woman's purse and I don't even know what I did to her."

Isabelle could not contain herself any longer. She busted out laughing as well as everyone around her, including her next customer. After Isabelle explained to the man what happened, the man did leave the grocery store with a smile on his face.

. . .

Friday night Isabelle put on a tight fitting beige skirt and a light tan blouse. She wore a beige scarf that matched the skirt around her neck. She applied makeup and lipstick, combed her hair, and inspected herself in the mirror. Isabelle heard Matt talking to Henry. She went downstairs and saw him in the living room waiting for her on the sofa. He rose the minute Isabelle entered the room. "Hello. Are you ready?"

Caroline came from the kitchen carrying a tray with four glasses of iced tea. "Have something to drink with us before you go."

Isabelle knew just how Sara felt when Jim picked her up for a date. Why do parents do that? "Mom, the movies are going to start soon. We don't want to be late."

Matt politely took a glass and handed it to Isabelle. He took one for himself and motioned for her to sit down on the sofa. "We have a few minutes."

Henry and Caroline asked Matt about his parents. They asked questions about the store and wondered how they liked living in Cleary. Isabelle was anxious and finished her glass of tea. Matt drank his down and looked at his watch. "Thank you for the tea. We should be going."

Caroline took the empty glasses from them and set them on the tray. "You're welcome."

Isabelle climbed in Matt's car and slid over next to him saying, "Sorry about that. I didn't expect Mom coming out of the kitchen with tea."

Matt started the car. "That's okay. You have nice parents."

Matt parked the car towards the back of the Drive-In Theatre lot where there were no other cars around them. He was hoping none of his friends saw the car, as he did not want to be bothered tonight. He rolled the window down far enough to put the speaker on it.

Isabelle rested her head on Matt's shoulder and sighed. "This is nice."

Matt lifted her chin to kiss her. "Alone at last. I brought sodas for us. They're in a cooler on the floor in the back seat."

"I'm fine, but thanks."

Matt put his arm around her. The advertisements were over and the movie started. They sat in the car for a while watching the movie until Matt moved his arm and lifted Isabelle's chin again. This time Isabelle shifted her hips to move towards him for a better kiss. He took that as an implication that she was not interested in the movie either. He reached over and turned the volume down on the speaker. Isabelle slid over to let Matt get out from behind the steering wheel. He opened her door and whispered, "Do you want to move to the back seat?"

Isabelle nodded affirmatively. She got into the back seat while Matt moved the cooler to the front. He slid in the back seat next to her. He gave her a kiss. He wasted no time before he opened the small box he pulled out of his pocket and revealed the wedding ring he bought for her. "Isabelle, will you marry me?"

Isabelle stared at it for a moment. She could not believe what she heard. "Oh Matt, of course I will marry you." He took the ring out of the box and put it on her finger. "Matt, I love you so much." Isabelle slid down on the seat. Matt gingerly lowered himself on top of her. Neither one of them paid any attention to the movie.

"Are you comfortable?"

"Yes."

Matt kissed her lips. Then he kissed her neck. He removed the scarf, unbuttoned her blouse, and roamed his hands over her midsection. Isabelle did nothing to stop him until he reached down under her skirt. "Matt we better slow down before we do something we shouldn't."

Matt removed his hand. "You're right." He buttoned her blouse and sat up. Matt stared at the movie screen without saying anything.

Isabelle sat up next to him, "Matt, what's the matter? Don't be upset with me." She was almost ready to cry. "I just thought we were going too far."

184

"No, that's not it. I have something else I want to talk to you about." He held her total attention while he informed her that he would be leaving to live in Lincoln. He told her about the job at the Lincoln grocery store. "Isabelle, I will be the manager someday." He went on and talked about the apartment his dad found that was close to the store. Matt told her that he and his parents were going to Lincoln to look at it on Monday. He stopped talking when he looked at Isabelle's face.

"But how long do we have to wait to get married?" Isabelle was about to cry.

"We can get married in the fall. After we're married you can live with me in the apartment."

"But that means I won't get to see you all summer." She broke out in tears.

Matt kissed her and wiped her tears away. "That's only a few months. I have a lot to learn at the Lincoln store. I will be working every day and at all hours. I'm afraid that you'll have to plan our wedding without me though."

Isabelle leaned back on the seat. She needed a minute to sort out all of what Matt just told her. Matt sat back and rested his head on the seat too. He continued to tell her that he would come back to Cleary whenever he could. He put his arm around her. "I promise you that I will call you every day, just to hear your voice."

Isabelle smiled. "Oh Matt, I love you. I am going to hate it when you leave. I loved going to work knowing that you are there too." She lifted her hand to look at the ring on her finger. The lights from the Drive-In Theatre made the ring sparkle.

"I know. I feel the same way, but this is our future. If I can prove to my dad that I can handle the job, we will have a life together. Then I know I can take care of you."

"Do your parents already know that you were going to ask me to marry you?"

"Yes. I showed them the ring."

"What did they say?"

"They adore you Isabelle. I told them that the wedding would be in the fall sometime."

They made plans to get married in October. Maggie would be the Maid of Honor and Sara would be a bridesmaid. Matt said that he would ask Jim to be groomsman. He told Isabelle that he wanted

185

to ask Kevin Davis to be the best man. He was a good friend in Lincoln and he has known him for a long time.

The movie ended and the cars were pulling out of the Drive-In Theatre. Isabelle and Mat moved back into the front seat. Isabelle reached into the cooler, "Now I could use a soda." She handed one to Matt and put the cooler in the back seat.

Matt parked the car in the Sims' yard. He reached into the glove compartment to get the ring box out of it. "Maybe you should hide this until you're ready to tell your parents."

"You want me to keep it?"

"Yes, of course. It's yours."

Isabelle took the box from him and placed the ring into it. "I want us to tell them together. I don't want to wait until you are already moved. Can you come to my house on Sunday?"

"I agree; the sooner the better." He opened Isabelle's door and kissed her before he escorted her to the house. "I just want to say that this summer will be tough without you. I will pour myself into my job. You are the best thing that ever happened to me and I am thrilled to know that I will be spending the rest of my life with you." He kissed her again.

Isabelle returned his kiss. She could only manage to whisper another "I love you" before she turned to walk in the house. She gripped the small box she had in her hand and cried. This time, the tears were tears of joy.

CHAPTER TWENTY-TWO

After work on Saturday, Isabelle bought some fresh vegetables for a relish tray. Then she went to the bakery and bought a package of dinner rolls and a cake to take home for Sunday dinner. She stopped at the flower shop and picked out a small bouquet of flowers for the dining room table. She was excited about her and Matt telling her family about the wedding. She drove home quickly, singing along to a tune on the radio.

At home, Isabelle was arranging the flowers in a vase in the kitchen when Caroline walked in. She said, "Those are pretty. What's the occasion?"

"I have invited Matt to come over after church tomorrow and have dinner with us. I hope that is okay. You won't have to do anything. I'll make a meatloaf in the morning before we go." Isabelle showed her the vegetables, dinner rolls, and cake she bought. "I will clean the vegetables for a relish tray too. I can cut the potatoes ahead of time for mashed potatoes."

Caroline was impressed. "Isabelle, that is so thoughtful. Are you sure won't need any help?"

"No, I have it all planned."

Sunday, Matt drove into the yard. He got out of the car wearing a nice shirt and slacks. He checked his hair in the rear view mirror. Isabelle ran out to meet him and gave him a kiss, "Come on in."

"Do they know why I'm here?"

"No. I didn't tell them anything."

Isabelle and Matt entered the house. Caroline and Maggie were setting the table for dinner. Henry was in the living room reading. Isabelle led Matt into the living room and they both sat on

187

the sofa. Henry lifted his head from his newspaper, "Hi Matt. How are you?"

Matt seemed nervous, "Couldn't be better, Sir."

Caroline came into the living room and sat down in her chair, "Isabelle's dinner will be a few more minutes. The potatoes are not done yet. Maggie will keep an eye on them."

Matt looked at Isabelle, "You made the dinner? I can't wait to eat it," he teased.

"It's just meatloaf." Isabelle said, and motioned for her mother to sit down. "We have something to talk about." Henry folded up the newspaper and put it on the lamp stand next to him. Both Caroline and Henry held their full attention to the young couple sitting on their sofa. Isabelle nervously sat on the edge of it fidgeting. She did not want to wait a minute longer. "Matt has asked me to marry him." She fixed her eyes on Caroline. Matt scooted closer to Isabelle and fixed his eyes on Henry. Isabelle could not stop fidgeting. Neither one of her parents said anything for a long agonizing minute.

Maggie was in the kitchen doorway. She came rushing into the room and blurted, "That's wonderful!"

Caroline stood up from her chair with a tear coming down her cheek, "Oh Honey, I thought that is what you were going to say."

Matt and Isabelle both rose from the sofa. Henry stood up and extended a hand to Matt. Instantly Matt had a smile on his face and his nerves calmed. He took Henry's hand and gave him a hardy handshake.

Isabelle could hardly contain herself with excitement, "We're thinking of an October wedding. After the harvest of course."

Caroline lifted her eyebrows, "Why so quick?"

Isabelle looked a little uneasy and sat back down on the sofa, "Well, Matt's parents are sending him back this summer to Lincoln to work in their grocery store there. Alfred wants Matt to learn everything about the grocery store business." Isabelle realized that she was doing all of the talking. Matt finished the conversation, telling them that he was hoping to be the manager of the store someday. He told them about the apartment they were going to look at on Monday.

Caroline looked as if she was in a daze. "That means we only have a few months to plan a wedding. I will need you to help with the arrangements."

"Oh yes. Every day I will be thinking of the wedding. We will have the most beautiful wedding Tranquility Lutheran Church has ever had." Isabelle reassured her. Matt sat down next to Isabelle expecting some opposition about the wedding held in just three and a half months. Henry congratulated him on his ability to think things through. Caroline did not say anything more and went into the kitchen to check on the midday meal. She mashed the potatoes and put the meatloaf on a platter. She busied herself with setting the food on the table and filling the glasses with water. Matt, Isabelle, and Henry gathered around the table. Maggie got a folding chair out of the closet for Matt to sit on. Confused by Caroline's sudden silence, Isabelle followed Caroline when she went into the kitchen with the empty water pitcher. Isabelle could not stand that her mother did not say anything, "Mom are you okay with this?"

Caroline put the water pitcher on the counter, turned around, and cradled Isabelle's face in her hands saying, "Oh I'm fine. I just needed a minute to absorb the news that my daughter is no longer a little girl." She let go of her face and fixed her eyes on Isabelle, "I just can't believe how fast the years flew by."

Isabelle relaxed and gave Caroline a hug. "Oh Mom, I thought you were upset about the announcement that we wanted to get married."

The family gathered at the table to enjoy Isabelle's dinner. Matt took a helping of the meatloaf, "This looks really good Isabelle. Mrs. Sims, I didn't know I was getting a girl that was not only beautiful, but also a good cook." Isabelle face turned as red as the radishes on her relish tray with embarrassment.

Caroline immediately corrected him, "You can call me Caroline now that you are one of the family."

"Sure thing." He said as he passed the meatloaf to Henry. "Shall I call you Henry?"

"Just call me Dad."

Everyone at the table laughed. Isabelle was getting over her jitters and Matt was relaxing. Maggie broke the ice by asking some questions about the wedding, "Will I be a bridesmaid."

Isabelle smiled at her, "Well of course. You will be my Maid of Honor. I was going to ask Sara to be a bridesmaid too. Is that alright Mom?"

Caroline replied, "Oh sure. Does Matt have anyone for the best man? I know you don't have any brothers."

Matt put his glass down, "I asked a friend from Lincoln that I've known since the seventh grade to be my Best Man. He said he would."

Isabelle added, "He asked Jim Perry to be a groomsman."

Henry smiled, "Sounds like you two have been planning this wedding awhile. Even before asking us."

This time Matt turned red with embarrassment, "I actually have been thinking about asking Isabelle to get married before graduation."

"I'll be right back." Isabelle quickly left the room and ran upstairs. She took the ring box out from under the scarves in her bottom drawer and went back downstairs. She opened the box and handed it to Caroline.

"Oh! Honey it's gorgeous." She handed the box to Henry.

Maggie walked over to Henry to look at the ring too. "Wow."

Henry gave the box back to Isabelle. "That looks really nice honey."

She took the ring out of the box and put the ring on her finger. "Now it's official. I'm engaged." She announced with a big smile.

They finished with the meal. Henry and Matt returned to the living room to talk. Henry wanted to know more about the Lincoln grocery store. Caroline and the girls sat around the table and talked about the wedding. Caroline asked Isabelle, "Have you thought about a color?"

Isabelle had been planning her wedding in her mind all day Saturday. In fact, she had been planning her wedding day since she was twelve, like any typical girl. "I thought I would like Maggie and Sara in peach."

Caroline was impressed with her choice, "That would be pretty for the fall. Do Matt and his friend have suits already? How about Jim, does he have one?"

"Jim and Matt do. I don't know about Kevin." Excitement drained from Isabelle's face. She put her head down and played with her hands in her lap while looking at the ring on her finger.

Caroline saw the sudden change in Isabelle's face, "Isabelle, what's wrong?"

Isabelle said solemnly, "I was just thinking. I wish Grandma was still here."

"Oh. I wish that too, but that was not God's plan." Caroline was trying to console her daughter.

Isabelle sadly said, "I know, but I feel cheated. Your parents are both gone; now Dads' are too."

Maggie was as solemn as Isabelle was, "Does Matt have grandparents?"

"His dad's mom is still living and his mom has both of her parents." The conversation saddened Caroline too. She did not want Isabelle or Maggie to see that she was almost in tears. She stood up to fill some glasses of lemonade for everyone.

Maggie tried to change the subject. "How about the flower girl? Who do you have for that?"

Caroline returned to the table with the lemonade, "What about Lillian? She will be three-years-old by then. If Julie practiced with her, I think she would do okay."

"Oh, Mom, that's a good idea. I was thinking it would be awesome if she could drop real leaves from a basket instead of flower petals."

Matt and Henry came into the dining room for some lemonade. They joined the women at the table. All afternoon they talked about the upcoming wedding. Isabelle wrote down some questions she needed to ask Matt's parents.

Matt stood up, "Well I should be heading home. I told my parents I would be home before supper." The afternoon was mentally exhausting. His nerves were getting the best of him.

Isabelle rose from her chair to walk him outside. She took his hand into hers. "Matt, I know that was a hard afternoon for you. It was for me too."

Matt kissed her. "It was okay. Now I know that they like me. I just didn't know what they were going to say."

"They admire you. I can tell."

"I will call you after Dad and I get back from Lincoln tomorrow. I will tell you all about the apartment. It may be late though."

"I won't care what time it is. I will wait for you to call me. I want to hear all about it."

. . .

Alfred was so impressed with Isabelle's work ethics at the store he increased her hours. Isabelle was now working full time. Isabelle did not mind, she was planning a wedding and needed all the money she could earn.

Isabelle left the grocery store on Monday and went to Sara's house. Betty answered the door, "Hi Isabelle. Sara is in her room."

"Hi Betty. Thanks." Isabelle went upstairs to find Sara. Sara had the record player blaring while lying on her bed looking at the papers she had from the Des Moines nurse's college. "I have an important question to ask you."

"What is it?" Sara looked up from her papers with a frown on her face.

Isabelle extended her arm and showed her hand with the ring on it. "I was wondering if you would be my bridesmaid."

"Oh my gosh!" Sara gasped. She leaped from her bed and turned down the volume of the record player. "Are you getting married?"

"Yes," Isabelle answered with a big smile on her face.

"When did this happen?"

"Just yesterday."

Sara grabbed Isabelle and gave her a hug, "A big congrats! The ring is beautiful. Of course, I will be your bridesmaid. When is this big event?"

"Saturday October 20th."

"I'll be away at college by then, but I promise I will be back that weekend. Sit down. You have to tell me how Matt proposed. Don't leave anything out, not even the juicy stuff."

Isabelle smiled at her. She knew Sara was going to ask her that. She only told Sara some of the details of the night at the Drive-In Theatre. She told her the plans she made about the wedding and that Matt was going to work in the Lincoln grocery store. "Mom and I were wondering if you think your Mom can make your bridesmaid dress and Maggie's Maid of Honor dress."

"Oh, I'm sure of it. Did you want to ask her right now?"

"Okay."

Both of the girls walked down to the sewing room where Betty was. Sara blurted out the news before Isabelle could speak. "Mom,

Isabelle is getting married!" Sara took Isabelle's hand and showed Betty the ring.

Betty got up from behind the sewing machine. She took Isabelle's hand for a closer look at the ring. She gave Isabelle a hug. "Congratulations! When is the big day?"

"Saturday October 20th." Sara said, then realized she was doing all of the talking. "Sorry, I should let you tell. I'm just so excited for you."

Isabelle laughed. "I would like Sara to be a bridesmaid. Maggie would be the Maid of Honor. Mom and I were wondering if you will make the dresses."

"Of course I will. It would be an honor."

Isabelle was relieved that Betty agreed to sew the dresses for the wedding. She explained to Betty that Caroline would call her and work out the details. Caroline just needed to know how much fabric to buy. Isabelle thanked Betty. The girls went back upstairs to Sara's room to talk. Sara showed Isabelle the new clothes Betty made for her. She held up a beige tweed skirt with a vest to match. "I really like this outfit. It will be nice for a cold winter day." Sara showed her a gray dress with a black belt. "I like this one too," she said as she held it front of her.

Isabelle was impressed with the dresses, blouses, and skirts she made. "They are so nice," she said.

Sara and Isabelle talked about the wedding. Sara was pleased that Jim would be walking with her in the ceremony. "Maybe that will spark a proposal from Jim." Isabelle teased.

"Not a chance." Sara replied. "He knows that I want to be a nurse. He told me he wouldn't stand in my way of my dreams." She ended the conversation with, "We're just friends."

Isabelle sat down on Sara's bed. "I am going to miss you Sara."

"I know, I will miss you too, but let's not talk about that yet. We have all summer to be together."

They talked the rest of the afternoon. Isabelle looked at Sara's clock and told her that she needed to get home.

Once she was at home, Isabelle informed Caroline that Betty agreed to make the dresses for Sara and Maggie. Caroline was relieved. She knew that the gowns would be much more expensive to buy. She was not sure they would be able to find two dresses alike and peach in color.

"We may have to go to Lincoln to get the yardage we need. I don't thing Cleary Department Store would have that much fabric in stock, especially in peach."

Isabelle told her that Matt wanted the family to meet his grandparents someday. "Maybe we could make a day of it."

Caroline liked the idea. She would look on her schedule at the hospital when the next time she was off on a weekday. Isabelle would need to make sure the same day would work for Matt and his family too. "After we visit his grandparents, we'll leave the men at the house and the women will go shopping."

CHAPTER TWENTY-THREE

On Monday, Isabelle went upstairs after supper to wait for Matt to call. She dozed off dreaming about the wedding. When she awoke, she realized it was dark and the clock beside her bed read 2:30 a.m. She was confused why Matt did not call. She wanted to wake up her parents to ask if he called and they did not let her know, but decided she would have to wait until morning. She laid there awake thinking of all the things that could have happened. She was scaring herself. She tried to close her eyes and get the bad thoughts out of her head, but to no avail. She looked at her clock again to see that it was only 4:00 a.m. She wished the time would go faster. She rolled over and finally dozed off.

The next morning, Maggie was up moving around getting dressed. She noticed that Isabelle did not even change out of her clothes she had on the day before. Isabelle opened her eyes when she heard Maggie open her dresser drawer. She jumped out of bed and ran downstairs. Caroline had already gone to work. Henry was not around either. She ran outside to find her dad, but the tractor was not there. Henry was already in the field disking. She went back in the house and asked Maggie if she heard the phone ring last night.

"The only phone call I heard was when Mom was talking to Betty. That was about seven thirty last night. Why what's the matter?"

"Matt was supposed to call last night after they came back from Lincoln." Isabelle was tempted to go to the store to talk to him, but decided not to. She wished she worked today. Isabelle was in agony waiting for Matt to call. She fixed some breakfast for her and Maggie. After Maggie ate, she went outside to attend to her garden leaving Isabelle alone in the house.

195

When the telephone rang, Isabelle rushed to answer it. "Isabelle this is Kathy from Cleary Grocery. We are wondering if you could come in to work today. We need someone to fill in for Karen. She called and said she was sick."

Isabelle was confused, "Why didn't Alfred Carson call me?"

"They're not back from Lincoln yet. He called and said that he and Matt wouldn't be at the store today."

Now Isabelle was worried. She felt a knot in the pit of her stomach. "Sure I can be there in a half an hour." She hung up the telephone. She was tired from being up most of the night. Isabelle got ready and walked out to the garden to tell Maggie she needed to go to work.

Maggie looked up from weeding her garden. "Did something happen to Matt yesterday?"

Isabelle replied, "I don't know," and walked away.

Once Isabelle got to work, she clocked in and went to the office to get her moneybag for her register. "Kathy, did Alfred say why they weren't coming to the store today?"

"All I know is that he called and said that they were still in Lincoln and that they would not be back today. Thanks for filling in for Karen." It was hard for Isabelle to keep her mind on her job. She busied herself dusting shelves and sweeping the floor. Kathy stopped Isabelle. "I have two home deliveries. Matt was supposed to take Mr. Barkley's order to him yesterday and I have Mrs. Marks' order, too. Can you deliver them?"

Isabelle was happy to. She looked at the addresses on the order sheet. Isabelle knew the one address, but did not know the other one. "Kathy, where does Mr. Barkley live?"

"He lives in the last house on the block before the cemetery. The house has blue shutters with an attached garage. You can't miss it." Kathy helped Isabelle load her car with the grocery orders. She had Matt on her mind and wondered what happened to the Carson's in Lincoln.

Isabelle stopped in front of the house of her first grocery order. She knocked on the door and yelled, "Cleary Grocery."

An elderly woman opened the door. "Hello." She smiled when she saw Isabelle. "I didn't think you sounded like Matt Carson." She led Isabelle into the kitchen. "You can just put the groceries on the counter. I can put them away."

Isabelle put the sacks of groceries on the counter and took out the bill. "This is the total Mrs. Marks." Mrs. Marks wrote a check for the groceries and handed it to Isabelle. Isabelle took the check from her and said, "We thank you for your business."

"Just a minute." Mrs. Marks stopped her before she walked out of the door. She handed Isabelle four dollars. "This is for you."

"Thank you." Isabelle went back to her car smiling to herself wondering how much extra money Matt makes in a month's time making home deliveries.

She knocked on Mr. Barkley's screen door. No one answered. She pounded louder and yelled, "Mr. Barkley? I'm from Cleary Grocery." She peered through the screen to see if she could see anyone moving about. She saw no one, so she opened the screen door and again yelled out. "I have a grocery delivery from Cleary Grocery." She stopped to listen. She could hear an engine running. It sounded like a car. She decided to go through a hallway to where she thought the kitchen might be. Isabelle could smell something strange coming through the kitchen door. She took another whiff of the odor and realized that it was a gas smell from an automobile. She put the groceries on the kitchen table and stopped to listen again. She saw a door off the kitchen. When she opened that door, a blast of exhaust fumes from the car that was running filled the kitchen. She had a sick feeling come over her as she tried to peer through the car window from where she was standing in the kitchen doorway, but she was afraid to proceed into the garage. She closed the door and tried to find a telephone. She searched in the kitchen and the living room, but could not find one. Isabelle just knew in her heart that Mr. Barkley was in that car in the garage. She panicked. Isabelle ran to the next nearest house. She pounded on the door yelling, "Is anyone home?" No one answered. She ran to the next house. She pounded on the door, "Is anyone home?" A toddler came to the door followed by a woman.

"Can I help you?"

"Do you have a telephone?"

"Yes"

"Call for emergency services quick. There is an emergency at Mr. Phil Barkley's house."

The woman hurried into the living room and dialed emergency services. She told the dispatcher what Isabelle had said. When she turned around to ask Isabelle what the trouble was, she saw the door shut and Isabelle was gone.

Isabelle ran back to Mr. Barkley's house. When she reached the front steps of the house, she stopped. She was afraid to go back inside, especially the garage. She waited by the street until the fire department arrived. Then she heard the siren of the fire engine Isabelle flagged it down with her hands. Fire Chief Saunders hurried out of the fire engine. "Are you the one who called for the fire department? Where is the fire?"

"There is no fire. I walked into that house and I could smell car exhaust coming from the garage. I could hear a car running. I ran to the neighbors to get help."

Fire Chief Saunders turned to the two firefighters who were dragging hoses from the fire engine. He immediately knew what the situation was. Mr. Barkley was a troubled soul. The fire department has been to his house before. Chief Saunders tried to get him some help, but Mr. Barkley refused to see anyone. "There's no fire, but take fire extinguishers for extra caution, just in case a fire breaks out when you enter the house," he said to the two firefighters. "The young lady said she could smell car exhaust coming from the garage." The firefighters gingerly opened the door and walked into the house. Each of them was holding a fire extinguisher. One of them yelled. "Mr. Barkley?" No one answered. The other firefighter kicked the door open to the kitchen, while holding on to the nozzle of the fire extinguisher. The door flew open. A blast of car exhaust fumes hit his face.

Fire Chief Saunders searched the rest of the house to see if anyone was inside. He heard one of the firefighters calling, "Chief Saunders, come, quick!" Mr. Barkley was lying unconscious on the front seat of the car holding an empty whisky bottle. The firefighter eyed the hose that was wedged in the passenger side window, filling the car with the deadly gas. He tried to open the car doors, but all of them were locked. Chief Saunders opened the garage door and ran to the fire engine to radio the dispatcher for an ambulance. He grabbed a crowbar and helped the two firefighters pry the car door open.

Isabelle heard another siren coming towards her. She saw the ambulance. The ambulance crew ran into the garage. She waited by the street wondering if she should go back to the store, but something told her not to move. Isabelle froze when she saw them carrying Mr. Barkley out on a stretcher. Fire Chief Saunders approached her with a clipboard in his hand. He clicked a pen and started writing on it. He asked Isabelle, "Did you see anyone around when you entered the house?"

"No. I called out for Mr. Barkley, but he did not answer. I didn't see him either."

"Can I get your name?"

Isabelle was shaking. Her voice cracked as she spoke. "I-I'm Isabelle Sims."

"What were you doing here, Miss Sims?"

"I-I work for Cleary Grocery. I was delivering him his grocery order." She was shaking uncontrollably.

Fire Chief Saunders continued to ask Isabelle questions while he was writing down her answers. He put down the clipboard to his side. "This is all I need from you Miss Sims. If we have any more questions, we will call you." Isabelle ran through the day's events in her mind. She kept thinking to herself; 'if only she would have gotten there sooner, she could have perhaps caught him before he did anything.' Chief Saunders could see that Isabelle was almost in tears. He put his clipboard under his arm, and put his hands on her shoulders. "You did all the right things Miss Sims."

"But if I would have gotten here sooner, perhaps..." She lowered her face and could not finish her sentence.

Fire Chief Saunders lifted her chin and looked right into her eyes. "He would have just done something else, or tried it again another time. Sometimes life is just too unbearable for some folks."

Isabelle still did not feel much better as she walked back to her car and drove back to the grocery store. Isabelle walked into the store through the back room. She went into the restroom and washed her face. When she came out of the restroom, Alfred was waiting for her. "What happened to you? Kathy said you have been gone for almost two hours."

Isabelle was relieved to see him. She explained to Alfred about the incident at Mr. Barkley's house. Alfred did not ask her any questions about Mr. Barkley. He did not want to pry into her personal feelings about the incident. Isabelle searched the backroom for Matt, but did not see him. "Where's Matt?"

"I sent him to the meat locker for the meat order."

Isabelle went back to her checkout register. It was hard for her to concentrate. She wanted to ask what happened yesterday, but she was on the clock and needed to go back to work. Isabelle decided she would talk to Matt at the end of her shift.

Isabelle entered the backroom to clock out when her shift was over. She felt physically and mentally drained from the day. Isabelle saw Matt breaking down boxes. "Hi!"

Matt looked up. "Hi Isabelle." Immediately he started to apologize for not calling her yesterday. He told her that George Gibbs had a stroke and could not return to work. They went to the hospital to see how he was. "Isabelle, I don't think he will ever work again. Dad went to the store to talk to Doug. They already need me. I'm going to move into the apartment on Friday."

Isabelle took a deep breath. "This Friday? Things are moving so fast."

"I know. I feel the same way. I'm afraid that I can't do what Dad expects me to do."

Isabelle assured him that he would be okay. Doug Ayker will help him learn what he needs to know. Isabelle told her story about the grocery delivery. Matt was apologetic when he heard what she had to go through. "I should have taken that order to him yesterday." was all he could say.

Isabelle left Matt to do his job. She just needed some time to unwind. It was a sleepless night and an exhausting day. Isabelle drove to Sara's house to talk to her. Sara was a good friend and she needed her right now.

CHAPTER TWENTY-FOUR

Alfred Carson parked the car in front of the nursing home in Lincoln. Alfred and his wife Bonnie went to the room where Alfred's mom, Helen, was sitting in her chair waiting for them to come. Bonnie found a sweater in her closet to bring for the day. She put Helen's glasses in her purse. Alfred positioned Helen's wheel chair in front of her asking, "Mom, are you ready?"

"I am."

Alfred and Bonnie helped her into the wheel chair and pushed her outside. Helen lifted her head to take in the sunshine. She has not gotten out much since Alfred moved to Cleary. Matt helped her into the front seat of the car and bent down to give Helen a kiss on her cheek. "Hi Grandma." He folded up Helen's wheel chair and placed in the trunk of the car. Helen was excited to see Bonnie's parents, Harold and Carrie Becker. It had been a couple of months since she last visited with them.

Bonnie's parents lived in a house by the airport in Lincoln. Just as Alfred parked the car, a plane was flying over. Bonnie opened her door. The plane was so loud that she put her hands over her ears. "I don't know how Mom and Dad can stand that day in and day out. I certainly don't miss the noise."

Matt got out of the back seat, looked up at the plane and stated, "Someday I would like to take a ride in one of those."

Alfred opened the trunk to get Helen's wheel chair out of it. He looked up at the plane saying, "Not me. I had enough of flying in the war." Alfred and Matt helped Helen into her wheel chair and the family walked up to the door.

Bonnie rang the doorbell just as Harold opened the door. "Hi Dad." Bonnie said to him while Carrie came to the entryway and greeted them. "Hello, Mom."

Alfred and Matt helped Helen into an easy chair in the living room. Bonnie followed Carrie into the kitchen. "Is there anything I can do to help?" she asked as she lifted the lid off the kettle on the stove.

"You can finish chopping these vegetables for the salad." Carrie handed the knife to Bonnie and sat on a chair in the kitchen. She folded the kitchen towel she had on her shoulder and placed it on the table. Carrie stayed sitting on the kitchen chair to let Bonnie finish the meal. Bonnie busied herself with the food; not paying any attention to the fact that her mother just assumed Bonnie would finish the meal for her.

Bonnie unpacked the box of food she brought. She had two apple pies and banana bread that Alfred picked up from the bakery. "Isabelle and her family should be here shortly. Mom, you are really going to like her. She is perfect for Matt."

Henry parked the car in front of Harold and Carrie Becker's home. The white two-story colonial-style home had a row of well-groomed shrubs on either of the sidewalk. A bed of roses surrounded six pillars that supported an upper deck. The deck spanned the width of the home. Two shaped pine trees stood on each corner of the home. The Sims' family was impressed. Caroline checked the address again to make sure they were at the correct house. Maggie exclaimed, "Wow, what a beautiful house!" Isabelle was awed.

Caroline got out of the car. She studied the landscape and said aloud, "I wonder if they have a professional gardener?"

The doorbell rang. Matt rushed to answer it. He let Isabelle and her family in. He introduced his grandparents to Henry, Caroline, and Maggie. "And this is Isabelle," he said as he took Isabelle's hand. "She is the love of my life."

Harold smiled and kissed her hand. "She sure is a looker." Isabelle blushed.

Isabelle and Matt walked over to Helen. Matt said, "Grandma, what do you think of Isabelle?"

"Hello Isabelle. I am very glad to meet you. You are the only thing Matt has been talking about for months."

Bonnie escorted everyone to the formal dining room. Carrie had the table set with a fresh flower arrangement as the centerpiece with candles on either side of it. The dishes were lead crystal and the silverware was freshly polished. Neatly folded white linen napkins were set near each plate. Everyone stood while Alfred and Matt helped Helen into her seat. Harold pulled out the chair for Carrie, Alfred did the same for Bonnie while Matt helped seat Caroline. Maggie and Isabelle exchanged glances. Henry stayed standing until Matt finished seating Isabelle and Maggie. Alfred seated himself after Harold sat down. Then Henry and Matt followed suit.

Carrie let Bonnie bring in the food from the kitchen. Bonnie handed the salad to Harold first, and then she returned to the kitchen for the rest of the food. Maggie was thinking to herself that she was acting like a butler rather than one of the guests. Bonnie took her place in her chair when the food was all on the table. She took small helpings for herself. Bonnie watched the guests at the table as she ate. She barely had time to finish what little food she had on her own plate before she rose, took everyone's dinner plate, and returned with a silver coffee server to fill the cups with coffee. Then Bonnie disappeared into the kitchen again and returned with a serving tray with desert plates of apple pie and a scoop of vanilla ice cream on top of each piece. She finally sat down with one for herself. Isabelle did not know what to think of the way Bonnie took control of the meal. She was not used to someone being so formal.

When Harold stood up, Carrie and Bonnie rose from their chairs. Alfred and Matt helped Helen out of her seat. Henry pulled out Caroline's chair and gave her a smile. Caroline acknowledged the gesture with a smile back. Once everyone was standing, Harold led everyone through a door off the dining room to the sitting room. The room had shelves of books lined on one wall and a grandfather clock that was eight feet tall with a pendulum swinging back and forth on the opposite wall. It chimed once, just as they were entering the room. Maggie's eyes grew big when she saw the books. She wanted to move closer to the shelves to read the titles.

Isabelle was nervous until Matt put his arms around her and led her to the settee in front of the east window. Bonnie stayed behind to clear the dining room table. Caroline was tempted to go back into the dining room to help her, but she decided against it. Harold motioned for Henry and Caroline to sit on the royal blue sofa in the middle of the room. Alfred helped Helen to sit on a blue tufted chair across from the sofa. Then he sat down on the matching one. Maggie sat down on a blue overstuffed chair next to the settee. The chair was so luxurious and big, it seemed to swallow her up. Harold and Carrie each sat on the wooden glider-rocking chairs on either side of the sofa.

They waited for Bonnie before the conversation started about of the upcoming wedding. Bonnie entered the sitting room carrying a tray with a pitcher of water and tall glasses filled with ice. She placed it on a buffet table in front of the west window. Caroline wondered if Isabelle's wedding plans would be up to the standards of the family she was getting into. Alfred and Bonnie did not seem to be that way until today. Matt was the one to break the silence. He told his grandparents of the plans that Isabelle had. When he mentioned that Isabelle wanted Lillian to drop real leaves down the aisle of the church instead of flower petals, Isabelle looked down at her hands in her lap, thinking that Matt's grandmother, Carrie, would not approve of the idea. However, Carrie surprised her. She put her hands together with a clap. Carrie adored the idea and thought it was a nice touch to a fall theme wedding. Isabelle was pleased to hear that and regained her enthusiasm.

Bonnie looked at the grandfather clock. She announced that it was time for the women to go shopping for fabric before the store closed. Carrie decided to stay with Helen and the men. Alfred handed Bonnie the keys to the car.

Maggie and Isabelle climbed in the back seat, while Caroline took the front passenger seat next to Bonnie. Before Bonnie started the car, she turned around to talk to Isabelle. "Isabelle, I sensed that you were uneasy at my parent's house. I am sorry about that. It is just that my mother grew up in the south on a plantation. She grew up with servants and maids. When she married my dad, he would not hear of hiring domestic assistants. So when I was old enough, I was brought up serving meals that way."

Isabelle did not know what to say. She appreciated Bonnie for taking the time to tell her why she acted the way she did. "I was impressed," was all Isabelle good manage to say back to her.

Bonnie went on to say, "There is no reason for you to be intimidated. Alfred and I are just regular folks. I just wanted you to know that."

"Thank you Mrs. Carson." Isabelle admired Bonnie for taking special consideration of her feelings.

"Oh, and by the way, you can certainly call me Bonnie."

Isabelle smiled and said, "Okay Bonnie."

Bonnie knew of a store in downtown Lincoln that sold fabric. Caroline had talked to Betty before she came and knew how much fabric she needed for two dresses. They searched through the rack of fabric. Isabelle was disappointed. She could not find anything that looked like the peach she had envisioned. A salesclerk came up and asked if she could be of any help. Caroline was the first to answer. "We are looking for a peach taffeta for wedding bridesmaid dresses."

The salesclerk exclaimed, "Oh, these fabrics are for the summer. We have not set out our fall fabrics yet. I'll be right back." She came back carrying three bolts of fabric still wrapped in paper. She laid them on a table and removed the wrapping paper from the first one. Isabelle gasped when she saw the first bolt. It was a color slightly darker than peach. "I really like that one."

"That's a new color." The salesclerk replied. "They call it 'Autumn Apricot'."

Caroline saw Isabelle's face light up when she saw the fabric. At that point, it did not matter what the cost was for the fabric, nor did it matter what the color the other two bolts were. She wanted Isabelle to have it for her wedding. She took the paper out of her purse and told the salesclerk the amount of yardage she needed.

"Do you want me to un-wrap the other bolts?" asked the salesclerk. The fabric mesmerized Isabelle.

Caroline looked at Isabelle. "You don't need to bother. I think Isabelle has picked the one she wants."

The salesclerk handed the cut fabric to Isabelle. "Your wedding will be beautiful."

Isabelle pressed the package to her chest and said with a big grin. "I think so too."

Maggie liked the color too. She commented, "If I were asked to a prom, I would wear my Maid of Honor dress."

Bonnie asked Isabelle if she already had a wedding dress. Of course, she did not, but she secretly wanted to pick one out with just her mother some other time. Caroline knew that was a personal thing for Isabelle. She answered Bonnie, "Isabelle and I will take another day out for that, but thanks for the offer."

"Okay. We'll now go back to my parent's house and rescue Henry." They laughed at her cynicism.

CHAPTER TWENTY-FIVE

Isabelle shut off the vacuum cleaner when she heard the phone ring. "Hello?"

"Hi sweet-heart. What ya doin?"

"Hi Honey. Just cleaning, I didn't have to work today. How's it going at the store?"

"Oh fine, but very busy. There is a lot to learn. I can't talk too long, but I heard that Cleary's fair is next week. I'm coming home for it." Isabelle was almost jumping up and down for joy. "I can't wait to see you. I love you."

"I love you too." Isabelle replaced the phone on its cradle, turned up the radio she was listening to, and finished her vacuuming with a dance to her steps and a song on her lips.

. . .

On a warm Tuesday morning in late July, Maggie pulled out the watering hose from Casey's shed and dragged it to her garden. She had never seen such a great crop of carrots before. Maggie was picking green beans every three days and the green bell peppers were the best she had ever grown. She spread the hose to the tomatoes and eggplant. When she turned on the water, it flowed down her trench she dug to each tomato plant. She thought to herself that she was getting good at directing the water to go where exactly she wanted it to go.

She put the pail on her arm as she stretched over the cucumber vines to search for some small cucumbers for dill pickles. Maggie spotted a large one that had already turned yellow. "Oops," she said to herself when she realized she missed that one several days ago.

The Cleary County Fair was coming up. She had been taking extra care of her garden this year. She was hoping to get some good ribbons on her vegetables she wanted to enter in the fair.

Caroline was in the kitchen washing some pint jars. In anticipation that Maggie would be bringing a pail full of cucumbers and green beans, she washed a few extra. Maggie put the pail on the kitchen counter for her mother to see. "Oh Maggie, those cucumbers are beautiful." Caroline lifted the large yellow cucumber out of the pail. "Except for this one."

"That's an 'oops'." Maggie giggled. "I was going to feed that one to the chickens, they can peck at it." Caroline smiled. She gathered all of her ingredients for the batch of dill pickles. Maggie and Caroline worked at getting the jars ready for the canner. Caroline was pleased that Maggie picked enough small cucumbers for eight pints.

Henry put down the newspaper when Caroline called him to the table to eat supper. Maggie set the plate of hamburgers in front of her father. The table was set with all the fixings for hamburger sandwiches from her garden. There was a bowl of sliced tomatoes, a jar of dill pickles, a plate of fresh boiled beets, and a steaming bowl of green beans on the table to eat. Henry was impressed with all of the fresh produce on the table. "Maggie, you're hard work on the garden sure paid off," as he loaded his plate. "The fair is coming up. Are you planning on entering anything from your garden this year?"

"Oh yes. I have been watching this one eggplant. It is already a good size. I staked it so the eggplant would not fall over on the ground. The carrots are looking good too." The family had gotten used to not having Isabelle join them at the supper table. Sometimes she would bring home something from the bakery for their dessert after she got off work from the grocery store.

. . .

Maggie flipped the calendar. August 2nd was entry day for the Cleary County Fair. All of the entries needed to be at the exhibit hall by Thursday before 5:00 p.m. Judging would take place the next day. Maggie got up early and went out to her garden. She picked the prize eggplant. It measured nearly eight inches across and was a beautiful color purple with no sun blemishes. Maggie dug up some of the carrots and was surprised to find three that were uniform in size and perfect shape. She picked through the beets and the green beans for the best ones. She saved the best vegetables for a '5 vegetable box' entry. She could not wait to find out what ribbons she would get at the fair for her vegetables.

After dinner, Caroline parked the car on the grass at the fairgrounds. She helped Maggie carry the boxes of produce to the Exhibit Hall. "Maggie, I think you'll do well with your vegetables. They really look nice." After Maggie submitted her vegetables, she and Caroline walked to the food stand. Caroline bought each of them a piece of cherry pie.

That Friday night, Isabelle was ready when Matt pulled into the driveway to take her and Maggie to the Cleary County Fair. Isabelle and Matt exchanged kisses and hugs while Maggie got into the back seat. Matt could not get very close to the gate of the fairgrounds to park. He finally found a parking place on the far west corner. The carnival rides were already busy with thrill seekers. There was a line of people in front of the Ferris wheel. Isabelle got out of the car. "Let's go see what ribbons Maggie received on her vegetables." Matt said, "Then we can eat."

Maggie liked that idea. She had been anxious all day to find out what ribbons she received. They walked through the Exhibit Hall, but they could only find the beets and the green beans she entered. She received a red ribbon for her beets and a blue ribbon for the green beans. Maggie was pleased, but confused that she could not find her eggplant, carrots, and the '5 vegetable box'. Matt discovered the rest of Maggie's entries. They were on a table set aside for the champion exhibits. Maggie could not believe it when she saw a Champion ribbon on both of her carrots and eggplant. She was thrilled when she saw the Grand Champion rosette attached to her '5 vegetable box', along with a money certificate worth $5.00, with Maggie's name on it.

Matt and Isabelle congratulated Maggie for a job well done. Matt treated both of the girls to a barbecued sandwich and a coke at the fair food stand. After they finished eating, they walked around the fair. Maggie spotted Susan and her brothers in line for the Tilt-A-Whirl ride. "I'll find you guys later. I'd like to hang out with Susan for a while."

Isabelle looked at her watch. "Let's say we meet back at the Exhibit Hall at nine o'clock." Maggie agreed and left. Matt and Isabelle headed for the Ferris wheel.

The fair was exciting with the lights, music, and laughter. Screams came from the thrill seekers on the carnival rides. The aroma from popcorn, hotdogs, and hamburgers on the grills filled the air. Maggie, Susan, Scott, and Nate rode several of the rides. They were having so much fun they did not realize that it was already after eight o'clock. They wondered through the midway watching the fair goers playing at the gaming tables. Scott wanted to play some of the games. Maggie, Susan, and Nate watched him play the ring toss game. Just as Scott tossed his last ring into the pit of empty coke bottles, Fred and Margaret came up behind them. To Scott's surprise, he hooked the ring around the prize winning red painted bottle in the center of the pit. The crowd around the game applauded and shouted their congratulations. Scott chose a pocketknife for his prize and showed it to everyone. Fred was impressed with the quality of the pocketknife when Scott showed it to him. Margaret congratulated Scott and then announced that it was time to go home. Nate complained that he did not get to spend all of his money yet. The family took him to the sales stand. He bought some cotton candy and a Cleary County Fair pennant to hang up above his bed in his room.

Maggie said goodbye to the Johnson family. She slowly walked back to the Exhibit Hall. Someone tapped her on her right shoulder. She turned around to find Allen Jones. "Hi Maggie."

"Hi Allen."

"Are you here alone? Where is your sister?"

"She and Matt Carson are around here someplace."

"Do you want to hang around with me for a while?" Allen asked with hopes that she would agree. He liked Maggie and has always wanted to get to know her better. Yes, he has flirted with her to get her attention at the corn-shelling day, but now, there was no one in particular around them.

"Okay. It's only eight thirty. I am supposed to be at the Exhibit Hall at nine o'clock."

"Do you like Bumper Cars?"

"They look like fun."

Allen bought two tickets for the Bumper Cars. Maggie chose to get into a blue car and Allen hopped into a red car. When the operator announced for the riders to go, Allen immediately bumped Maggie into the middle of the arena. Maggie laughed and hollered,

"I get you back for that." She turned her bumper car around and chased him. Just when she got close enough to bump him from behind, Allen made a sharp right turn. Maggie slammed into a ten-year-old boy in a yellow bumper car. "Oops. Sorry about that!" she yelled. The boy just laughed and spun around to hit someone else.

Then Allen smacked Maggie again from behind. "I'm not sorry about that!" he yelled, flirting with her.

"I'll get you!" Maggie yelled back. She knew she was flirting back, but she did not care. She was having a good time. Maggie tried to chase Allen down again, but she could not catch him to hit his bumper car. After that, it seemed that all of the bumper cars in the arena were after Maggie. Bumper cars bumped into her no matter which way she turned. At one point, she was laughing so hard she thought she was going to pee in her pants.

Allen enjoyed watching Maggie. When the ride was over, he helped Maggie get out of her bumper car saying, "It looked like you were having fun."

"I loved it. Thank you for the ticket to ride it."

"You want to try something else?"

"I'm sorry, but I should be heading to the Exhibit Hall."

"Okay." Allen replied.

As Maggie and Allen walked through the midway towards the Exhibit Hall, they could hear the attendant for the darts game yelling, "Step right up, step right up, everybody is a winner." At the ball throw the attendant yelled, "Prizes, Prizes, Prizes." Allen and Maggie kept walking until they approached the shooting gallery. The attendant yelled at Allen, "Who is next? How about you, son? Show the lady what you could do." Allen was good at shooting a gun. He wanted to try it. "Yeah, I'll try it." He put $1.00 on the counter and asked the attendant for a gun. The attendant informed Allen that he could shoot five shots for twenty-five cents. Allen aimed for the ducks that were on a conveyor belt. He missed the duck on his first shot, but hit four ducks after that. The attendant asked if he wanted to spend another twenty-five cents for a bigger prize. Allen agreed and was able to hit three more ducks out of the next five shots. Maggie was impressed and congratulated him on his shooting ability. The attendant pointed to the prizes and asked Allen what prize he wanted. Allen chose a brown teddy bear. He handed it to Maggie saying, "For the lady who is having so much fun."

"You want to give this to me? Thank you."

Allen sat on the bench with Maggie in front of the Exhibit Hall waiting for Matt and Isabelle. It was nearly nine o'clock. They sat and watched the fair goers carrying their prizes and tired children back to the parking lot to go home.

Matt and Isabelle were walking up to the bench where Maggie and Allen were sitting. Matt leaned over to Isabelle asking, "Who is that sitting next to Maggie?"

Isabelle replied, "I don't know. He looks familiar." She was searching her mind.

Allen and Maggie stood up from the bench when Isabelle and Matt came up to it. Immediately Maggie said, "This is Allen Jones."

Then Isabelle remembered he was the boy that came to help shell corn. "It's nice to see you again Allen. This is Matt Carson." They all exchanged hellos.

Allen excused himself saying his goodbyes. He turned to face Maggie and bowed while saying, "Good night my lady."

Maggie was glad it was semi dark where they were standing, as her face was a crimson red. "Thank you Allen for the Bumper Car ride and for the bear".

After Matt parked the car in front of Maggie and Isabelle's house, Maggie opened the door of the car. She took the teddy bear saying, "Thanks Matt for taking me to the fair. I had a great time."

"You're welcome. Congratulations are your vegetable exhibits," he said back to her.

"Thanks," Maggie said as she shut the car door. Maggie went into the living room to talk to her parents. She told them about the money certificate and the ribbons she received for her vegetables at the fair. They were excited for Maggie and told her congratulations. Maggie was surprised they did not ask her where or how she got the teddy bear she was holding. She said goodnight to her parents and went upstairs. Henry and Caroline did not bother asking about Isabelle. They knew she and Matt were still outside. They left them alone.

Matt and Isabelle got out of the car and walked to the grove of trees. It seemed forever since they last saw each other. There were no words spoken, just passionate kisses between them.

CHAPTER TWENTY-SIX

Isabelle and Caroline found a beautiful wedding dress in a bridal shop in the town of Morgan. Isabelle especially loved the small white beads sewn into the neckline. She was pleased that the dress fit her perfectly and did not need any alterations. Caroline, Bonnie, and Isabelle were busy with wedding announcements, flowers, hair appointments, and decorations for the wedding. Bonnie made sure the wedding cake was on order at the bakery. She surprised Isabelle when she told her she ordered peach colored mints and that they would be her treat.

The days were flying by. Isabelle was so busy that she forgot her own birthday, until Matt called, wishing her a happy day. Even Henry, Caroline, and Maggie did not realize that it was Isabelle's birthday until she hung up the phone from talking to Matt. Caroline remembered that she purchased a photo album book for her birthday several months ago. Caroline retrieved it from her closet in the bedroom and handed to Isabelle. "Happy Birthday! This is for you. I didn't have time to wrap it though."

"Gee thanks. We have been so busy around here."

Isabelle walked into the bedroom carrying the photo album book. Maggie asked, "What's that?"

"It's a birthday present from Mom and Dad."

"Oh. Is today your birthday? I'm sorry, Isabelle, I forgot. Happy Birthday!"

"Thanks, but I forgot too, until just now. We have been so busy, as a matter of fact; Betty wants you to go to her house tomorrow to try on the dress she made you for the wedding."

Maggie was surprised that Betty was already finished with it. She knew that they drove to Des Moines last weekend to have Sara try hers on. "Okay. I will go over there after school on Wednesday. Can you meet me there then?"

"Yes," Isabelle said. "I can be at Sara's house after five o'clock to pick you up."

. . .

Isabelle flipped the calendar to October. Her butterflies in her stomach fluttered when she saw Maggie's red heart she drew on October 20 and wrote 'Wedding Day'. It was only three weeks away. Isabelle took a deep breath while going over in her head all of the things she still had to do.

Julie called and told Caroline that Lillian was excited to be 'leaf girl'. They started to call her that instead of flower girl. She said that Lillian would even correct anyone saying she was a leaf girl, not a flower girl. Julie informed her they were letting her practice dropping leaves while walking down the aisle in their church.

Isabelle and Maggie searched the farm grove for the prettiest colored leaves they could find. It did not take long before they filled Lillian's basket with leaves. They found enough to scatter on the serving table with the wedding cake.

Jim found out that Matt and Kevin both had brown suits, so Jim talked his dad into buying him one. Jim told Matt that he was dating a girl from Omaha, and that he told Sara about her. He said Sara was not too disappointed. By the end of the summer, Sara and Jim had parted as friends.

On October 20, Isabelle was awake waiting for her alarm clock to go off. She could not wait any longer. She pressed the off button ten minutes before it was going to ring. Isabelle opened the top drawer for the one set of clean undergarments she did not pack, and crept down the stairs to take a bath. She heard her mother roaming around in the living room. She stood in the doorway watching Caroline inspecting a set of white pearls. Caroline was going to surprise Isabelle with them before she walked down the aisle. Isabelle had never seen them before. "Mom, what do you have in your hand?"

Caroline abruptly turned around. "You startled me," she said as she tried to hide the string of pearls behind her back. "I wasn't going to show you these until we were at the church." She opened her hand to reveal the pearls. "They are my mother's. My mother gave them to me on my wedding day." She had a tear streaming down her face.

"Mom, they're beautiful." Isabelle had tears swelling up in her eyes too. "I'll give them back to you after today."

"Oh no, they are yours to keep."

Isabelle took the pearls and gave her mother a hug. A tear dropped on her mother's shoulder. Isabelle whispered, "Thank you. They mean the world to me."

There was a light sprinkle of rain coming down, before the clouds parted to let the morning sun shine through them. It was going to be a glorious day for a wedding. Henry went into the kitchen to make himself some breakfast and coffee. He would fend for himself. He knew the best thing for him to do on this day was to stay out of the way of the women in his life, until they needed him at the church to walk down the aisle to give his daughter away.

Isabelle sat in front of her mirror adjusting to every detail of her makeup and hair. When she was satisfied, she opened her closet door. Her wedding dress was the only garment hanging in her closet. She stood there looking at it for a moment before she took it out. "Maggie can you help me? I don't want to mess up my hair." Maggie held the dress high above Isabelle's head while she slipped her arms into it. Maggie buttoned the row of buttons in the back and adjusted the skirt of the dress over the cancan. Isabelle smiled at the image in the mirror. She applied lipstick on her lips. "Well, what do you think, Maggie?"

Maggie stepped back from Isabelle, smiled and said, "Wow!"

Isabelle handed the string of pearls to Maggie. "Can you help me put these on?" Isabelle was waiting for Maggie's reaction to the pearls, but she did not show any emotion. "Do you know where these come from?"

"Yeah, Mom showed them to me yesterday. They are Grandmother Anne's; I was not supposed to tell you about them. They are beautiful. I thought Mom was going to wait until we were in the church to give them to you."

"I saw Mom in the living room with them earlier this morning. I think I surprised her."

Maggie came down the steps first. Henry and Caroline were waiting in the living room for the girls. Caroline was holding a hair clip adorned with peach roses on it. She took a deep breath when she saw Maggie in the doorway. "Maggie, you are very beautiful." She affixed the clip to her hair, and helped her put on a necklace that she bought for her.

Henry hugged Maggie. "I agree."

Isabelle entered the living room. Caroline cleared the lump in her throat before she could speak. "Oh! Isabelle how lovely you are!"

Henry smiled. "I wish you all the happiness in the world my dear," and gave her a hug.

"Thank you." She stood still to let her family admire her for a minute. Henry opened the door to watch the three beautiful women of his life walk passed him, all dressed in their finest.

Caroline, Maggie, and Isabelle entered the church though the back entrance. Bonnie, Carrie, and Helen greeted them with adoration and many compliments. Julie walked in holding Lillian's hand with her basket of leaves. Julie put Lillian's hair up in a bun with a ring of white flowers around it. She was so cute in her white floor length dress and her little white shoes. The women were fussing over her and complementing on how cute she was. Maggie gave Lillian the doll that Isabelle bought her for being a 'leaf girl' to keep her occupied.

Betty and Sara walked in. Sara immediately grabbed Isabelle. "What a gorgeous bride you are!" Betty adjusted the bows on Maggie and Sara's dresses. Caroline, Helen, Bonnie, and Carrie praised Betty for her exquisite talent as a seamstress.

Alfred knew that Kathy was good at taking pictures. He offered to buy her a camera and several rolls of film. Kathy took several pictures of the bride and the women, before she walked upstairs to take pictures of the men. Matt looked as nervous as a cat stuck up in a tree, until Alfred put his hands on his shoulders and told him to relax.

Family, friends, and neighbors filled the church. When the church bells sounded, the guests hushed. Matt, Kevin, and Jim walked in and stood in their places in the front of the altar. Matt looked like he was going to faint until he caught sight of his Grandmother Helen sitting in her wheel chair in front of the first pew. She smiled, winked at him, and mouthed, "I love you." Matt relaxed and smiled knowing that he will remember that for the rest of his life.

Sara marched in, followed by Maggie to take their places in front of the altar. All eyes were on Lillian as she carefully dropped a leaf with every step she took. When she reached the front, she noticed that she still had leaves in her basket. She looked at Maggie wondering what she was supposed to do with the rest. She decided to dump them all out and joined Maggie and Sara with her empty basket. The guests chuckled.

The organist began to play the 'Wedding March'. Everyone rose from the pews and turned to look at the bride coming from the back of the church. Henry smiled at Isabelle. He squeezed her hand, and then took her arm. He walked her down the aisle with such pride. Isabelle caught a glimpse of Caroline in the first pew and gave her smile just before she saw Matt. Matt seemed to be paralyzed, as he stared at Isabelle with such adoration. By the time Henry reached him, he still did not move. Kevin gave him a gentle shove to get his attention. Matt blurted out, "Oh!" and turned a bright red. Again, the guests chuckled.

Isabelle had a lump in her throat trying to keep tears from streaming down her face as she recited the wedding vows. The emotions were getting to Matt too, as his voice cracked when he recited his vows and placed the wedding ring on Isabelle's finger. Matt and Isabelle faced the congregation while Reverend Ahlmann said, "Ladies and gentlemen, I present Mr. and Mrs. Matthew Carson. You may kiss the bride."

When the newlyweds reached the lobby of the church, Matt turned towards Isabelle saying, "There is no turning back, you're mine now. I love you."

Isabelle smiled and leaned in to kiss him again. "I love you too, and I would not want to turn back."

It took a while for the guests to get through the receiving line. Most of Matt and Isabelle's senior class attended. Maggie loved all of the attention she was getting from several of the boys. Isabelle glanced over to her just as Allen Jones gave her a kiss on her hand. She smiled knowing that Allen was a big flirt. The guests gathered outside the church waiting for Matt and Isabelle. The newly wedded couple paused at the door of the church for the guests to clap and cheer. The unmarried females in the crowd gathered at the bottom of the steps waiting to catch Isabelle's bouquet. Isabelle turned around and tossed it behind her. Maggie stepped behind Sara just in time for Sara to catch it. Mark shouted, "You're next sis!"

She turned and held up the bouquet shouting back, "Not this gal. Not for a long time."

Rice showered Matt and Isabelle as they weaved through the crowd. When they reached the end of the sidewalk, Matt saw a grocery cart adorned with ribbon and streamers. He scooped up Isabelle and put her into the cart before Isabelle knew what was happening. Attached to the cart were tin cans. They clanked as Matt pushed her in and out of the crowd.

The guests were getting into the spirit of the moment shouting comments. "Isabelle, don't let Matt push you around the rest of your life." "Matt, did you get her with green stamps?" "Well, that's one way of saving gas money. That's cheap transportation", and so on. Matt and Isabelle joined in the laughter.

Matt finally stopped to let Isabelle out of the grocery cart. They led the guests into the church reception hall for some wedding cake and mints. Matt and Isabelle wondered around the tables greeting guests. Everyone complemented on how lovely the wedding was and gave their congratulations. There were lots of well wishes and toasts to the happy couple. Finally, Matt lifted his glass to Isabelle and said, "To my beautiful wife." He kissed her in front of everyone. They both waved goodbye and left the church to start their married life together.

Matt had the honeymoon planned. He had saved his money to take a road trip to the Black Hills in South Dakota. They stopped at Isabelle's house so that she could change out of her wedding dress. She hung it back up in her closet. Isabelle buried the pearls in a pocket of her cosmetic suitcase. She took out a tablet from Maggie's dresser and sat down to write her a note.

Maggie:
I give you full control of this entire room. You can finally spread your clothes out to both of the closets and to both of the dressers. I give you all of my teen magazines, so enjoy. Call me often. As even though you may not think so, I will miss you.
With Love,
Isabelle.

She put the note inside the cover of a novel that she bought for her and placed it on Maggie's pillow.

Isabelle took one last look around the room that she and Maggie shared all of their life. All of a sudden, she realized that things would never be the same. The next time Isabelle would come to the farm and enter this room, she would be a guest. Isabelle had mixed emotions. She was sad for leaving the past, afraid of what is to come, and excited to start a new chapter in her life.

CHAPTER TWENTY-SEVEN

Maggie sat on the couch to watch television with her parents. She waited for the commercial to air before she asked if she could have Susan Johnson stay over for a weekend. Caroline said, "Why don't you ask her for the weekend of November 3rd. I don't work that weekend."

"Thanks Mom. I will ask her tomorrow in school."

Before the bell sounded, Maggie shoved her coat in her locker before she slammed it shut. She approached Susan, "Did you have a happy birthday? What did you get?"

Susan retrieved her books that she needed for the first class. "I got records, nail polish, and the boys gave me drawing supplies. My grandparents came on Sunday to help celebrate. We had a cake and ice cream."

Maggie invited Susan for a sleepover on the next weekend. Susan was sure they were not doing anything, but she would let Maggie know tomorrow in school if she could come. "I'll bring the records I got for my birthday," Susan said."

Caroline brought home some bottles of coke and a bag of popcorn that Maggie and Susan could pop. She bought some cupcakes from the bakery and a bag of apples. Maggie cleaned her room and put fresh linens on Isabelle's bed for Susan. She was ready for her sleepover.

On Friday, November 2, Henry parked the pickup in front of the school. Susan handed her overnight bag to Maggie before she climbed into the pickup beside her. On the way to Maggie's house, the girls were already talking a mile a minute and giggling about some of the boys in their class. Henry listened to their chatter while smiling to himself.

Susan and Maggie immediately went upstairs to change into their jeans. Maggie pointed to the bed on the other side of the room. "You can sleep in Isabelle's bed."

Susan unpacked her bag and took out the records. "Wow Maggie, I wish I had a big room like this."

Maggie put one of the records that Susan brought on the record player. She started dancing to the music. "Yeah, it was big enough to not get into each other's way, but at times we still annoyed each other. Sometimes I wished Dad would have built a wall between us and made it into two rooms, but he never did."

The girls talked and flipped though the magazines that Isabelle left, while listening to the music blaring from the record player. Maggie took Isabelle's wedding dress out of the back of Isabelle's closet and showed it to Susan. She also showed Susan the bridesmaid dress that Betty Parker made for her. Susan was impressed. Maggie decided to tell her about the kiss on the hand that Allen Jones gave her at the wedding. Maggie blushed and said, "He sure likes to flirt, but I was flattered." She pointed to the teddy bear she had on top of her dresser. "Do you know that after you left the fair with your family, Allen bought tickets for us to ride the Bumper cars? He also shot a gun at the shooting gallery at the fair and won this teddy bear. He gave it to me."

Susan laughed at Maggie and said, "You are blushing." Maggie turned and touched her hot cheeks.

Caroline hollered up the stairs announcing that supper was on the table. Susan told Maggie that her favorite meal at school was beef stew, so Caroline graciously obliged. She added a salad to the meal and served cupcakes for dessert. There was a smile on the girl's faces when they came into the dining room. When they finished eating, they headed back upstairs, leaving Caroline to do the dishes. The girls talked until the alarm clock on Maggie's dresser said 2:00 a.m. The girls finally stopped talking and fell asleep.

The girls slept until Caroline knocked on Maggie's bedroom door, "Breakfast is ready. Are you awake?"

Maggie yawned and asked Susan if she was awake. The girls slowly got dressed with sleepy eyes and went downstairs to eat breakfast. Caroline informed Maggie that she needed to feed Casey and make sure he had fresh water. Susan followed Maggie outside. She was a farm girl too, and was familiar with the corncob pile in the yard. Susan had one in their yard too. Maggie showed her where the smoke house used to be before it burned down. Susan expressed her sincere sympathy for the loss of the meat. Maggie gave Casey a scoop of his dog food and put fresh water in his dish. The girls walked around the farm until lunchtime.

After lunch, Susan and Maggie played cards and board games while listening to the radio. Maggie had several bottles of nail polish that Isabelle left on her dresser. They painted each other nails and waved their hands in the air to let them dry.

After supper, they popped some popcorn and took it upstairs to munch on along with bottles of coke and apples. Susan talked about the country school that her brothers Scott and Nate still attended. She gossiped about a girl that she graduated with in the eighth grade. Susan told Maggie she was not very nice to anybody there. She was glad that the girl's family moved to Iowa so that she would not go to Cleary High School. The alarm clock on the dresser said 3:15 a.m. before the girls finally fell asleep. They learned so much about each other.

Sunday morning, Caroline did not bother waking the girls up for breakfast. When she woke up in the middle of the night, she could hear them still talking and giggling. She left them sleep.

Caroline put a roast in the oven, thinking the aroma would drift upstairs and wake the girls up. The scheme worked, but it was nearly eleven thirty in the morning before they emerged and went downstairs. Maggie set the table for dinner. Susan admitted that she was hungry. Henry asked them what they were going to do today. He informed them that it was going to be a nice day with the temperature reaching 60 degrees. Maggie thought they would walk to the country school and show Susan where she went to school. "Just make sure you don't walk into the school yard. Even though it is Sunday and there is no school, you could be deemed as a trespasser."

Susan and Maggie walked past the school and continued to walk to the one-lane bridge. They peered over the bridge at the river. The river was high and moving swiftly. Maggie pointed to the spot where she and Isabelle found a wallet. She told Susan about the money they found in it.

Casey started barking to get Maggie's attention. The girls ran to the end of the bridge to get out of the way of an oncoming pickup.

The pickup stopped when the driver recognized Maggie. Ed Jones rolled down the window, "Hey Maggie. How are you?"

Maggie walked up to the pickup to say hello. She introduced Susan to Ed and Allen and explained that they were just out for a walk. Susan said hello to them. Allen replied with a hello and tipped his hat. Susan just smiled. Ed put the pickup back in gear and hollered, "Have fun girls."

Maggie told Susan that Allen flirted with her the day of corn shelling too. Susan and Maggie walked back to Maggie's house talking about how much of a flirt Allen was, but giggled when they both admitted that he was good-looking.

After supper, the girls played another game of cards while listening to more of the records. When they were tired of playing cards, Susan picked up a drawing tablet she saw on Isabelle's dresser. She drew a picture from memory of the one-lane bridge at the river. She drew a dog on the side of the bank representing Casey and a girl tossing a rock into the water. She showed the picture to Maggie. "Susan, I want to keep that. Is that girl supposed to be me?"

"Yes it is, and the dog is Casey." Maggie had her sign the picture on the bottom. Susan flipped it over and wrote 'To Maggie: best friends forever' and dated it November 4, 1962.

Maggie got out her diary from the bottom of her dresser. She wrote about the weekend with Susan and how much fun it was having her stay over. Susan and Maggie fell asleep early that night. They finally had talked each other out and had nothing more to say.

CHAPTER TWENTY-EIGHT

Maggie rushed down the stairs to answer the telephone. "Hello."

"Hi Maggie, its Isabelle. How are you?"

"I'm fine. I put up the Christmas tree today. Mom and I made decorated Christmas cookies yesterday. It's nice not to have school for a week. How are you guys?"

"We're fine too. Is Mom there?"

"No she had to work today. Dad went into town to get some fencing and dog food."

"Well, tell them that Matt and I will be coming home on Saturday for Christmas. We will be staying overnight and then going to Alfred and Bonnie's on Sunday. I cannot wait to see everyone. We've been so busy."

"Okay. I will tell them. Bye and drive safe." Maggie hung up the phone. She really was excited to be seeing Isabelle. She wished she had told her so.

. . .

Matt locked the door to the apartment. He looked up at the sky, "Not a bad day for a drive." He and Isabelle were on their way to Cleary.

Isabelle put the last gift in the trunk of the car and slammed it shut. "I hope the weather stays this way for a while. You never know in the month of December in Nebraska. It won't bother me if we don't have a white Christmas." She tuned the radio to a station that was playing Christmas music. Before long, she was singing with the music. As Matt drove through towns, they saw poles with Christmas banners attached to them, decorated trees with lights, and many Santa's standing on street corners ringing their bells for charity.

225

Matt drove up the lane to the Sims' farmhouse. Isabelle felt strange to come to this house as a guest. Matt took as many suitcases and packages out of the trunk as he could carry. Maggie ran out of the house to greet them. She helped Isabelle carry in the rest of the packages from the car. When Isabelle came into the kitchen, she dropped her cosmetic case on the floor and grabbed her Mother for a hug. "Merry Christmas, Mom."

"Oh it's so good to see you two. You can have the entire upstairs. Maggie agreed to sleep on the couch."

Matt set the gifts under the tree. All of a sudden, Isabelle turned ghostly white and rushed to the bathroom. She vomited, washed her face, and ate two soda crackers she had in her purse. She returned to the living room looking pale. Matt studied her face to see if she was okay. Just a couple of minutes went by before Isabelle left to rush to the bathroom again. Caroline followed her this time to see what the matter was, but Isabelle closed the door before Caroline got there.

"Are you alright Isabelle?" Caroline asked through the closed door.

Isabelle assured her that she was fine and she would be out in a minute. Matt rose from the couch when Isabelle came back. "Did you get sick again?"

Caroline figured out right away what the matter was. She went into the kitchen to get her a glass of water. Henry was concerned. He asked Isabelle, "Do you have the flu? Maybe we should call Doc Parker and have you checked out."

"No Dad, that's not necessary. I had already been to see a doctor."

Caroline was beaming from ear to ear. "When are you due?"

Isabelle face turned red. "Matt, did you tell Mom while I was in the bathroom? We were going to tell them together!"

Caroline gave her the glass of water. "No he didn't say anything. He didn't have to."

Isabelle smiled. "Yes, we're going to have a baby. I'm due in late July, early August."

Henry shook Matt's hand. Caroline grabbed Isabelle and gave her a hug. Maggie clapped while hollering, "Congratulations!" Isabelle went on to tell them that she just found out this week and they had not told Matt's family yet.

Caroline set the pot of chicken and dumplings in the middle of the table. She served it with fresh baked bread and vanilla pudding for dessert. The family spent the evening opening the gifts. Caroline handed Isabelle a gift to open. "I wish I would have known that you were pregnant. I would have gotten you something for the baby instead."

Isabelle opened the gift to reveal a tailored blue suit. "Oh, it's gorgeous." She held it up in front of her. "I can wear this several times before it won't fit me." She put on the jacket of the suit and modeled it. "I will wear it tomorrow."

Matt admired Isabelle. "That looks nice on you. I just wish we could stay longer. We will be leaving tomorrow afternoon, after we visit my parents."

"That's the way the holidays will be for you and Isabelle from now on." Caroline said with a bit of sadness in her voice. "We'll have to get used to sharing you two on the holidays."

The next morning Maggie opened the curtains in the living room and saw that ice covered the bare branches of the trees and shrubs. She put on her clothes, coat, and hat to go outside to attend to Casey. She stopped on the cement steps to take in the heavenly sight before her. The morning sunshine made the trees glisten, making them look as if they were encased in glass. Henry approached her. "Be careful going down those steps. It's icy."

Maggie hung onto the railing while going down the steps. "Will we get to church?"

"No. We can't take the chance; the highway might be too icy. Matt and Isabelle will have to wait until it burns off before they go into Cleary, too."

By mid-morning, the sun had melted the ice. Matt and Isabelle said their goodbyes. Caroline handed Isabelle a box of soda crackers for their trip home. Henry warned Matt to leave early enough in the evening to get home safely.

Alfred and Bonnie were also thrilled to hear that Isabelle was going to have a baby. Bonnie took out the family album from the bureau. Isabelle had never seen Matt's baby pictures before. She laughed at the picture of Matt inside a big hollowed out pumpkin when he was little.

Before long, it was time for Matt and Isabelle to go back to Lincoln. Bonnie was in tears when she hugged Matt goodbye. "We just don't see you often enough. You take care of Isabelle." She turned to hug Isabelle. "If you need anything, make sure you call us."

Matt put the suitcases in the trunk and shook his dad's hand before he got into the car. Alfred stood still watching his son back out of the driveway thinking to himself, 'how grown up he was'. Now Matt has a job, living away from home, married to a wonderful girl, and has a baby on the way. It seemed that those baby pictures they were looking at were not so long ago. Where did all those years go?

CHAPTER TWENTY-NINE

Henry hollered upstairs to remind Maggie of the time. He did not want her to be late for school. She drudged downstairs to get breakfast. Henry honked the horn of the pickup to get Maggie's attention. She grabbed the toast that Henry put in the toaster for her, spread butter on it, and went out the door. Maggie threw her schoolbooks on the seat and climbed into the pickup.

A light snow had fallen during the night. Henry tapped on the brake to test the highway to see how slick it was. The highway did not seem to be icy, so he sped up the pickup to get Maggie to school on time. Maggie got out of the pickup just before Henry said, "Remember, Mom is going to pick you up from school today."

"Okay." She hollered back as she shut the door to Henry's pickup.

Maggie walked into the school. Susan greeted her with a bubbly, "Good Morning!"

"Hi Susan. What makes you so happy this morning?"

"Oh, nothing. Why are you so glum?"

"I don't know. I stayed up late last night and woke up tired this morning."

"Well cheer up. Your birthday is Friday, right. And you're going to be sixteen."

"Yeah. So?"

"So, you might get something really great. Maybe even a car."

"Fat chance of that, Isabelle didn't get a car until she was a senior." She took her English book out of her locker just before the first bell rang.

After the last bell sounded for the end of the school day, Maggie waited outside the school for Caroline. She took out her science book and sat on the cement step. Tomorrow was a science test and that was a big part of her grade. Caroline pulled up to the curb. She apologized to Maggie for being late. "We have to go to the courthouse before we go home." She announced. Maggie reached behind her to put her schoolbooks on the back seat, as Caroline drove to the courthouse.

Caroline and Maggie walked to the second floor of the courthouse. Maggie followed Caroline to the first office. She saw the sign on the door that read 'Department of Motor Vehicles'. A receptionist greeted them and asked, "May I help you?"

Caroline put her purse on the counter and took out a piece of paper. "This is my daughter, Maggie Sims. We are here to apply for a driver's permit. I have her birth certificate with me." Maggie was shocked. She had no idea that is why they were there.

The receptionist handed an application to Maggie. "Please fill this out and sign it." She made a copy of the birth certificate and handed it back to Caroline. Maggie filled out the application and handed it to the receptionist. The receptionist stapled the copy of the birth certificate to the application and gave Maggie a driver's permit. "Here you are. Remember you must have a licensed driver with you before you can legally drive. This is good for one year or until you get a driver's license. Have a nice day."

Maggie smiled. "Thank you."

Caroline headed out of town. Just before she reached the last house, she pulled the car over. "Maggie would you like to drive home?"

"Really, can I?" Maggie and Caroline switched places. Maggie's heart fluttered has she gripped the steering wheel. She did have a little driving experience. She drove Henry's pickup around the farm on several occasions. Sometimes she drove it to the hay meadow to help her dad with the cattle. Last fall she drove the tractor to help Henry with the harvest, but this was different. Caroline instructed Maggie to go slow at first to get the feel of the car on the road. Maggie put the shift in drive and eased away from the curb. She was nervous on the highway, but relaxed after she turned onto the gravel road. By the time she parked the car in front of their house, she felt at ease.

"How did I do?"

"Very good." Caroline said. "You seem confident. You're a natural."

"Thanks Mom."

Maggie ran into the house and called Susan to tell her all about it. "You were right Susan. There was no need to be glum this morning. It turned out to be a super day." She said goodbye, hung up the phone, and went upstairs to study for her science test.

. . .

Henry drove into the school parking lot to pick up Maggie from school. He was driving a 1954 Buick. Maggie stopped at the top of the school steps when she saw her dad standing in front of a car she did not recognize. "Dad, are you driving that car?"

"Yeah, get in. Let's go get Mom from the hospital."

Maggie had butterflies in her stomach. "Whose car is it?"

"I borrowed it," he fibbed. Henry looked at Maggie's face and saw the excitement fade away. He grinned to himself and put the car in gear. Caroline was waiting outside the hospital for Henry and Maggie to come around the corner. When Henry stopped, Maggie left the front seat and got into the back.

Maggie was still confused. "Mom, where is your car?"

"Dad brought me to work this morning. It's at home."

There was silence until Henry parked the car in the yard. All three of them went into the house. Maggie went upstairs to change out of her school clothes. She put her homework on her dresser and went back downstairs.

Caroline answered the telephone, "Hello. Hi Isabelle. How are you? Are you showing yet?" She continued to talk to Isabelle a long time before she handed the telephone to Henry.

Henry wished Isabelle well before he handed the telephone to Maggie. "Hi Isabelle."

"Hey. Happy sixteenth birthday, Sister."

"Thanks. When are you coming home again?"

"Well I told Dad that we thought we would in a couple of weeks, if the weather is good. Matt has been real busy at the store." Isabelle and Maggie talked for a few minutes before Maggie said goodbye and put the telephone receiver back on the wall.

Henry asked Maggie to come into the living room. She was sure her parents were going to give her a birthday present, but she did not know what it could be. Maggie had not dropped any hints about anything she wanted. Maggie sat down on the sofa while Caroline handed her a small box. Maggie did not want to seem disappointed, but she really thought the car was hers. Maggie assumed it was jewelry in the box. When she opened it, there was a note inside. It read 'Ask Dad for the keys'. Maggie did not know what to say. "Keys to what?" she asked.

Henry pulled out the keys for the car they drove home in. "Yes the car is for you. Happy Birthday!"

"Wow, really?" Maggie was shocked. Of course, Maggie had to hear the same speech Henry gave Isabelle when she got her car. He reminded her that she would need to practice driving a few more times before she tries to get her driver's license. He also reminded her that it is wintertime and she would not be driving the car to school in bad weather. Maggie did not mind. She understood all of what he was saying, especially after hearing about Matt sliding in the ditch in the snowstorm and Isabelle almost hitting a deer in the fog.

After supper, Isabelle called back and asked for Maggie. "Well, did you get what you wanted for your birthday?"

"Yeah, I got a car. Did you already know about it?"

"Yes, actually it's Kevin's old car."

"You schemers, how come no one told me about it?"

"Because you know how Dad likes to surprise everyone." Both of the girls laughed before Isabelle said another 'Happy Birthday' then said, "Goodbye."

Finally, in March, Maggie went to the courthouse to get her driver's license. She felt somewhat free. She drove her car to school and showed it off to her friends.

Susan was jealous. "I'm sixteen too, and I don't get to drive to school. We even live ten miles out of town. You'd think my parents would let me drive, so they don't have to come to get me every day."

Maggie could tell Susan was jealous. She did not know what to say, so she just left the conversation drop. Maggie changed the subject and asked Susan if she liked the substitute teacher they had in English today.

Susan replied, "Yeah, he looked so young. I wonder if he will be teaching at our school next year."

"I don't know, but I liked him better than Mrs. Reed."

"That's for sure." Susan saw Margaret pull into the school parking lot. "I'll see you Maggie."

Maggie drove her car home with pride. She was thinking to herself that Susan would eventually get a car to drive to school, too.

CHAPTER THIRTY

Principal Jackson got on the loud speaker announcing that school will be dismissing early. The temperature had dropped and the mist in the air had turned into sleet. He reminded everyone, "Those of you that are driving home, please take your time. The roads may be icy."

Maggie saw Susan waiting in line to use the school telephone to call her mother to come get her. She figured it would take a while before Susan got home. Maggie walked out of the school and saw two girls fall down the school steps. She helped them up and asked if they were okay. She realized just how slippery the parking lot was, when she took a tumble also. She managed to get into her car with her back hurting. She was nervous and drove slowly out of the parking lot. Maggie approached the first intersection past the school and stepped on the breaks to stop. She could not get the car to stop and she slid through it, nearly hitting another car. She decided that was enough. She drove the car to the side of the curb and parked it. Maggie shut off the engine and decided to walk to the hospital.

Caroline was surprised to see her. "Why are you here?"

Maggie told her how slippery the street was and that she fell in the parking lot at school. She said, "I got too nervous to drive when I couldn't stop the car on 3rd Street." Caroline was impressed with her daughter for making such a gown up decision, although she did not realize the weather was that bad. She called Henry and told him that they were going to stay in town for the night. She was glad that they had decided not to sell Marie's house until next summer. It had been almost a month since they had been there to check on the house anyway.

Caroline went to work at six o'clock the next morning. The streets were still icy. She suspected that Maggie would not have school. She learned that Margaret Johnson was in the hospital with a broken leg. She found out that Margaret had slid off the road the day before. Her car rolled then hit a tree before coming to a stop. Caroline also learned that Susan was in the car with her. She was devastated to find out that Susan's door came open and she fell out of it pinning Susan underneath the car. She did not survive the accident. Caroline did not know how she was going to tell Maggie. She would be grief stricken.

After Susan's funeral, Maggie seemed to be lost in a world of her own. She became so reclusive she did not talk to anyone at school. Maggie did not even want to drive her car anymore. She did not care about her schoolwork or her grades.

When school was out, Maggie waited for Henry to drive her home. Henry would try to ask Maggie about her day, but she would not answer him. Every day they would head home in silence.

Two weeks had gone by before the guidance counselor called Henry and Caroline into the school to talk about Maggie. "Mr. and Mrs. Sims, we are worried about Maggie. She eats alone in the cafeteria, and she is failing in her schoolwork. How does she act at home?"

Caroline replied, "Same thing. She seems so distant. She does not want to talk to us. When Isabelle calls, she doesn't want to talk to her either."

"I know of a doctor that deals with children that have gone through trauma such as this. We are sending for him to talk to the students about Susan Johnson. Would you be willing to have Maggie talk to him on a one-to-one basis? We would ask that he talk to her in my office. None of the other students would need to know." Henry and Caroline agreed with the arrangement. They knew that Maggie needed help before she had permanent repercussion.

A couple days later Maggie entered the Guidance Counselor's office. "Did you want to see me?" she asked the Guidance Counselor.

"Yes Maggie," said the Guidance Counselor. "Have a seat. This is Dr. Nabity. As you know, he gave a talk to the sophomore class this morning. He would like to talk to you, if that's okay."

"I supposed so." Maggie slouched down in a chair, crossed her arms on her chest, and extended her legs.

Dr. Nabity escorted the guidance counselor out of her office and shut the door. He pulled a chair closer to Maggie instead of using the chair behind the desk. He began slowly, asking Maggie how she felt. At first, Maggie just gave short answers to his questions, but Dr. Nabity kept probing her. The study of psychology told Dr. Nabity to keep Maggie talking, no matter how long it would take. Finally, Maggie opened up when he asked her if she had a pet. Maggie uncrossed her arms and sat straighter in her chair. She told Dr. Nabity about the time when she thought the family lost their dog, Casey, in the flood. Dr. Nabity knew that he found something that was dear to Maggie. Before long, he had Maggie talking about Isabelle's wedding. She started to talk about the good times she had in school. However, Maggie did not mention anything about Susan. Dr. Nabity did not pressure her into talking about her either. He knew that would take some time for Maggie's feelings to heal. By the time the bell rang, Maggie was smiling. Before Dr. Nabity opened the door to let Maggie leave, he said, "Maggie, I know that life can throw difficulties in your direction, but the main thing is to remind yourself of what you still have and enjoy."

Maggie turned towards Dr. Nabity and whispered, "Thank you."

When Maggie returned home after school, she went upstairs and changed out of her school clothes. She took a picture down from the wall that was above Isabelle's bed. Maggie replaced the picture of flowers with Susan's drawing from when the two girls were at the river. She hung it on the wall with tears streaming down her face.

CHAPTER THIRTY-ONE

Matt parked the car in the Sims' farmyard. He helped Isabelle out of it and walked over to Maggie's car. Matt opened the car door to look inside it. Maggie came out of the house saying, "Happy Easter!"

Isabelle turned to face Maggie saying, "Well, well. I can't believe my baby sister is driving."

"I haven't driven much, but I will." She opened the jacket Isabelle was wearing to inspect her belly. "You're getting fatter."

Isabelle pulled the jacket back around her, frowning. She scornfully said, "That was rather rude."

Maggie ignored Isabelle and took a box from Matt. "What's in here?"

"Isabelle baked an Easter cake."

Caroline was in the kitchen preparing the dinner. She invited Alfred and Bonnie out to the farm to join them. As soon as she greeted Matt and Isabelle with hugs, she also opened Isabelle's jacket. Isabelle protested. "Don't you dare say what Maggie said! It wasn't very nice." Caroline had to ask what she said. She frowned at Maggie, but Matt told her he thought it was funny.

Alfred and Bonnie came into the house. Alfred set the casserole that Bonnie made on the kitchen counter. Caroline thanked them and led them into the dining room. Maggie had set the table before they arrived. Bonnie complimented on how lovely it looked. Maggie was sure she was just being nice, as it was not nearly as pretty as Carrie's, Bonnie's mom, dining table.

They spent the day catching up on what everyone was doing. Matt talked endlessly about the store until Isabelle told him it was time to change the subject. Henry asked about the plans for the new baby and wondered if the apartment was big enough for them.

Matt assured him it was. Isabelle rearranged the walk-in closet for the baby's room. It was just off the bedroom. Maggie expressed how excited she was to be an aunt. When she asked Matt and Isabelle about baby names, Isabelle nudged Matt and shook her head saying, "we haven't decided about that yet."

The day went by so quickly. Bonnie helped Caroline and Maggie set some sandwiches and left overs on the dining table for their supper. The time approached seven o'clock; Matt stood up from the table and announced that they needed to head back to Lincoln. Both sets of parents expressed how disappointed they were because they did not get to see them often enough. Henry, Caroline, and Maggie arranged to come to Lincoln to visit. Alfred and Bonnie agreed that Isabelle would be getting too far into the pregnancy to be traveling.

Isabelle said, "Okay, all of you can come, if you bring the food with you."

"That's a deal," Alfred said. He turned towards Bonnie saying, "We should be getting home too."

Bonnie said, "Thank you for a wonderful Easter. I can't wait to hold that grandchild and celebrate the holidays with all of us for many years to come."

CHAPTER THIRTY-TWO

It was spring again and planting season was in full swing. It was already into the month of May. Henry had only one field left to plant, then he could leave the tractor in the tool shed until he had to cultivate, once the weeds came up.

Henry left the breakfast table saying, "Maggie, I will just take a couple of sandwiches and some water with me today. I don't want to stop planting and come in for lunch. I'd like to finish before it rains."

"Okay Dad." Maggie filled his water jug with water and wrapped up two sandwiches to put into his metal lunch box. She added three cookies too. She handed the lunch box to Henry, "Here, it's ready." Henry took the lunch box from Maggie. As he was heading out the door, Maggie yelled, "Love you Dad." Maggie heard the porch door slammed shut behind him.

Henry looked up at the clouds that filled the sky. He noticed a soft south breeze that felt warm to the touch. Henry walked to the north field where he had left the tractor the day before. He filled the planter boxes with seed corn. Henry only had one more bag of seed corn, but he had enough experience to know that would be all he needed. He put the tractor in gear. From one end of the field to the other he went. Henry could do this is his sleep. In fact, some nights he did. He would wake up in the morning feeling the aches from the jarring of the tractor seat as if he had been on it all night. Henry put the tractor in neutral, took a drink from his water jug, and took out one of the sandwiches from his lunch box. He smiled when he noticed the cookies Maggie had put with the sandwiches. He finished a sandwich and two of the cookies before he shut the lunch box and set it down beside him. He took another swig of the water, set the water jug down on the other side of him, and put the tractor back in gear. Henry stopped the tractor to fill the planter boxes with seed corn once again. When he looked up at the clouds in the sky, he noticed that the clouds were darker. Just as quickly, as the clouds grew dark, the breeze shifted and blew from the west. He felt the cool west breeze and knew that rain was coming his way.

Henry scanned the field to count how many rows he had left to plant. He thought he could still finish the field before the rain came. Henry quickly started up the tractor again. He reached the south end of the field and turned the tractor to go north. He was nearing the north end of the field where the small creek separated his field from his neighbor's field. All of a sudden, the breeze turned into a forceful wind. The wind blew a small tree branch in front of the tractor. The wind picked up the branch and carried it, nearly hitting Henry. Henry looked up at the clouds above and spotted a tornado in the west sky. Henry had his eyes fixed on the tornado when he realized that he was coming very close to the creek. He cranked the wheel of the tractor abruptly. Henry was too close to the bank of the creek. As the bank gave way, the tractor slid downwards. The force of the wind and the bank of the creek made the tractor roll over into the creek.

The lunch box and water jug tumbled out of the tractor. The seed sack dropped to the bottom of the creek and spilled open. Henry fell against the tractor fender and then plunged into the creek, hitting his head on a rock. He moaned with pain. He tried to move, but could not. He felt a sharp pain from the back of his neck rush down his spine. Then he was silenced.

. . .

Meanwhile, Maggie put the meat away that she had made Henry's sandwiches with, cleared the table from breakfast, and washed the dishes. Planting season arrived for Maggie too. It was time for her to work her magic in the garden. She went into Casey's shed to get the red wagon that Isabelle and she had played for hours with when they were young. Now she used it to carry a garden spade, hose, a pint jar, hoe, marking sticks, and a ball of string. Maggie also put her packages of seeds and her flat of tomato seedlings into the wagon. She pulled it out of the shed to the garden. Maggie punched one of the sticks into the dirt, tied the end of her string to it, walked several feet, and punched another stick in the dirt. She wrapped the string around that stick. Maggie watched

Caroline do this at a very young age. She would tell her, "This way the rows would be straight with the world." Maggie hoed out a trough next to the string. The first row was for beets. She carefully sprinkled the beet seeds into the trough, gently sprayed them with water, and covered the seeds with dirt. Maggie planted two more rows of beets. She hoed out another trough using the same method for the green beans. Maggie strategically planted the green bean seeds two inches apart in the next three rows. She proceeded to plant cucumber seeds and carrot seeds. The tomato seedlings would take more time to plant. Maggie remembered her transistor radio and went back into the house to get it.

When she returned to her garden, she knelt down on her knees with the flat of tomato seedlings beside her. With the radio tuned to a rock and roll station, she went to work putting each tomato seedling into a hole. She poured a pint jar of water onto the seedling, and covered it with dirt. Maggie was singing along to the radio, knowing every word, as she was moving down the row. In the middle of the song an announcement aired on the radio, "We interrupt this regularly scheduled program to bring you a tornado watch for Cleary County until four o'clock this afternoon. In the event of a tornado, take cover in a basement. . . ." Maggie stopped planting and looked up into the sky. She looked in all four directions and did not see anything. She could not see beyond the grove of trees to the west of her, but she did not see any reason to stop what she was doing and go into the basement. It was just cloudy. She ignored the warning and continued her gardening.

Suddenly the wind became brisk and changed from the south to the west. The sky grew darker. Again the announcement on the radio aired, "We interrupt this regularly scheduled program. There has been a tornado spotted three miles west of Cleary and heading east. If you are travelling in the path of this funnel cloud, take cover immediately in a deep ditch. If you are in a house or a public building, go to the inner most bathroom . . ." Without listening to the rest of the newscast, Maggie quickly gathered her gardening tools, the rest of the tomato seedlings, and put them into the wagon. Pulling the wagon, she ran for Casey's shed. The wind was so strong that Maggie was having trouble getting the door open to the shed. She used all of her strength, but the wind was too strong. A tree limb flew by Maggie, almost hitting her in the head. She gave up on the door to the shed. Maggie left the wagon outside of the shed and ran into the house. She thought that Henry was already there. She turned on the lights in the kitchen but realized the power was off. She yelled, "Dad!" There was no answer. She could hear the wind howling as she went to the porch to get a flashlight from the cupboard and went down the steps to the basement. She yelled again, "Dad, are you down here." Again, there was no answer. She shined the flashlight in the basement until she found an old chair to sit on. It was strange to her that she was so calm. The family had been in the basement numerous times during tornado threats. Never has there ever been one touch the ground. She just sat there listening, waiting for it to dissipate. Maggie wished she remembered to take her transistor radio out of the wagon. She just wondered why her dad was not in the house with her. Wasn't he worried about her safety?

A few minutes went by before she realized the wind had died down or completely stopped, she was not sure which. She listened. Sure enough, the wind had stopped and it had started to rain. She cautiously proceeded up the basement steps. When she reached the porch, she could hear hail coming down and hitting the west window. She went into the house and yelled again for Henry, "Dad!" There was no answer. Maggie put on her coat and boots and proceeded to go outside to look for him. There were tree limbs down everywhere. The hail stung Maggie's face as she crossed the yard to go into the barn. "Dad!" she yelled out. She listened but Henry did not answer. She zipped up her jacket, put her head down, and ran to the tool shed where Henry housed the tractor. She noticed that the tractor was not in it. Panic started to settle upon her. She yelled from the top of her lungs, "Dad!" Again, she received no answer.

The hail stopped, but the rain was coming down hard. Maggie knew which field her dad was in, but for some reason she was afraid to go out there. She opened Casey's shed and shined her flashlight around, but did not see Henry in there either. She found Casey burrowed in his hay in the corner. He immediately came to her side. She petted him, told him to stay, and shut the door.

Maggie put her fears aside and ventured to the north field. She came to the edge of the field and squinted through the rain. She scanned the field to the west, then to the east, but did not see the tractor anywhere. Maggie turned and headed back to the house. All of a sudden, Maggie froze in her tracks. Terror came upon her as she remembered the creek at the north end of the field. She walked towards it with caution. The rain was coming down so hard it was difficult for Maggie to see. As she came closer to the creek, she saw the wheel of the tractor sticking up. Maggie put her hands above her eyes to shield them from the rain as she rushed through the mud towards the tractor. She hastened her pace yelling, "Dad! Dad!"

As she neared the overturned tractor, she could see Henry's body. She screamed, "Dad! Oh God!" Maggie ran closer to him. She saw her dad's head resting on the rock. Maggie stood paralyzed for a moment before she ran as fast as she could back to the house. Her boots were caked with so much mud she could not lift her feet. She stopped, kicked them off, and ran the rest of the way in her stocking feet to the house.

Once inside the house, Maggie ran to the telephone and dialed the emergency number.

The dispatcher on the other end said, "Emergency services."

Maggie wasted no time, "I need an ambulance."

"Who is calling, please?"

"I'm Maggie Sims." Maggie continued in a panic, "My dad is injured."

"Do you know your homestead number?"

"Um," Maggie stammered. She had heard it only a couple of times. Then she remembered what Caroline said when she called for the fire department. "F827."

"Okay Miss Sims, an ambulance is on its way."

Maggie hung up the phone and dialed the hospital.

The receptionist answered, "Cleary General."

Maggie was crying hysterically, "C-Can I talk to Caroline Sims?'

"Sure. Please hold while I get her." The receptionist put the phone down and ran down the hall. She found Caroline in one of the rooms assisting a patient into a wheel chair. "Caroline come quick, I think it's Maggie on the phone. She is crying. Something is wrong."

Caroline set the patient into the chair and hurried down the hall. She took the phone from the receptionist, "Maggie, what's wrong?"

"It-It's D-Dad." Maggie was trying to fight the tears.

"Maggie, settle down and talk to me!"

"D-Dad had an accident."

"What kind of accident?"

"Oh Mom!" Maggie broke out in tears and could not finish talking,

"Maggie, talk to me!"

"I-I didn't know what to do." She said through her sobs. "I-I called for an ambulance."

"Maggie, I coming right home."

"O-Okay." Maggie hung up the phone and sat in the kitchen. She did not know what to do next. Maggie was afraid to call Isabelle. She did not think she could talk through her tears anyway. Maggie was afraid to go out into the field again. She felt so helpless. The vision of finding her dad laying on that rock with the rain falling down on him was just too much for her to bear. The few minutes that went by seemed like hours. Maggie heard the ambulance come into the driveway. She ran out of the house.

The paramedic asked, "Are you Maggie Sims?"

"Yes." She broke out in tears again, "M-My dad is in the creek."

The paramedic put his hands on her shoulder, "Maggie, calm down. You'll have to show us."

Maggie pointed towards the north field, "At the end of that field."

Can we get there by the road or through the yard? Which way is faster?"

"Through-through the yard."

The paramedic rushed back to the ambulance, "He's in a field. We will have to go out to him. Bring the stretcher and the kits." He ran towards the north field dodging the tree limbs. Maggie started to follow, but the paramedics stopped her. One of them said, "Maggie we ask that you stay back." Maggie stood in the middle of the yard feeling even more helpless than before. She stayed standing as the heavy rain was pouring down on her.

. . .

Caroline gave the phone back to the receptionist, "Mary, did you hear anything about Henry being brought in by the ambulance?"

"No."

"I'm going home. Please tell Doctor Parker."

Caroline pulled into the driveway and saw Maggie standing in the rain in the middle of the yard, sobbing.

Maggie ran to Caroline's car as Caroline stopped the car and got out, "Maggie." She took her into her arms. "Where is Dad? What's going on?"

"They're-they're still out in the field." Maggie would not let go of Caroline.

"Maggie, let go of me!" Caroline ran out towards the cornfield with Maggie following right behind her.

When Caroline got closer to the creek at the north end, one of the paramedics came towards her. He put his hand on her shoulders, "Caroline, don't. Let them bring Henry up."

"Oh God!" Caroline screamed.

She put her head in her hands and fell down on her knees into the mud. Maggie came running to her mother and held her. Neither one of them could move.

The paramedics brought Henry out of the creek on the stretcher. They were not moving very fast because their boots were caked with mud also. They carried Henry out of the field to the ambulance in the yard. The other paramedic stopped and helped Caroline and Maggie stand up, "We are taking Henry to the hospital."

Caroline just nodded. She knew that the paramedic would not answer any questions about Henry. Caroline regained her composure, "Maggie and I will follow you to the hospital."

"Only if you are able to drive," said the paramedics.

Caroline did not answer. She and Maggie walked arm in arm back to her car. The paramedic put on the siren of the ambulance and drove away with Caroline following behind them.

The ambulance drove up to the emergency door of the hospital. Doctor Parker and a nurse were there waiting. Doctor Parker removed Henry's jacket and shirt to check his vital signs as they wheeled Henry into the emergency room. He could not detect a heartbeat. He did everything he could do to try to bring Henry back to life, but to no avail. He looked at the nurse and shook his head.

Caroline and Maggie were in the waiting room when Doctor Parker came in. Caroline knew by the look on his face that Henry was already gone, but she just did not want to hear him tell her so. Maggie could sense it too, and buried her face in her Mother's chest and sobbed.

Doctor Parker said in a solemn voice, "I'm sorry. We did everything we could."

"Wh-What happened?" Caroline managed to ask.

"The paramedics said that the tractor rolled into the creek. Henry fell off the tractor and hit his head on a rock. They think the tractor rolled when the tornado came up. Caroline, when the paramedics arrived, Henry was not breathing. They could not get a pulse."

"Oh God." Caroline slumped down in a chair. Caroline and Maggie hugged each other and cried. Caroline lifted Maggie off her chest, "Maggie I have to call Isabelle."

"O-Okay," Maggie said through her sobs.

Caroline went to the receptionist desk. "Mary, I need to use the telephone."

Mary put the telephone on the counter, "I am so sorry Caroline." Caroline dialed Isabelle's number.

"Hello?" Isabelle answered.

"Isabelle, it is Mom." Caroline said as calmly as she could manage.

"Mom?" Isabelle could sense that something was wrong with Caroline by the tone of her voice.

"Isabelle. Dad had an accident with the tractor." Caroline was silent again.

"But he's okay right?" Isabelle questioned her. Matt came into the room and stood closer to Isabelle.

"No Isabelle."

"Mom, what are you saying?" Isabelle panicked.

"He's gone Isabelle."

"What do you mean, he's gone?"

"Dad rolled the tractor in the creek and hit his head."

"What do you mean, he's gone?" Isabelle repeated. She dropped the receiver and left it dangling to the floor, slammed the bedroom door shut behind her, and buried her face in a pillow to cry.

Matt picked up the receiver, "Caroline, this is Matt."

"Can you and Isabelle come home?"

"Of course. We will leave right away. We will be there in a couple of hours."

. . .

At Henry's funeral, Caroline paused in front of Henry's casket. She looked down at him in his gray suit. She put her hands together saying silently to herself all of her thoughts. "What am I going to do without you? How will I manage to live alone and take care of Maggie by myself? What am I going to do about the farm? How will I be able to take care of the house? Oh, I will be so lost. I do not know what to do first. Whom will I turn to for help? You were my pillar of strength." Caroline just stood there looking at Henry until Reverend Ahlmann put his hands on her shoulder. He helped her to a chair in the family viewing room.

Maggie stopped and gazed at her dad. She whispered, "I will never forget you. I will be strong for Mom. I will remind her, what Dr. Nabity told me. Remember the good things. I love you Dad, forever." She sat down next to her mother. Maggie took Caroline's hand and held it in hers.

Matt looked down at Henry. "Good-bye Henry. You will be missed." Matt drew Isabelle closer to him. He placed his arm around her shoulders.

Isabelle leaned her head on Matt's chest and stared down at her dad, saying silently to herself, "I love you Dad. I wish you could have met the little baby I have inside me. I will make sure it knows how wonderful and kind you were, every day. Good-bye." She pressed two fingers to her lips and then put them on Henry's lips.

Tranquility Church bells sounded. It seemed that everyone from Cleary County was there to pay respects to Henry. Following the service, everyone showered Caroline with well wishes and kind words. Louise was by her side throughout the day. It seemed that she could help her somehow. Caroline expressed several times to Louise how much she appreciated her staying with her.

Young people surrounded Matt, Isabelle, and Maggie. They were expressing their condolences to them. Isabelle melted in Sara's arms when she came up to her. "Sara, I am so glad you came."

Sara lifted her chin. "I am here for you."

Matt and Isabelle followed Caroline and Maggie back to the farm when the church service was over. There was a long procession of cars following them. Cars were parked everywhere in the yard, as well as the entire length of the lane. People brought sandwiches, salads, cakes, pies, etc. There was so much food; the girls did not know where to put it all.

It was nearly eight o'clock in the evening when the last of the mourners left. Caroline, Matt, and Maggie sat in silence in the living room too drained to talk. Isabelle fell asleep on Caroline's bed. Matt finally broke the silence saying, "Well, I will wake Isabelle and we will go upstairs for the night."

Caroline protested. "No, leave her sleeping on my bed. I will just lie on the couch for the night. I don't know how much sleep I'll get anyway."

Matt went to the car to get the suitcase. He gave Casey some fresh water and food before he came back into the house. He took the suitcase into Caroline's bedroom and closed the door.

Maggie plodded up the stairs and fell asleep with the lamp still on.

CHAPTER THIRTY-THREE

Matt kissed Isabelle just before he left the apartment to go to the store. He was thinking that Isabelle looked more tired today than usual. When he asked her if she was feeling okay, she assured him she was. Isabelle watched Matt drive away, and decided to lie back down on the bed. As she was lying there, the baby was kicking and keeping her awake. She felt nauseated. Isabelle got back up and put some bread in the toaster. Suddenly, she doubled over in a sharp pain and wondered if she should call for an ambulance. Isabelle waited a few minutes. The sharp pain went away, so she stood in the kitchen and ate one piece of toast. Isabelle walked into the living room to sit in the recliner when she realized that her water broke. She reached for the telephone, dialed the store, and asked if Matt had gotten there yet. Doug said, "He just walked in. Do you want to talk to him?"

"This is Isabelle. Tell him to come back home. My water just broke."

Matt drove as fast as he legally could to get back to the apartment. He rushed into the apartment yelling, "Is this the real thing?" He did not wait for her to answer before he grabbed the packed suitcase from the closet and rushed back out to put it in the car. When he came back in, Isabelle was standing in the living room laughing at his haste. She reminded him that there was plenty of time before the birth of their first child and there was no need to panic. Matt helped Isabelle into the car, still not slowing down his pace. He rushed through a yellow light, but then he had to stop behind another car at the next stoplight. When the stoplight turned green, that car did not pull out fast enough for Matt. In disgust, he honked his horn.

Isabelle started laughing again. "Matt, relax! You're as jittery as a pig in a butcher shop."

Matt turned towards Isabelle and laughed at her comment.

Matt pulled up to the emergency door of the hospital. The hospital staff helped Isabelle into a wheel chair and wheeled her into a room. A nurse asked Isabelle how far apart her contractions were. "I really don't know," replied Isabelle. "Maybe fifteen minutes."

Based on that information, the nurse knew that Isabelle had some time before the baby was born. She prepared the delivery table and dressed Isabelle in a hospital gown. She told her to try to relax until the doctor could come and get a closer look. Just then, Isabelle had another contraction. This one was more severe. Isabelle took Matt's hand and squeezed until the contraction was over. Doctor Manze came in and inspected Isabelle. He announced, "We have a ways to go yet. Just relax."

Isabelle scorned, "Easy for you to say." Doctor Manze chuckled. Isabelle did not have any more contractions for a while. Doctor Manze had her walk up and down the halls to try to speed things up. Matt and Isabelle were in front of the nursery when Isabelle doubled over again with a harsh contraction. The nurse helped her back into her room. She ran to get the doctor. An orderly told Matt that he needed to wait in the waiting room. He looked behind him at Isabelle as he left her room.

The nurse helped Isabelle onto the birthing bed. Doctor Manze inspected Isabelle again. "Well, this is it Isabelle. You can push now." Isabelle pushed as hard as she could. The baby fell into Doctor Manze's hands. "Stop pushing Isabelle! It's a girl." Doctor Manze handed the baby to the nurse while he finished with Isabelle. Isabelle heard her baby cry when the nurse wrapped her up in a blanket. The nurse handed the baby to Isabelle. Then the nurse went to the waiting room to get Matt.

Matt came running into the room and stopped when he saw a tiny baby wrapped in a blanket lying in Isabelle's lap. He had tears coming down his cheeks. Isabelle smiled, "Look. Isn't she beautiful?" Isabelle had tears streaming down her face too.

Doctor Manze presented Matt with a healthy baby girl and assured him that Isabelle did a fine job. It was hard to leave Isabelle and his baby in the hospital that night. He returned to the apartment and called his parents. He called Caroline's number, but no one answered. He then called Cleary General.

Caroline answered, "Hello?"

"Congratulations Grandma." Matt said. "It's a girl. Six pounds three ounces and she has Isabelle's eyes." Caroline was beaming from ear to ear. She congratulated Matt and told him that she and Maggie would travel to Lincoln to the hospital to see Isabelle and his new baby tomorrow.

. . .

Maggie folded the baby blanket and put it in a paper sack along with a package of sleepers that Caroline got for the baby. She also put in the paper sack the baby rattle she bought. She placed the sack on the back seat. Caroline was still smiling as she drove down the lane and headed for Lincoln to see her new grandchild.

At the hospital in Lincoln, the nurse showed Caroline and Maggie to Isabelle's room. Caroline opened the door and saw Isabelle sitting up in an easy chair near the window. Caroline stopped to look at her. All of a sudden, Isabelle looked older to her. She was not the little girl she remembered. The nurse was behind Maggie carrying in the baby. Maggie stepped to the side so that her mother could see the baby first. Caroline took the baby from the nurse. She was overjoyed as she gazed at the little baby girl saying, "Hello, I am your grandma. Oh, she is just beautiful."

Caroline held the baby closer to Maggie so that she could see her. Maggie put her sack of the baby gifts on the bedside table to observe the baby. She touched the baby's hands saying, "Hi. I am your aunt, Maggie."

Shortly after, Alfred and Bonnie came in. Caroline was gracious enough to hand the baby over to Bonnie. Alfred gave Matt a handshake saying, "Congratulations Son!" He had a beautiful bouquet of flowers in a vase. Alfred announced that the flowers were from his mom, Helen. He laid a package of cloth diapers and a baby book on her table. Isabelle thanked them for the gifts. Matt stated that he would call his grandmother Helen and thank her for the flowers.

Caroline turned towards Isabelle and asked if she had a name for the baby yet. Isabelle got up from the easy chair. She took Caroline's hands in hers and said. "Mom, her name is Henrietta. Henrietta Marie."

Caroline could not contain the tears. She hugged her daughter so tight it was hard for Isabelle to breathe. She finally let go of her and looked directly into Isabelle's eyes. "Your dad would have been so honored."

Everyone in the room was in tears when Harold and Carrie walked into the room. Carrie was worried that something dreadful happened to the baby, but Matt immediately took hold of the conversation. He said that the baby was fine, as well as Isabelle. Then he announced that his daughter's name was Henrietta. Carrie was relieved and walked over to Caroline. She hugged her saying, "That's what her name should be." Harold handed Isabelle and Matt each a wrapped gift. Isabelle opened hers first. It was a pair of gold plated baby shoes. She thanked them, saying it was precious. Matt un-wrapped a silver-plated bank in the shape of a child's block. He turned it over and saw the engraving. It read 'To Baby Carson'. Matt thanked his grandparents for the gift. Isabelle expressed that she had never seen anything like it.

CHAPTER THIRTY-FOUR

It was corn-shelling day. Caroline looked out the kitchen window when she heard Casey barking at Joe and Alice driving into the yard. Caroline was told not to worry about the meal for the day as Alice had it all arranged. She brought in a box of food and set it on the counter. Tom Anderson and his wife Diane drove into the yard. Maggie held the kitchen door open while Diane came into the house carrying a picnic basket. Donna Shields, Virginia Jones, and Connie Drake were right behind her, each carrying a box. Before long, Caroline had six women in her kitchen preparing the meal for the farmers. Maggie was getting out the table service and gathering chairs around the table. Caroline was feeling useless until Louise surprised her when she walked into the house. She chased Caroline out of the kitchen and led her into the living room. Louise asked how she was doing and complemented to her about how well she had adjusted. Caroline confided to her that she really was not doing very well, but she was keeping up her smiles for Maggie's sake. She told Louise that she was so thankful for Maggie. "I don't know what I would have done without her. When I am down, she brings me back up."

Louise replied, "I would bet that you return the favor to her."

"Well I suppose you're right." Caroline fixed her eyes on the floor. "Louise, can I tell you something?"

"Sure. You can tell me anything."

"I have decided to sell the farm." Caroline looked straight into Louise's eyes saying, "I haven't even told the girls yet." She went on to tell her that she would not be able to manage the farm without Henry. Joe has been coming over to cultivate and to take care of the cattle. He informed Caroline that she needed to buy hay before the winter. "Louise, I just don't know about such things. Henry always took care of everything. I did not even realize that the corn needed to be shelled today. Joe and Alice made all of the arrangements."

Louise knew that was a big step for Caroline to take. She could tell Caroline had contemplated the decision to sell the farm for quite some time. "I know what you are going through. That is why Alice called me to come over today."

"Well I wondered." Caroline smiled. "I have decided that Maggie and I will be moving to Marie's house after the farm sale."

Louise rejoiced with joy saying, "We will be neighbors."

. . .

Caroline and Maggie had moved what they needed from the farm into Marie's house in Cleary. It was hard for Caroline, but she knew that was the only way. She and Maggie were a family and Caroline was going to do her best to make them feel undivided. Joe Miller, Bill Drake, Tom Anderson, and Ed Jones helped Caroline organize the farm sale. Joe hired an auctioneer from Morgan.

The day of the farm sale, Isabelle saw Maggie walking on the other side of the yard. She handed Henrietta over to Matt, "Matt, can you take her? I'm going to talk to Maggie."

Matt took his daughter saying, "Sure." Matt was listening to the auctioneer. "I'll stay here. I want to hear how much money they bid on the planter and the tractor."

Maggie stopped to look at the wringer washing machine. She ran her fingers through her hair just as Isabelle came up beside her, "Maggie do you remember that day your hair got caught in those rollers?"

"Oh I'll never forget that. I was so scared that I would have to go to school with short hair."

Isabelle brushed a strand of hair away from Maggie's face. "Maggie you are so beautiful."

"Thanks."

"I really mean that. You are way prettier than I am."

Maggie smiled. "I think we both are. After all that's why Matt fell in love with you the first day he saw you in the gymnasium."

They walked back to where Matt was standing with Henrietta. Caroline came up to join them. The auctioneer had just sold the planter. The next item was the tractor. All four of them stood with solemn faces with their eyes affixed on the tractor. Matt knew the story of the winter flood they had. Caroline touched her wrist and flexed it while remembering that day, that seemed so long ago. Caroline could still see Henry sitting on the seat of that tractor, taking the family away from the flooded farm to seek shelter. She remembered him sitting on it going up and down the fields disking, planting, cultivating, and harvesting the crops. She remembered how some days he would come in after a long day in the field so exhausted he could barely walk. Then he would get up early the next day and climb back on it. Sadness swept her face when she remembered the day that piece of machinery took Henry's life. Tears were swelling up in her eyes. She reached over to take Henrietta from Matt. Matt saw her tears, without saying a single word, he handed Henrietta over to her. Caroline walked away with her to sit on the cement steps of the house. Matt completely understood why she left at that moment.

Maggie walked away too. She went behind the house and sat up against the cottonwood tree in the backyard. Isabelle saw her leaving, "Matt I'm going to see if Maggie is doing okay."

Matt nodded, "I understand."

Alice took Gregory's hand and walked with him to where Caroline and Henrietta were. She sat down beside her on the cement steps in front of the house with a sigh of relief, "Oh I needed to sit down." She saw that Caroline had been crying. Alice touched her shoulder. "This is a hard day for you, isn't it Caroline?"

"Oh, I'll be fine. A lot has happened in the last couple of years."

"Yes it has. If you ever need anything, don't hesitate to call."

"Thanks Alice. Maggie and I are getting settled."

"Caroline, I want to tell you something." She paused to make sure that she had Caroline's full attention. "Joe is going to buy your farm." Caroline instantly broke down into tears. Alice was concerned about her decision to tell Caroline at this time. "I didn't mean to upset you."

"Oh." Caroline was wiping her face with Henrietta's cloth diaper she had on her shoulder. "You don't realize how happy that makes me. You and Joe have been the best neighbors we could have ever had."

"Well, we rent the house and the ground we live on now. The owner's son is coming back to Nebraska to farm it. We have been searching for a farm to buy. Joe made some trips to Iowa and Kansas, but we just were not ready to leave Cleary County. We stalled on making a purchase when we found out that you were going to sell." Henrietta let out a wail. Caroline smiled and switched her to the other arm. Alice was concerned, "What happened to her all of a sudden?"

"I think I was holding her too tight."

Alice laughed. "Do you want to know something else?" Alice looked straight into Caroline's eyes and said, "I'm pregnant again."

Caroline smiled. "Alice, congratulations! It has been a long time since there were children running around in this house."

Casey was making his presence. Gregory took after him to chase him into the yard. Alice immediately ran after Gregory and brought him back. "Well Caroline, I think there will be kids running in the yard too. Casey will be happy staying here."

Caroline grinned, "Maggie will be pleased to hear that. She has been worried about him."

"Well he's home where he belongs. Maggie can come out to see him anytime she wants."

Caroline said, "God always works things out doesn't he?"

"Yes He does."

Meanwhile, Isabelle sat down next to Maggie. They sat in silence for a moment before Maggie spoke. "I just couldn't watch Dad's tractor being sold."

Isabelle put her arms on Maggie's shoulders, "I know. I felt the same way."

"Isabelle, I know that Mom is with me and she says that I can talk to her anytime, but sometimes I feel so alone."

"It will take time to adjust to everything. A lot has happened."

"Sometimes I look at Mom and see how sad she is. It breaks my heart."

"Give her time too. When I am sad, I turn to Matt. Then I give an extra hug to Henrietta."

"Henrietta is so lucky to have you. You really are good at being a mom."

Isabelle smiled. "I think Mom had something to do with that. She has taught us a lot."

The two girls were silent again. Isabelle kept her arms around Maggie's shoulders as each of them collecting their own thoughts while sitting side by side *against the cottonwood tree.*

About the Author

Linda Jensen has lived in Nebraska her entire life. She grew up on a farm near Pierce, Nebraska, a small town of 1,700 people. There her roots were sown. Her character Maggie, in this novel, is much like Linda when she was a teenager. She liked the farm life and reading her novels.

Forty years ago, Linda married Leslie Jensen and moved to Central City, Nebraska. Central City is a slightly larger town of 3,000 people. Leslie and Linda have one daughter Lacey, a son Landon, and his family, Kimmera and Lillian.

Linda has been employed in the City Clerk's office of Central City for 35 years.

If she is not curled up in her easy chair with a book in her hand, she is sitting alongside her camper in a lawn chair, facing a lake, and pounding the keys on her laptop.

"The best time to create is in the early morning," Linda says, "when my mind is clear of any distractions."

Made in the USA
Lexington, KY
30 October 2018